THE ALAMO'S FORGOTTEN DEFENDERS

The Remarkable Story of the Irish
During the Texas Revolution

D1426938

Phillip Thomas Tucker

SB

Savas Beatie

California

2016 © Phillip Thomas Tucker

Library of Congress Cataloging-in-Publication Data

Names: Tucker, Phillip Thomas, 1953- author.
Title: The Alamo's Forgotten Defenders : The Remarkable Story of the Irish During the Texas Revolution / Phillip Thomas Tucker.
Description: First edition. | El Dorado Hills, California : Savas Beatie LLC, 2016. | Includes bibliographical references and index.
Identifiers: LCCN 2015044716 | ISBN 9781611211917 (alk. paper) | ISBN 9781611211924 (ebk. : alk. paper)
Subjects: LCSH: Alamo (San Antonio, Tex.)—Siege, 1836. |
Texas—History—Revolution, 1835-1836—Participation, Irish American. |
Irish American soldiers—History—19th Century. |
Irish Americans—History—19th century.
Classification: LCC F390 .T829 2016 | DDC 976.4/03—dc23
LC record available at: http://lccn.loc.gov/2015044716

SB

Published by
Savas Beatie LLC
989 Governor Drive, Suite 102
El Dorado Hills, CA 95762

Phone: 916-941-6896
(web) www.savasbeatie.com
(E-mail) sales@savasbeatie.com

First edition, first printing

ISBN 13: 978-1-61121-191-7

Savas Beatie titles are available at special discounts for bulk purchases in the United States by corporations, institutions, and other organizations. For more details, please contact Special Sales, Savas Beatie LLC, 989 Governor Drive, Suite 102, El Dorado Hills, CA 95762, or you may e-mail us at sales@savasbeatie.com, or visit our website at www.savasbeatie.com for additional information.

Proudly published, printed, and warehoused in the United States of America.

To the proud descendants
of the Irish across Texas

The largest concentration of Mexican soldiers attacked the north wall of the Alamo on the morning of March 6, 1836. Artist Lajos Markos caught the drama and horror of the Mexican surprise attack in his fine painting. *Courtesy of the State Preservation Board, Austin, Texas*

Table of Contents

Prologue—"Will you go?"

From his desk in San Felipe de Austin on January 19, 1836, and nearly five weeks before Antonio Lopez de Santa Anna's army reached San Antonio de Béxar to catch the Alamo garrison by surprise, Acting Governor James W. Robinson penned a desperate appeal for Texians to come to the assistance of the diminutive garrison. He explained in an open letter how "an immediate attack was expected" and that "only seventy-five men are in the Alamo [and] provisions are scarce. Under these circumstances they ask for your aid, to defend the fortress against the enemy. Will you go?"[1]

While the cold winds howled across the prairie, the Alamo remained little more than a deadly trap, especially for a small garrison held by those with inadequate defensive preparations, lack of training, and little war-waging capabilities. Although the sprawling complex spanned nearly three acres, with a huge main plaza and a lengthy defensive parameter of a quarter mile, the fort itself was small and in poor shape. Even with better prepared forces, these details ensured that the old Spanish mission simply could not be held for any length of time, especially if attacked on all four sides at once. Green B. Jameson, the Alamo's chief engineer, emphasized as much in a letter dated January 16, 1836, showing a recognition of the seemingly endless defensive liabilities of the

---

1 *Telegraph and Texas Register*, San Felipe de Austin, Texas, January 23, 1836.

ancient mission: "the Alamo never was built by a military people for a fortress."[2] It was confirmed in February 1836 by a Mexican Tejano defender who said the "Alamo was old and gray and tumbling," a wreck of its former self.[3]

Truly, in terms of the final decision to make a last-ditch defensive stand, the Alamo garrison at San Antonio de Béxar was of no real strategic importance. The words of a volunteer captain from Mobile, Alabama, from an October 22, 1835 letter, revealed the extent of the lack of strategic insight among the Alamo's homespun leadership. He said that the southern garrison, Presidio La Bahía near Goliad, was "of vastly more importance in a military point of view than Béxar, as the latter is in a valley upon the banks of the river and commanded by the hills on each side; it is therefore indefensible."[4] The defensive advantages of making a stand at Goliad rather than at San Antonio were common knowledge to the people across Texas by early 1836. Even the *New Orleans Bulletin* published an insightful article that elaborated on the superior strength of the Presidio la Bahía at Goliad, noting that "a garrison of three hundred and fifty patriots in the war of 1812-13, withstood a siege of an army of more than two thousand Spanish troops and forced them to retire–discomfited."[5]

The commander of the garrison, Lieutenant Colonel James Cinton Neill, had been requesting assistance for weeks. Neill lamented the overall situation of the Alamo that continued to deteriorate, warning the government of Texas as early as January 6, 1836 that, "we know not what day, or hour, an enemy of 1000 in number may be down upon us, and as we have no supplies of provisions within the fortress we could be Starved out in 4 days by anything like a close Siege."[6] By this time, as reported by a New York journalist who had gained firsthand information of the Texas situation, much of the country had been

2   Bill Groneman, *Alamo Defenders, A Genealogy: The People and Their Words* (Plano, TX, 1990), 63-64, 141; Todd Hansen, ed., *The Alamo Reader: A Study in History* (Mechanicsburg, PA, 2003), 654; William C. Davis, *Lone Star Rising: The Revolutionary Birth of a Texas Republic* (New York, NY, 2004), 213-214.

3   Hansen, ed., *The Alamo Reader*, 113.

4   *Maryland Gazette*, Annapolis, Maryland, December 3, 1835; Davis, *Lone Star Rising*, 213-214.

5   Jerry J. Gaddy, *Texas in Revolt: Contemporary Newspaper Account of the Texas Revolution* (Fort Collins, CO, 1973), 35; Jay A. Stout, *Slaughter at Goliad: The Mexican Massacre of 400 Texas Volunteers* (Annapolis, MD, 2008), 74.

6   Hansen, ed., *The Alamo Reader*, 649.

depleted of resources, because the "vast number of emigrants and volunteers, who have gone to Texas, during the past fall and winter, have made supplies scarce."[7]

Neill remained the most responsible for the ultimate leadership decision to make a defensive stand at the Alamo, based partly upon the mistaken belief that his increasingly desperate appeals to the government would garner adequate reinforcements, and that he possessed sufficient artillery to defend the mission. Yet in the same desperate letter, the Scotch-Irish commander and Creek War veteran complained with ample justification of the impossibility of simultaneously defending both San Antonio de Béxar and the Alamo [because in] "our alarming weakness We have 104 men, and two distinct fortresses to garrison [but] we have no Provisions nor clothing in this garrison."[8] He was to be sorely disappointed in his expectations, because of the pervasive "state of apathy" among the Texians, in Governor Henry Smith's words.[9]

Even a last-minute appeal, again from Robinson, failed to have the desired effect on the apathetic Texians: "the Mexicans had advanced as far as Larado and the Rio Frio river. Col. Neill has but 75 men with him in the Alamo. . . . I regret to make you at this season of the year, when the case of your domestic concerns [on the farm and ranch], claims all your attention; but I am compelled to do it by the imminet [sic] danger which menaces your brothers in arms, by risks to which the inhabitants of our frontier will be exposed if we do not fly to their succor. . . . Fly then to the protection of our household goods; hasten to the west, where you will be organized for a short and glorious campaign. MARCH!! Victory awaits you."[10]

But the people of Texas, now engaged in early spring planting and farm and ranch work, ignored the patriotic call. They simply would not "march" to reinforce the Alamo. Unlike the recent United States volunteers, and as reported in the Telegraph and Texas Register, the vast majority of Texians who were "possessed of lands and other property [including slaves] are staying home to take care of their substance" rather than serve in the military in defense of their own homeland. Two Texians, Thomas Gay and John R. Jones, chastised: "We regret to hear of the backwardness of some of our fellow citizens, in

7   *New York Herald*, March 29, 1836.

8   Hansen, ed., *The Alamo Reader*, 648.

9   Ibid; *Texas Republican*, Brazoria, Texas, March 2, 1836.

10 Gaddy, *Texas in Revolt*, 43.

turning out in defense of their wives and children [as the men of Texas] are not willing to turn out" to defend Texas.[11]

Even as far away as New York City, Wall Street investors speculating in commodities, were concerned if profits would be reaped from a bountiful Texas corn harvest with the knowledge that Santa Anna's Army was moving north into Texas: "it is probable, that the Texians can gather the coming crop of corn, as corn ripens in that country in July [but now] there is very little that can be safely relied on—and the corn crop is precarious, as the force of the country will be called out" to defend Texas.[12]

As hundreds of United States volunteers flooded into Texas, the relatively small number of Texian settlers became increasingly concerned about the war effort dominated by newcomers—politically, militarily, and economically. The "Old Texians" knew that these newly arrived volunteers would gain large amounts of lush, bountiful Texas lands if they emerged victorious. By early 1836, therefore, an ever-increasing number of Texians actually "preferred returning Texas to the Mexicans to turning it over to U.S. volunteers," many of whom were responsible for the Alamo garrison's defense.[13]

Like the people of Texas in general, Sam Houston, the commander of the Texas Army, possessed strong vested interests (personal, economic, and political) and abandoned the Alamo when the garrison most desperately needed assistance. With the goal of restoring his lost status as Tennessee's governor, Houston had a host of pressing reasons for the elimination of his greatest political rivals—the increasingly popular William Barret Travis, Jim Bowie, and David Crockett. Instead of rallying the Texians to the Alamo's defense, Houston delayed his help, and instead inconsistently advised that the fort be demolished and its ammunition removed.

Indeed, when Dr. Amos Pollard, the 32-year-old chief surgeon of the Alamo garrison, wrote on February 13, 1836 that, "I wish Gen. Houston was now on the [western] frontier to help us," he was hoping in vain. Like others in

---

11 *Ibid; Paul Lack, The Texas Revolutionary Experience: A Political and Social History, 1835-1836* (College Station, TX, 1995), 215; the *Telegraph and Texas Register,* March 5, 1836.

12 *New York Herald,* March 29, 1836.

13 Lack, *The Texas Revolutionary Experience,* 110-155, 208-218; Bruce Marshall, *Uniforms of the Alamo and the Texas Revolution and the Men Who Wore Them: 1835-1836* (Atglen, TX, 2003), 6-7; Shackford, *David Crockett,* 224-227, 233-234; Stephen L. Moore, *Eighteen Minutes: The Battle of San Jacinto and the Texas Independence Campaign* (R&L, 2003), 10-17, 41.

the Alamo, he carried naïve beliefs, and would never again see his home or his precious daughter.[14]

And even when he belatedly returned to the center of government, Houston spent most of the time at Washington-on-the-Brazos playing politics, angling to be named commander-in-chief of all Texas forces, and drinking corn whisky to excess. Houston, the Texas government, and the Texian colonists all but abandoned the small band of soldiers at San Antonio, leaving them to fend for themselves in a no-win situation.[15]

In a January 14, 1836 letter to Houston, a desperate Neill described the garrison's shocking condition and an even more disastrous strategic situation: "The men all under my command . . . are almost naked . . . and almost every one of them speak[s] of going home [while the Mexican Army] . . . at Laredo [is] now 3,000 men. 1,000 of them are destined for this place, and two thousand for Matamoros."[16]

With such nagging concerns in mind, Neill had wisely decided to concentrate his forces in a single defensive structure, the Alamo, which was then commanded by Captain William Ridgeway Carey. Jameson described the garrison's dilemma that resulted in the hasty reshuffling of troops in a letter: "We have too few to garrison both [the town and the Alamo], and will bring all our forces to the Alamo."[17]

Neill ordered the mounting of the 18-pounder at an elevated point of a rooftop barbette at the southwest corner of the sprawling compound, facing San Antonio (west) where Santa Anna was expected to enter the town. Even with these preparations, however, the lack of adequate weaponry, manpower, supplies, and munitions—virtually everything necessary for a solid defense— ensured the defeat of the garrison. In a January 18, 1836 letter, the pragmatic engineer, Jameson, described his ever-growing apprehension about the garrison's forlorn situation in the low-lying San Antonio River valley, because "I

---

14 Groneman, *Alamo Defenders*, 91-92, 154.

15 Lack, *The Texas Revolutionary Experience*, 53-155, 208-216; Stephen L. Hardin, *Texian Iliad: A Military History of the Texas Revolution, 1835-1836* (Austin, TX, 1996), 107-108; Groneman, *Alamo Defender*, 141; Davis, *Land!*, 17-19; Sam W. Haynes and Cary D. Wintz, eds., *Major Problems in Texas History* (Belmont, CA, 2001), 98-104.

16 Hansen, ed., *The Alamo Reader*, 652.

17 Groneman, *Alamo Defenders*, 142.

[have no] doubt but there are 1500 of the enemy [under Santa Anna] at the town of Rio Grande, and as many more at Laredo."[18]

Yet when James Bowie arrived mid-January, he was impressed with the preparations Neill had made to the garrison, and confidence among its members remained surprisingly high. Even Jameson wrote Houston crowing that the Béxar garrison could "whip [the Mexican Army] 10 to 1 with our artillery."[19]

Unfortunately for the Alamo soldiers, the dysfunctional Texas government was in complete chaos, torn by dissension, jealousy, and seemingly endless in-fighting. The provisional government's collapse in early 1836 guaranteed that these squabbling politicians, who were more concerned about their own egos and promotion of personal interests rather than the Alamo's fate, failed to send the timely assistance needed to reinforce the garrison now stuck out on a lengthy limb on the isolated frontier. As evidence, the bickering General Council politicians in San Felipe de Austin could not even raise enough money for monthly pay for garrison members, not to mention the purchase of powder and munitions that Neill requested in vain.

Perhaps no Alamo garrison member was more disgusted by the pervasive apathy and general collapse of the Texas provisional government than Joseph M. Hawkins. He advised the governor on January 20, 1836 that Texas could be only won by the uniting of two groups of soldiers, who drew upon two distinct revolutionary heritages and legacies: "the sons of Washington and St. Patrick." Increasingly angry at the folly that sabotaged any chance of successfully defending not only the Alamo but also Texas, the 37-year-old Irishman bitterly complained in this same letter of "the disorderly and anarchical conduct of the council" of Texas.

Hawkins outlined his "indignation at this post" and its member forces in San Antonio. Indeed, the garrison was defended almost exclusively by non-Texian soldiers, and too few at that. To the Alamo defenders, it seemed as if they were only serving as a remote western outpost, little more than expendable cannon fodder—not for the everyday citizens, but for the wealthy landowners and the large slave-owners, who remained far from the front lines.[20]

18 Grady McWhiney and Perry D. Jamieson, *Attack and Die: Civil War Tactics and the Southern Tradition* (Tuscaloosa, AL, 1982), 174-187; Groneman, *Alamo Defenders*, 141.

19 Hardin, *Texian Illiad*, 111.

20 Lack, *The Texas Revolutionary Experience*, 58,149-150; Groneman, *Alamo Defenders*, 4-125.

Of course, the Alamo defenders were unaware that a good many disgruntled United States volunteers had already returned home completely disillusioned by their recent experiences in Texas. Once back, they complained loudly how the Texians "care not a fig under what Government they live."[21] Worst of all, the Alamo men had no idea how united the Mexican nation had become in regard to Texas. With steely determination, a finely-uniformed aide to Santa Anna predicted how, "there revolutionists [of Texas] will be ground down" and destroyed. Santa Anna, who wanted most of all to save his splintered republic before it was too late, swore that he would "conquer Texas or lose Mexico."[22]

While the Texas government was divided by the war's demands, priorities, and even objectives, Mexico's liberals and conservatives were now united in a war against the Texans, in no small part because of the steady flow of those who arrived to secure Texas land for themselves. Consequently, no one was more eager to strike a blow against these armed "foreigners" on Mexican soil than generalissimo Santa Anna.[23]

One of Santa Anna's top lieutenants, Colonel Juan Nepomuceno Almonte, had belatedly warned the top leaders in Mexico City in 1834 of the inevitable conflict: "we must recognize that these American settlers could never unite with us [and] no one but Mexicans should be allowed" to settle in Texas. Santa Anna was most desirous of inflicting an overwhelming punishing blow not only upon the rebellious settlers of east Texas but also "the foreigners [from the United States] who wage war against the Mexican Nation [and who] have violated all laws"—Mexican law, United States law, and international law. It was time to address, once and for all, the colonies claimed by Texians and United States volunteers in arms.[24]

Benefitting from the advantage of excellent intelligence from "worthy spies" and the Mexican Tejano community of San Antonio, Santa Anna knew all about the Alamo garrison's dismal plight and lack of combat capabilities at a

21 *Albany Evening Journal*, Albany, New York, March 23, 1836.

22 John Edward Weems and Jane Weems, *Dream of Empire: A History of the Republic of Texas, 1836-1846* (Newark, NJ, 1995), 29; *The Telegraph and Texas Register*, February 27, 1836.

23 Edward L. Miller, *New Orleans and the Texas Revolution* (College Station, TX, 2004), 150; Santos, *Santa Anna's Campaign Against Texas, 1835-1836*, 9-11.

24 Luis Geraldo Morales Moreno, Jesus V. Marquez, and Kristyna Libura, *Echoes of the Mexican-American War* (Toronto, ON, 2005), 26; Richard G. Santos, *Santa Anna's Campaign Against Texas, 1835-1836* (Waco, TX, 1968), 11.

relatively early date. Therefore, the commander pushed north with a powerful army of mostly Indian and mestizo troops. Under blackened skies, the Mexican Army's relentless advance benefitted from the element of surprise and a well-designed pincer movement. Santa Anna led the main force, or the left wing, while his capable top lieutenant, General Jose de Urrea, commanding the right wing, swept up through the low-lying mesquite country of the gulf coast to the east. Santa Anna launched what was essentially a preemptive strike, before either the Texas settlements or armed citizens from the United States were ready to meet a mighty invasion, and the Alamo's soldiers were caught by fatal lack of support and miscalculations of their own military and political leaders.

The Alamo's Hawkins early understood the strategic reality that spelled disaster. He knew that only massive assistance from the United States could save Texas. In a January 24, 1836 letter he wrote, "Let a copy of [Santa Anna's threats] . . . of today be published, and circulated . . . throughout the United States and Sta. Anna will boast no more, America will be triumphant, and Texas free." Meanwhile, the Alamo garrison's best hope, James Walker Fannin, Jr. and his many volunteers, remained stationary at Goliad southeast of San Antonio near the gulf coast.[25]

In truth, a host of ugly realities finally caught up with the over-optimistic men at the Alamo. A deluded member of Captain Harrison's Tennessee Mounted Volunteers, North Carolina-born Micajah Autry, penned: "it is thought that Santa Anna will make a descent with his whole force in the Spring, but here will be soldiers enough of the real grit in Texas by that time to overrun all Mexico."[26]

Perhaps most indicative of the confusion surrounding the Alamo and its continued lack of support are two different letters sent around the same time. On February 2, Bowie wrote to Governor Smith that he and Neill had resolved to "die in these ditches" before they would surrender the post.[27]

Yet with Santa Anna bearing down on them, "Buck" Travis penned a pathetic plea to Sam Houston, imploring in vain: "For God's sake, and the sake of our country, send us reinforcements."[28]

---

25 Groneman, *Alamo Defenders*, 144; Santos, *Santa Anna's Campaign against Texas*, 9-56.

26 Groneman, *Alamo Defenders*, 7-8, 130

27 Hansen, ed., *The Alamo Reader*, 20.

28 Ibid., 150; Bill Walraven and Marjorie Walraven, *The Magnificent Barbarians: Little Told Tales of the Texas Revolution* (Woodway, TX, 1993), 60-62.

Gary Zaboly's "Travis's Vigil." Alamo commander Lt. Col. William Barret Travis, a former lawyer of partially Scotch-Irish descent, on his lonely nightly watch along the Alamo's stone and adobe wall during the cold early morning hours of March 6, 1836. Near the beginning of the siege, Travis, a twenty-six-year-old South Carolinian, promised in an eloquent letter dated February 24, 1836, that he would "never surrender or retreat." Travis kept his word—and perished. *Courtesy of Gary Zaboly*

Introduction

The Alamo, surely one of America's greatest and most iconic stories, has evolved into one of the most the defining moments in American history. The fact that a large percentage of the doomed Alamo garrison consisted of Irishmen (either born on the Emerald Isle, or the sons and grandsons of Irish immigrants) seems entirely incongruous to what generations of Americans have been told about this dramatic story.

Texas has been blessed with a colorful, stirring, and dramatic history that has been explored in great detail in books, movies, and documentaries. However, in one of the most striking ironies of Texas history, the important roles played by the Irish in the story of the birth of Texas and the Texas Revolution have been long overlooked. Representing a significant and most glaring omission in the Texas historical record, the many notable Sons of Erin have been the forgotten players in the fascinating story of the Texas Revolution of 1835-1836. No distinct ethnic group played a larger role in fueling, sustaining, and ultimately winning the Texas Revolution than did the Irish and their descendants.

The Irish were not only at the center of revolutionary activities across Texas, but at the very forefront of the struggle for the heart and soul of Texas, leading the way in a peoples' revolution. Indeed, in the struggle for Texas liberty, the Irish faithfully and splendidly fulfilled the ancient Gaelic battle-cry of "Faugh A Ballagh," or "Clear the Way," for their disproportionate and important roles in securing a new republic's independence. Nevertheless, no story of Texians (or Texans) has been more thoroughly ignored and forgotten by generations of American and Texas historians (ironically including those of Irish descent) than the Irish and their disproportionate and meaningful contributions to the creation of an infant republic on the untamed southwestern frontier. Quite simply, a forceful argument can be made that neither the establishment of a new Texas republic nor the one-sided decisive victory at San Jacinto on April 21, 1836, would have taken place without the many achievements and sacrifices of the Irish and the larger number of soldiers of Irish descent.

Scholarship in the Texas Revolutionary period has been extensive and often outstanding, especially in regard to the Alamo's unforgettable story. The important role played by the Irish in winning the Texas Revolution and in creating of a new sovereign nation, however, has not been part of that impressive body of work. Because of this glaring historical oversight, this remarkable story will be presented here for the first time.

This forgotten chapter of the Texas Revolution and the Alamo might be said to have begun on the other side of the Atlantic. During the early spring of 2004, an Irish nationalist shrine was slated to be torn down by a demolition crew. The distressing eyesore to the aesthetically minded and urban elite was about to be demolished in the name of progress and urban development. The ramshackle house was located at Number 16, Moore Street, Dublin, Ireland. There, in the historic heart of old Dublin beside the gently flowing Liffey River, courageous Irish nationalistic leaders of the doomed 1916 Easter Uprising saw their most fervent nationalistic dreams of an independent Republic of Ireland succumb to an early death.

Outgunned and outnumbered, the surrounded Irish revolutionaries unconditionally surrendered, bringing to a tragic end the six-day Easter Uprising. This bloody closing curtain of yet another failed nationalist Irish revolt against British domination centered around this nondescript house on Moore Street and its heroic finale, which thereafter became known to generations of Irish as "Ireland's Alamo."

The historical parallel played out in dramatic fashion on Dublin's streets 4,700 miles from the rolling grasslands of the central plains around the little town of San Antonio, Texas, and yet the story of the Alamo has long struck a resonate chord with Ireland's history-minded citizens. For good reason, the Irish have long identified with the Alamo's heroic symbolism of a spirited defense of cherished republican principles and a tenacious last stand by defiant citizen-soldiers against arbitrary centralized authority, dictatorial rule, and impossible odds.

While the Alamo has become an iconic symbol of liberty to freedom-loving people around the world, few Americans today have ever heard of the equally dramatic story of "Ireland's Alamo," located in an urban setting not like today's Alamo in San Antonio's congested center.

The widespread obscurity of so many significant Irish contributions to the creation of a new Texas Republic developed, in no small part, because of the common but incorrect assumption that the Alamo garrison was homogeneous. In the annals of traditional historiography, the most generalized and stereo-typical labels—Nordics, Norteamericanos, Anglo-Saxons, Americans, Texians, and Texans—have been long applied to describe the demographics of the Alamo's garrison. The truth is something different. In fact, the Alamo's demographics were much more diverse than previously recognized or acknowledged by generations of historians.

Because of the traditional and popular telling of the Alamo's story, the Texas Revolution's multi-layered levels and complexities, especially in terms of ethnicity, have been routinely homogenized and simplified to fulfill traditional Texas and American nationalistic, cultural, and racial requirements. Such pressing, deep-seated requirements called for a glorified struggle of a heroic band of self-sacrificing Anglo-American (Anglo-Saxon) settlers battling for liberty (just like their revolutionary forefathers of 1776), to fit neatly into the supposed homogenous fabric of America's story.

What few Irish or American citizens realize is that the idea of "Ireland's Alamo" can and should be turned on its head: It took place not during the Easter Uprising in Dublin in 1916, but at the Alamo itself. No place in all of Texas was more Irish than the Alamo, from its founding to the famous 1836 battle. Other than Tennessee and Virginia, no region offered more native-born sons to die within the old limestone and adobe mission of the benevolent Franciscans than Ireland.

Known as Hibernia to the ancient Romans (who never conquered the Emerald Isle, thanks largely to geography's protective blessings that initially sheltered the Irish people until the English arrived), Ireland was thoroughly represented in the bloody struggle at El Alamo along the San Antonio River. If the large number of Scotch-Irish and the descendants of those hardy Protestant immigrants, who migrated much earlier to America from northern Ireland or Ulster Province, are counted among the defenders, no group of soldiers more thoroughly dominated the Alamo garrison's ranks—and the Texas Revolutionary Army's citizen-soldiers from 1835 to 1836—than determined fighting men of Irish and Scotch-Irish descent.

In his ground-breaking work entitled *Cracker Culture: Celtic Ways in the Old South*, historian Grady McWhiney correctly emphasized the overwhelming dominance of the distinct Celtic cultural and societal roots, composition, and traditions, especially in regard to fostering strong anti-centralized government sentiments and proclivities of the South, including Texas. However, in a perplexing omission McWhiney overlooked the vital role these same Celtic, or Celtic-Gaelic, legacies and traditions played in laying a central foundation for the rise of self-determination and revolution on American soil. Most of all, he ignored the pivotal roles these key factors played in fueling, sustaining, and winning both American and Texas revolutions—ironically the most convincing argument and best evidence available to substantiate McWhiney's thesis. By the mid-1830s, both the colonial South and Texas were peopled with large numbers of settlers of Irish or Celtic descent, who in turn helped set the stage for the rise of republicanism and fiery resistance to centralized authority.

In perhaps an almost natural, if not inevitable, development, American historians have long overlooked Irish contributions at the Alamo at least in part because Texas has long been perceived as more western (the Old West) than Southern. The distinguished history of the Lone Star State, especially its stirring creation story, has been long interpreted from this relatively narrow Old West perspective devoid of "Irishness." And the long-existing chauvinistic and xenophobic interpretations of traditional Texas history leave no room for the telling of the story of the culturally dissimilar, Gaelic-speaking in some cases, and ever-clannish Irish—especially Catholic Emerald Islanders.

Indeed, in a classic irony and thanks to the pervasive influence of the northeastern school of history, American historians in general have also long overlooked the depth of America's distinctive Celtic-Gaelic roots that served as a solid foundation for the resistance effort, not only in the American Revolution from 1775 to 1783, but also in the Texas Revolution from 1835-1836. Like the notable absence of the importance of Irish contributions in Texas Revolutionary historiography, so too have American historians overlooked the most distinguished early chapter of Celtic-Gaelic contributions to America's saga in regard to its own creation story, the American Revolution.

A rich Irish revolutionary heritage and tradition from the Atlantic's east side paved the way for early agitation and then open rebellion against the arbitrary rule of centralized government—first on American soil against the

British Empire (as so often on Irish soil) in 1775, and then against the Republic of Mexico sixty years later. Celtic-Gaelic revolutionary traditions, aspirations, and legacies from Ireland that fueled the nationalistic Irish Revolution of 1798 and Robert Emmet's abortive 1803 revolt (that most immediately influenced the revolutionary generation of Irish settlers in Texas) were brought to Texas from across the Atlantic as the cultural and ideological baggage of Irish immigrants.

These vibrant Irish revolutionary legacies and aspirations were faithfully resurrected by the Irish in a new land—first in America and then in Texas— to play key roles in the winning of not one but two distinct revolutionary struggles in consecutive centuries (although separated by barely half a century).

For generations, many have mistakenly viewed the Texas Revolution, including the Alamo's dramatic story, as primarily an Anglo-Saxon and Protestant struggle against Mexican Catholics, part of the much-celebrated but largely mythical "Texian Illiad" without significant Irish, and especially Catholic, antecedents and contributions. Indeed, a dark legacy of anti-Irish, anti-immigrant, and anti-Catholic sentiment has often dominated the story of America and Texas. A long host of ugly persistent racial stereotypes, long as popular with Americans as with Texans, about the alleged shortcomings of the much-maligned Irish character (drunkenness, quarrelsomeness, depravity, immorality, etc.) have denied the Irish their well-deserved place in the creation story of two independent republics.

Detested as "foreigners" as the result of a traditional xenophobia and racism that first began in America with the intolerant Puritans, the lower-class Irish immigrants led America's vanguard toward the setting sun, hacking out homes in the primeval wilderness, battling the Indians, and burying their dead family members (from disease and Indian attacks) along the way. During the colonial period, the Irish, both Catholic and Scotch-Irish, were looked upon with contempt by the refined revolutionary planter elite of English descent (and of course Protestants) of the Virginia Tidewater, including George Washington. Before the American Revolution, Washington was an established member of Virginia's upper class elite who lived like a proper English gentleman of the ruling class at stately Mount Vernon overlooking the Potomac River and the tree-lined southern Maryland shore. He was the antithesis of a lowly Irish (and especially Catholic) immigrant with little means and even fewer expectations.

The distinguished Irish contributions in the American Revolution brought little change or improvements for the Irish people in America, primarily because of prevailing anti-Irish prejudice. Deep-seated anti-Irish stereotypes were as commonplace in colonial America before during, and immediately after the American Revolution as they were on the frontier in Texas in the early 1830s. This, in turn, ensured the Emerald Islanders would win no distinguished or well-deserved place in the revolutionary annals and Texas Revolutionary memory. Besides prejudices, a host of other factors as diverse as class, race, culture, education, place of birth, and religion played roles in denying patriotic Irish proper recognition for their disproportionate contributions in the American and Texas revolutions. As noted earlier, all of this conspired to make their story one of the best remaining little-known and largely untold episodes of the Texas Revolution and the Alamo.

At long last, the well-deserving Irish patriots of Texas are placed in the forefront of the remarkable story of the birth of Texas and a common people's struggle for liberty from 1835-1836, including at the Alamo. It is one of the few untold stories of this era and place, and one of the most distinguished chapters in Texas and American history.

Chapter 1

A Natural Revolutionary Union

Second to none, the story of the bloody struggle for possession of an old Franciscan mission known as the Alamo on March 6, 1836 has become a cherished legend and a Texas and American icon. The dramatic showdown at the Alamo between the band of defenders and a formidable Mexican Army has provided one of the most celebrated chapters in American history. In addition, the 13-day siege of the Alamo has served as the very foundation of the highly-romanticized revolutionary saga known as the "Texian Iliad," as christened by at least one admiring Texas historian. But in fact, the name "Irish Odyssey" actually far better explains the course of the Texas Revolution and its Celtic-Gaelic roots and antecedents that have been long ignored.

The traditional telling of this memorable life-and-death struggle for possession of the mission, nestled in the shallow valley of the San Antonio River just outside the dusty Tejano town of San Antonio, has long overlooked the considerable ethnic contributions, as well as the extensive cultural diversity of the Alamo garrison long, and incorrectly, viewed as homogenous. In total, 15 Ireland-born Alamo defenders killed at the Alamo during Antonio Lopez de Santa Anna's surprise attack on the early morning of March 6, 1836 exceeded the number of Tejano defenders who fell. As important, these young men and boys from Ireland died beside a good many sons, grandsons, and great-grandsons of Irish immigrants, who were mostly Scotch-Irish Protestants from Ulster Province, northern Ireland. In fact, the Alamo garrison was predominantly Irish, Scotch-Irish, and Celtic—consisting of members from Wales, Scotland, Cornish (all Celtic)—and those of Anglo-Celtic descent, and whose Irish ancestors had been in America for generations.

Indeed, the Alamo's doomed garrison's mostly volunteer soldiers, who possessed scant military experience and training—a classic case of amateurs and rustics in rebellion—were made up of Celtic-Gaelic composition. Even the most famous combat unit of the Texas Revolution, the New Orleans Greys, consisted of a large percentage of Ireland-born soldiers, who had volunteered to assist the Texians in their righteous "struggle for liberty," according to one Alexandria, Louisiana journalist, including those citizen-soldiers who were killed on that cold, late-winter morning at the Alamo.

Even the Alamo's famous leadership trinity of William Barret Travis, David Crockett, and James Bowie possesed Celtic-Gaelic roots like the garrison that mostly consisted of men of either Ireland-born, Scotch-Irish, or of Scotch-Irish ancestry. These men hailed mostly from the South, a cultural and ethnic demographic that mirrored the overall dominant Southern (Celtic-Gaelic) composition of Texas Revolutionary soldiers, both the Texians and volunteers from the United States. Providing a representative example of personal Celtic and revolutionary legacies, Bowie's ancestral roots went back to fiery Scottish Jacobite rebels, who stood against England with a nationalistic and Celtic fury. Therefore, from beginning to end, the last-ditch defense in the Alamo, nestled amid the central plains dominated by Tejano ranching culture that was Mediterranean in origin and a legacy from Spain, was primarily a Celtic-Gaelic one.[1]

The disproportionate and important Irish contributions throughout the course of the Texas Revolution, including at the Alamo, should not be surprising because of not only the realities of the longtime demographics of

---

1   Grady McWhiney, *Cracker Culture, Celtic Ways in the Old South* (Tuscaloosa, AL, 1988), xiii-257; Paul D. Lack, *The Texas Revolutionary* Experience (College Station, TX, 1992), 122-123; *Arkansas Advocate*, Little Rock, Arkansas, November 20, 1835; Hardin, *Texian Illiad, A Military History of the Texas Revolution*, xiii, 138-148; Groneman, *Alamo Defenders, A Genealogy: The People And Their Words*, 4-125; William C. Davis, *Three Roads to the Alamo, The Lives and Fortunes of David Crockett, James Bowie, and William Barret Travis* (New York, NY, 1998), 9-10, 35, 194; Clifford Hopewell, *James Bowie, Texas Fighting Man* (Austin, TX, 1994), 1-2; Gary Brown, *The New Orleans Greys, Volunteers of the Texas Revolution* (Plano, TX, 1999), v-309; Edward L. Miller, *New Orleans and the Texas Revolution* (College Station, TX, 2004), 154; "The Alamo: The Irish Heroes of the Alamo, *Irish Connection* (2004), internet; *New York Times*, January 27, 1895; Mark Derr, *The Frontiersman, The Real Life and Many Legends of Davy Crockett* (New York, NY, 1993), 37.

America's western expansion and its largely Celtic-Gaelic composition, but the overall story of the Irish experience, including its role of the "westering Irishmen," in America.[2] In the words of one historian, "No larger nation did more to spark the cause of independence in America, indeed round the world," than Ireland.[3] Unfortunately, in regard to the Alamo's story, generations of Americans (including historians) relied primarily on "John Wayne [in his Cold War-inspired film The Alamo and others in Hollywood] to get it right." Instead they failed miserably, creating new falsehoods, distortions, and stereotypes to obscure the historical record.[4]

Irish immigrants and settlers were the third highest population group and the largest white ethnic group in Texas when the Texas Revolution erupted in early October 1835, comparable to numbers of overall United States settlers, who were likewise mostly of Scotch-Irish descent, and Tejanos. When combined, the number of Irish, Scotch-Irish, and those of Scotch-Irish descent—or Anglo-Celtic—made-up the vast majority of the Texas population by the time of the Texas Revolution's beginning in early October 1835. Although underestimating the overall Irish and Scotch-Irish contribution, gifted historian T. R. Fehrenbach correctly described the early fundamental make-up of the Texan people by 1836 as "Anglo-Celtic." Therefore, throughout the Texas Revolution, the self-styled "Army of the People" of Texas was thoroughly dominated by its Scotch-Irish and Irish composition, character, and flavor and until the final decisive victory was reaped by Sam Houston's forces on the sun-baked plain of San Jacinto on April 21, 1836. In the end, an Anglo-Celtic army won one of the most dramatic victories in the annals of American history at San Jacinto.

An historic Celtic-Gaelic restlessness, a burning desire to escape Old World political and economic oppressions and abusive central government, heavy taxation, high rents paid for laboring like slaves on the land of wealthy landlords, and a dreary existence as humble tenant farmers largely explained why so many Irish and the Scotch-Irish had pushed west and eventually settled in Texas by 1835—the same catalysts that led to the first exodus to America

---

2 McWhiney, *Cracker Culture*, viii-257; James Webb, *Born Fighting, How the Scots-Irish Shaped America* (New York, NY, 2004), 3-184; Irish, *The Texas* Handbook Online, internet; Myles Dugan, *How The Irish Won the West* (New York, NY, 2011), 2.

3 Walter Bryan, *The Improbable Irish* (New York, NY, 1969), 23-25.

4 Dugan, *How the Irish Won the West*, x.

from Ireland before the American Revolution. For the Scotch-Irish and their descendants who had already surged beyond the imposing forested barrier of the Appalachians, the fertile lands of Texas loomed as the enticing southwest frontier in the 1820s and 1830s. Earlier migrations spilled into the rich lands of the Ohio Valley and the Old Southwest (the Deep South), and then across the Mississippi River was only part of America's overall historic migratory process; this continued as they moved yet farther west and across the Red and Sabine Rivers, the Texas-Louisiana border, and entered Mexico's northern province of Texas

This fundamentally Scotch-Irish experience—members of the lowest class (after blacks) in American society—was rooted in the religious-like conviction the God had chosen this land specially for their own possession. The seemingly limitless natural bounty and beauty of Texas' virgin lands embodied the fulfillment of those same lofty dreams that had first inspired the relentless push of the Celtic-Gaelic people across America in successive generations.[5] In the words of one writer about the Irish: "Those who had settled in Texas a few months, really enjoy more comforts (and these, in addition to the opportunity of realizing a handsome property) than any peasantry with which I am now acquainted."[6]

In the early 1820s, Stephen Fuller Austin first settled the original "Three Hundred" norteamericanos on Texas soil. Among these first settlers in Texas were Ireland-born Humphrey and Alexander Jackson, Arthur and Peggy McCormick, a married couple, and Martin Allen. However, other Irish names among the settlers were Kelly, Fitzgerald, Callaghan, Kennedy, Lynch, Moore, Cummings, and others. Irish Protestants, perhaps even including women, were among the first schoolteachers of the children in the Austin Colony, and they played a leading role in bestowing education in this frontier setting. One of

---

5   T. R. Fehrenbach, *Lone Star, A History of Texas and the Texans* (New York, NY, 2000), 81-92; Moore, *Eighteen Minutes: The Battle of San Jacinto and the Texas Independence Campaign*, 435-462; Graham Davis, *Land!, Irish Pioneers in Mexican and Revolutionary Texas* (College Station, TX, 2002), 3-257; Webb, *Born Fighting*, xii-184; James Leyburn, *The Scotch-Irish, A Social History* (Chapel Hill, NC, 1962), xi-316; Marshall, *Uniforms of the Alamo and the Texas Revolution, 1835-1836*, 13; Mark Mayo Boatner, III, *The Dictionary of the American Revolution* (New York, NY, 1966), 620-632; "The Alamo: Irish Heroes of the Alamo," *IC*, internet; McWhiney, *Cracker Culture*, xiii-257; Irish, The Texas Handbook Online, internet.

6   *Commercial Bulletin and Missouri Literary Register*, St. Louis, Missouri, June 15, 1835.

these Irish schoolteachers, a man named Cummins, would later be killed in battling Mexicans who threatened the life of Texas.[7]

But the vast majority of Irish in Texas were never settlers of the Austin Colony, coming to Texas as either individuals or in like-minded groups. John Joseph Linn was one of the early pioneers of Texas, and an early soldier of the Texas Revolution. In his own words that revealed pride of ancestry, he "was born in the county of Antrim, Ireland, on the 19th day of June, A.D., 1798."[8] Like so many Irish, Linn fell in love with Texas, describing the land as a "garden in the wilds of nature . . . a terrestrial paradise."[9]

Thanks in part to the influence and sound advice of another County Antrim emigrant, early Texas trader and War of 1812 veteran John McHenry, Linn became a successful trader on the sprawling Gulf of Mexico coastal plain. With merchandise from New Orleans, the enterprising Irishman, who had learned to speak Spanish, traded with local Tejanos and also journeyed to Mexico to trade. Later joined by his two Ireland-born brothers, Linn also brought his parents to Victoria, Texas during the spring of 1831, where he made his new home.[10] Victoria evolved into a thriving Irish community by the time of the Texas Revolution. The call to arms resulted in the Victoria Irish playing distinguished roles, with "every man going who could shoulder a gun."[11]

More importantly, Linn represented the Irish community of Victoria (formerly Guadalupe Victoria) as a delegate of the revolutionary assembly known as the General Consultation (formed in early November 1835), which, in his words, was the "first organized movement in Texas in opposition to the despotic measure pursued by [Antonio Lopez de] Santa Anna. " He then represented the same community (along with other Ireland-born representatives like James Power and John Malone of the Refugio Colony) when the Texas provisional government was organized from the Consultation.[12]

7   John Brendan Flannery, *The Irish Texans* (San Antonio, TX, 1995), 25-26.

8   John J. Linn, *Reminiscences of Fifty Years in Texas* (Austin, TX,1986),

9   Ibid., 23.

10 Ibid., 10-13, 24; McHenry, John, The Handbook of Texas Online.

11 Linn, *Reminiscences of Fifty Years in Texas*, 12-14, 56; Flannery, *The Irish Texans*, 91.

12 Linn, *Reminiscences of Fifty Years in Texas*, 44.

In fact, Irish calls for independence predated the Consultation. Patrick Usher, an immigrant from County Cork, Munster Province, in the south of Ireland, who was destined to fight at the battle of San Jacinto, issued a call for independence from Mexico as early as July 17, 1835, galvanizing the people of Lavaca Navidad.[13]

Other groups of Irish settlers found their dreams coming true in Texas on the fertile lands near the Brazos River west of the Guadalupe River, both of which flowed lazily southeastward into the Gulf of Mexico, in an Irish community named Staggers Point. Established as an "Irish town" in 1833, the town's name was based on the word "striver," which alluded to the Irish settler's sense of determination to conquer the land and succeed. Here, in a pretty wooded tract that looked more like the Deep South lands from which they had departed, these pioneers created their own Scotch-Irish community, with migrants arriving from 1829 to 1834. A dozen years before 1829, eight Scotch-Irish families originally had departed Ulster Province and settled in South Carolina. They then moved on to Alabama, before making Staggers Point their permanent home. To fend off Indians, Ireland-born James Dunn and his fellow Emerald Islanders built a fort for protection, even before they constructed their small Presbyterian Church.

The Irish prudence paid dividends because the Scotch-Irish settlers, such as the McMillan, Dunn, Henry, Scale, Dixon, Payton, Henry, Seale, and Fullerton families, were threatened from the beginning. The most devastating Indian attack came in 1839. The shedding of Irish blood caused the Scotch-Irish, under the command of Ireland-born Benjamin Bryant, to grab rifles, shotguns, and muskets and set off in pursuit of the raiders. However, the eagerness of the Scotch-Irish to strike back led them directly into an ambush. While the Texas frontier would prove to be a harsh land won by force against both the elements and the Indians, the overall experience in battling Indians was put to good use by these Scotch-Irish in 1835-1836. Among Sam Houston's men at San Jacinto were Staggers Point settlers, led by Bryant, who served with distinction as a captain. The well-armed Irish of Stagger Point, like those across Texas, knew how to defend themselves and to live off the land by the ancient ways of the Fiacra (Gaelic), or Hunter.[14]

---

13 Flannery, *The Irish Texans*, 133.

14 Linn, *Reminiscences of Fifty Years in Texas*, 222; Flannery, *The Irish Texans*, 12, 26-27; Owen B. Hunt, *The Irish and the American Revolution: Three Essays* (Philadelphia: PA, 1976), 22.

Located on Aransas Creek, the town of Corrigan (in today's southern Bee County, Texas) was established by Irish immigrants Jeremiah O'Toole and James O'Reilly in 1835. O'Toole migrated from Ireland and journeyed to New York City in 1825. Four years later, O'Toole brought his family to Texas aboard the *New Packet*, and embarked upon a new life on the southwest frontier.[15]

When the sophisticated Colonel Juan Nepomuceno Almonte, educated by scholars at a fine Jesuit Catholic school in New Orleans, Louisiana, was dispatched by the Mexican government on a secret expedition to inspect Texas in 1834, he found the land not only teeming with norteamericano settlers of Celtic descent, but also Irish immigrants. He was pleased to report that two of the colonies—those of John McMullen and Martin de Leon—had "progressed the most" and consisted "of Irish and Mexicans."[16]

But Almonte also discovered a nascent Irish revolutionary ferment, especially in the form of Father Michael (Miguel) Muldoon, who was born around 1780 in County Cavan, in north central Ireland, Ulster Province. He was the son of an Irishman who had earlier fled the Emerald Isle, perhaps for revolutionary reasons, for Spain, where he married a Spanish woman. Here, at the Irish College in Seville, Spain, the younger Muldoon was ordained and entered the priesthood. However, he was not content to remain in Europe and requested transfer to the New World, where he became the chaplain to the New Spain's last viceroy, Irishman John O'Donoghue. Then, in the early 1830s, Muldoon obtained a transfer to the northern frontier of the new Republic of Mexico, which won independence from Spain in 1821: Texas.

Muldoon was not only the parish priest of the Stephen Fuller Austin Colony, at the capital of San Felipe de Austin, but also the vicar general of all foreign colonies on Texas soil. He was the only priest assigned to administer to the non-Latino settlers. Jovial, lively, and fun-loving, the Irishman was not only well-liked but also respected by the mostly Protestant settlers. In fact, he bonded with them far too closely, identifying with their freedom-loving and revolutionary inclinations. As early as 1832, the good Irish priest was siding with the norteamericanos, drafting in Spanish their 1832 protests that were sent to Mexico City against the recently established customs house at Anahuac on Trinity Bay. Almonte penned about what he saw and learned: "In this capital,

---

15 Corrigan, TX (Bee County), The Handbook of Texas Online.

16 Jack Jackson, ed., *Almonte's Texas, Juan N. Almonte's 1834 Inspection, Secret Report and Role in the 1836 Campaign* (Austin, TX, 2005), 224-225.

there is also an Irish priest who came to this country [and] is making many efforts for the separation of Texas" from Mexico.[17]

However, other Protestants in the Austin Colony were less than receptive to the concept of a Catholic priest. A young North Carolina-born settler, who migrated to Texas in 1827, Noah Smithwick was one such opinionated individual, although his reminiscences and memory are suspect because they came more than a half century after the Texas Revolution's conclusion. Of Scotch-Irish descent and a Protestant, Smithwick based his description on the usual negative Irish stereotypes, describing "Padre Muldoon" as "a bigoted old Irishman, with an unlimited capacity for drink."[18]

Unfortunately, Smithwick's views about Irish, Catholics, and priests were only too common among the Protestant Anglo-Celts (at least before Father Muldoon changed their minds with his winning ways), who generally looked upon Irish Catholics with disdain, and inherited their ancient prejudices from those before. After all, Father Muldoon was a Texas patriot and most sympathetic to the hard-working settlers so far from their own native homeland like himself. After the Texas Revolution, the good priest spent the rest of his life in an independent Texas that he had helped to create.[19]

Like others, this dynamic revolutionary Irish man of God had merely continued the dual traditional role of priest and warrior, including those who led Irish fighting men into the heat of battle. During the Great Irish Rebellion of 1798, which was partly inspired by the American Revolution, Father John Murphy led a "huge popular uprising" in County Wexford that was as much religious crusade as a revolution. In addition, Father Michael Murphy led another contingent of liberty-loving Irish rebels from County Wexfordi n bold offensive operations carrying green battle-flags emblazoned with the words "Liberty or Death." In encouraging a headlong charge against a row of British cannon at Arklow, Ireland, Father Michael Murphy was killed before his followers.[20]

---

17 Jackson, ed., *Almonte's Texas*, 216, 262-263; Flannery, *The Irish Texans*, 21-26; Muldoon, Michael, The Handbook of Texas Online.

18 Noah Smithwick, *The Evolution of a State* (Austin, TX, 1983), xiii, 46.

19 12 Irish Texans, Institute of Texan Cultures, San Antonio, Texas.

20 Michael Kenny, *The 1798 Rebellion, Photographs and Memorabilia from the National Museum of Ireland* (Dublin, Ireland, 1996), 5-6, 25, 38-39; A. T. Q., *The Summer Soldiers, The 1798 Rebellion in Antrim and Down* (Belfast, Ireland, 1996), 59.

Before the Rebellion of 1798 was crushed, the Irish revolutionaries under such fiery priests sang nationalist songs like The Wearin' of the Green, which offered solace if defeated: "I've heard whisper of a county that lies beyond the sea, Where rich and poor stand equal in the light of freedom's day, Oh Erin, must we leave you, driven by a tyrant's hand?"[21] Clearly, the Irish revolutionary experience on the Green Isle was a searing one for the average Irishman. Andrew Jackson has proved a notable example of this phenomenon. Engendering a lifelong hatred of the British, which was only natural for the son of an Irish immigrant from Ulster Province, northern Ireland, who migrated to the South Carolina Piedmont, President Jackson was early shaped by the trauma of the Irish experience. His own "grandfather fell at the siege of Carrickfergus [in County Antrim], a victim of the progress of British aggression" and imperialism.[22]

Northern Ireland-born John Joseph Linn explained the significance of the bitter Irish revolutionary experience—not in Texas, but in Ireland—and one that predated the Rebellion of 1798 by centuries. He wrote how his "ancestors incurred the displease of [Oliver] Cromwell, and were summarily dispossessed of their landed estates and forced to pay an alien [English] landlord rent for the occupation of a few of their patrimonial acres [and my] father, John Linn, of course identified himself with the patriotic movement and acted as a member of the 'United Irish' brotherhood of 1798." Then, he continued, "Despairing of success for the patriots, and detesting the tyrannous misrule of the English, he, with his wife and one child [John Joseph Linn] took passage on a ship bound for New York . . . Several years were spent in that city, and fourteen subsequent years in Dutchess County of that State, when the family again returned to New York City."[23]

Likewise, because of the dark legacies and never-forgotten lessons of the traumatic Irish experience, Ireland-born Thomas John O'Brien, from County Wexford, Ireland, and a member of the Irish Refugio Colony, was one of the youngest volunteers who fought for the great dream of Texas Independence.

21 Danny Doyle and Terence Folan, *The Gold Sun of Irish Freedom, 1798 in Song and Story* (Boulder, CO,, 1998), 20.

22 McWhiney, *Cracker Culture*, 35; Lalor, ed., *The Encyclopedia of Ireland*, 160-161; Robert V. Remini, *Andrew Jackson and His Indian Wars* (New York, NY, 2002), 7-9.

23 Linn, *Reminiscences of Fifty Years in Texas*, 9-10.

He was age thirteen and already a soldier when the Texians, including many Irish, captured Goliad in November 1835.[24]

With so many natural revolutionaries, both Ireland-born and those of Irish descent, in Texas, Mexican military leaders and officials grew increasingly worried and for good reason. Fearing for the future of Texas within the Mexican republic, an astounded Almonte warned his government of the warlike qualities of the hardy Anglo-Celts, including the Scotch-Irish, who were so unlike Mexicans and Tejanos: "The rooms of the colonists do not feature saints [as in Tejano and Mexican homes], but their place is taken by rifles, sabers, and pistols. Each colonist is a general in his house. All of his dependents, including the women, handle weapons with skill, and it would take an army to dislodge them" from Texas soil.[25] This was no exaggeration by an astute military man. After migrating to Texas in 1829, Ireland-born John Joseph Linn was soon able to hit a bull's eye at 200 yards with well-aimed fire from his trusty flintlock musket. In fact, Linn's skill was sufficient for him to demonstrate his uncanny accuracy in ad hoc firing exhibitions that amazed onlookers far and wide.[26]

What Colonel Almonte reported to Mexico City was a merely fact-of-life about the Celtic settlers, which was learned the hard way by the British Government during the American Revolution, when tens of thousands Irish and Scotch-Irish served the cause of liberty. By any measure and especially in regard to combativeness, those settlers of Celtic descent were no ordinary people who could be bullied, threatened, or easily pushed aside. After all, the people of Ireland, Scotland, and Wales were descendants of the ancient Celtics, embodying a distinctive "Celtic character." A well-known fighting prowess of the ancient Celts of Europe had early won the respect of first the ancient Greeks and then the Romans, including the well-trained legionnaires, who faced their fierce headlong charges and called them Gauls. However, in the language of this much-feared warrior society—that wandered as much as its men fought—they called themselves Celts.[27]

24 Flannery, *The Irish Texans*, 49, 71.

25 Jackson, ed., *Almonte's Texas*, 264; Irish Texans, Texas Almanac, Texas State Historical Association, internet.

26 Linn, *Reminiscences of Fifty Years in Texas*, 34.

27 Barry Cunliffe, *The Ancient Celts* (Oxford, NY, 1997), 1-2, 20; Hunt, *The Irish and the American Revolution*, 1-101.

This woodcut shows impoverished Irish immigrants living in squalid conditions in a cold winter cellar at the infamous Five Points, lower Manhattan Island, New York City. *Author's Collection*

Historically, the ancient Celtic fighting man—long-haired, generally tall when compared to the Romans, and extensively tattooed), had early acquired well-founded reputations as "wild fearless warriors, irrationally brave [especially] in the first onslaught," who were "easily roused to battle fury," in Europe. As the Roman Legions learned the hard way, the Celt's greatest skill in the art of war was the tactical offensive, often launched as sharp surprise attacks or ambushes.[28]

The Celtic warrior was the ideal, consummate fighting man, as the "whole race [was] madly fond of war, high spirited and quick to battle," wrote one contemporary, especially against invaders. Therefore, it was all but inevitable that the historic "cultural conflict between English and Celt not only continued in British North America," [but] "shaped the history of the United States." The consequence, in the estimation of a distinguished scholar of the Irish experience, Jay P. Dolan, was that "as many as one third of the Continental Army was Irish" during the American Revolution.[29]

28 Cunliffe, *The Ancient Celts*, 5-6, 10, 103.

29 Jay P. Dolan, *The Irish Americans, A History* (New York, NY, 2008), 22.

This early, disproportionate Celtic-Gaelic presence in the foremost ranks of revolutionary agitation and wartime activities applied as thoroughly to the American Revolution as the Texas Revolution; the Celtic, Gaelic-Celtic, and Scotch-Irish people shaped the very essence and character of the early settlement and history of Texas, especially in regard to independence. As during the American Revolution, this widespread Irish participation in the Texas Revolution developed primarily from the lengthy military and political tradition of so many earlier Irish revolts against the British conquers and occupiers of Ireland: a bitter struggle that had always ended in defeat and exile for Irish rebels, who failed to establish their own independent nation.

Under the threat of a centralized, arbitrary government, this spirited response was a natural, if not inevitable, development on Texas soil because these native Irish—who possessed a distinctive Catholic military tradition—and Scotch-Irish—who possessed a distinctive Protestant military tradition—had been America's original rebels and revolutionaries long before ever reaching her shores. In this sense, the Texas Revolution was little more than a repeat performance of the Sons of Erin in America's earlier struggle for independence.

Indeed, as part of their unique cultural baggage that was decidedly anti-central government, those migrating Irish brought heightened attitudes of an open defiance and a martial spirit, including traditional warrior virtues, that had been long highly revered in Celtic-Gaelic culture. These characteristics included well-honed skills of guerrilla fighting, a propensity for political agitation against abusive authority (especially the British on both sides of the Atlantic), a cultural inclination to engage in armed conflict and even a distinctive, well-known propensity for taking the tactical offensive. This was exhibited during the battle of San Jacinto in April 1836 when more than 100 Ireland-born soldiers served in Houston's ranks. These distinct Celtic-Gaelic qualities were directed not only against the initial English conquest, but also against the ruling British and their Anglo-Irish elite in Ireland—militant paramilitary organizations like the Steel Boys, Oak Boys, and Peep of Day Boys, who defended Protestant interests—and their equally militant counterparts known as the Catholic Defenders in the early 1770s.

The Irish people possessed cultural characteristics that inspired them and made them generally more responsive to the appeals of the highest and noble motivations, either patriotic or in regard to social and religious sentiments: ingredients that made for early political agitation in peacetime and a determined moral soldiery in wartime, which fueled their combat prowess in battles on both their home soil and across the Atlantic. And in 1835 and 1836, all of these unique qualities, characteristics, and tendencies of this distinctive Celtic-Gaelic people were directed against the invading Mexican Army.

Additionally, the Irish people, who had been frontiersmen and borderers for generations before coming to America's shores, had been long seemingly made for war against arbitrary, upper class rule and dictatorial dictates from the elite. Especially after hundreds of years of England's subjugation and occupation of their island homeland, the Irishman early made for the ideal revolutionary. Throughout the course of history, the Irish people had fought and defended their beloved isle against one invader after another, who crossed the seas with conquest in mind. The earliest invasions began with the Vikings, who were defeated at the battle of Clontarf, Ireland, by the united Gaelic clans led by King Brian Boru in 1014, and then later by the relentless English who succeeded in their imperialist venture.

This enduring legacy of battling invaders and oppressors—practically a way of life for the Irish for generations—was faithfully continued by Ireland-born soldiers and men of Irish descent on the Atlantic's other side, from the battles of Lexington, Massachusetts to the bloody showdown at the Alamo. Besides a militant culture and lingering warrior ethos, even the cherished religious faith of the native Irish reinforced a host of deep-seated martial values and virtues of a traditional warrior society.

Just as recently, newly discovered primary evidence reveals that a far larger percentage of Irish served in Washington's Continental Army during key times of the American Revolution than previously believed by American historians, the dramatic story of the Alamo and the Texas Revolution cannot be fully understood without appreciating and understanding the long-overlooked nature, complexities, and nuisances of the Irish experience, in both Ireland and Texas. And just as America today owes more to Ireland and thousands of her patriotic sons for the ultimate success of the American Revolution than any other European country (save perhaps France), so the same appreciation for the winning of independence also applies to the Irish in regard to the Texas Revolution.

The Irish who had migrated to America's shores from Ireland before the American Revolution drew upon the earlier revolutionary experiences, like David Crockett's father, John, who served with John Sevier's Tennessee Long Rifle-toting, buckskin-wearing volunteers (long-haired and looking more like Indians than white men); these men were from the Appalachian's west side—today's west Tennessee and Kentucky—and helped to defeat Major Patrick

Ferguson's Loyalists on the densely wooded hillsides of Kings Mountain, in the South Carolina Piedmont, October 7, 1780. They won the most surprising victory of the American Revolution at Kings Mountain, and were mostly citizen-soldiers with "recent immigrant roots" from Ireland.

Without orders and authority, the Celtic-Gaelic clans, experienced in Indian fighting, made up a sort of "shadow army" that emerged like magic from the wilderness and unleashed a masterful preemptive strike that destroyed the Loyalist force. In addition to the Pennsylvania Long Rifle, the western frontier victors were primarily armed with the lethal Dickert flintlock rifle, and one weapon found inside the Alamo after its fall was a well-crafted Dickert rifle.

As demonstrated by the amazing victory at Kings Mountain—which helped turn the tide and paved the way for the final British and Hessian defeat at the little tobacco port of Yorktown, Virginia in October 1781—the Irish and Scotch-Irish understood the necessity of standing up and fighting for their God-given and natural rights (without ever having read a word from Tom Paine's *Common Sense*). This was especially true in regard to resisting foreign invaders, like their nationalistic ancestors had done against British troops in both Ireland and in America.[30]

But it was far more than Irish "Texians" who came forth from scattered settlements to defend their adopted homeland. By 1836, the Texas Revolutionary Army drew its primary manpower from a sizeable "little

30 Thomas Bartlett and Keith Jeffery, *A Military History of Ireland* (Cambridge, MA,1996), 1-373;Webb, *Born Fighting*, 9-184; Buddy Levy, *American Legend, The Real-Life Adventures of David Crockett* (New York, NY, 2005), 5-8; Linn, *Reminiscences of Fifty Years in Texas*, 9-10, 41-44; Derr, *The Frontiersman*, 39-40; James Haltigan, *The Irish in the American Revolution and their Early Influence in the Colonies* (Washington, D.C., 1908), 9-619; Charles Murphy, *The Irish in the American Revolution* (Groveland, MA, 1975), 1-99; Davis, *Land!*, 3-257; Moore, *Eighteen Minutes*, 435-462; Hunt, *The Irish and the American Revolution,* , vii-101; Irish Texans, Texas Almanac, Texas State Historical Association, internet; Thomas Fleming, *Washington's Secret War, A Hidden History of Valley Forge* (New York, NY, 2005), 140-142; James K. Swisher, *The Revolutionary War* in *the Southern Back Country* (Gretna, LA: Pelican Publishing, 2008), 211-241; David Nevin, *The Texans* (New York: Time-Life Books, 1975), 84-85; Dolan, *The Irish Americans*, 22; Groneman, *Alamo Defenders*, 136, 143; McWhiney and Jamieson, *Attack and Die: Civil War Military Tactics and the Southern Heritage*, 172-190; Jackson, ed., *Almonte's Texas*, 216; Wallace Nutting, *Ireland Beautiful* (New York, NY, 1975), 62, 265; David Noel Doyle, *Ireland, Irishmen and Revolutionary America* (Dublin, Ireland, 1981), xv-151; Terry Golway, *For the Cause of Liberty, A Thousand Years of Ireland's Heroes* (New York, NY, 2000), 9-34; Billy Kennedy, *The Scots-Irish in the Hills of Tennessee* (Greenville, SC, 1995), 29-30, 43-57; Terry Golway, *For the Cause of Liberty, A Thousand Years of Ireland's Heroes* (New York, NY, 2000), 9-92; Moore, *Eighteen Minutes*, 435-462; "The Alamo: The Irish Heroes of the Alamo," *IC*, internet; R. F. Foster, editor, *The Oxford History of Ireland* (Oxford, NY, 1992), 97-155; McWhiney, *Cracker Culture*, xiii-257.

Ireland," located in the South's largest city and the closest major American city to east Texas: New Orleans, Louisiana. Multicultural New Orleans contained the South's largest Irish population and was second only to New York City as "the Irish capital" in the 1830s. The Southern city replaced Philadelphia, the gateway of generations of Irish immigrants long before the American Revolution, and an estimated 20,000 Irish immigrants poured into Louisiana, mostly by way of New Orleans, in 1836.

Further, a good many Irish migrants continued west for the greener pastures of Texas and to escape the urban ghettos. In a Celtic-Gaelic exodus, the Irish journeyed to Texas by foot, horseback, and wagon, following their hopes, dreams, and prayers. Other Irish, especially immigrants, purchased cheap deck space on the many merchant ships that plied the waters between the east Texas settlements and New Orleans, which was the Texans' primary trading partner over Mexico City; this was to be an ominous economic and commercial development for Mexico that helped to set the stage for political maturation among the Texians. Many Irish immigrants from New Orleans found employment as common laborers on Texas soil, before the Texas Revolution made them soldiers in a struggle for liberty.[31]

As explained in an article published in the *New York Sun*, during the spring of 1836 "[t]he enthusiasm in New Orleans in behalf of the Texians, is said to be so great that the city resembles a military barracks [and] crowds of volunteers were every day marching to their aid."[32] But this enthusiasm for Texas came at a high price for many Irish. Ireland-born John Joseph Linn described the sad fate of a boatload of immigrant Irish of the Refugio Colony in the spring of 1834: "The cholera here [at Aransas Pass, where they landed] broke out among the colonists in an epidemic form, and many of the unhappy people died ere transportation could be procured to convey them" to the colony.[33]

In a striking paradox, while the dominance of Celtic-Gaelic roots in America's westward expansion and in frontier and Southern society have been written about extensively and generally accepted by American and Irish historians, this same historical, demographic, and ethnic interpretation has not

31 David T. Gleeson, *The Irish in the South, 1815-1877* (Chapel Hill, NC, 2001), 14-34; Alan Barber, *David Kokernot, Rogue Soldier of the Texas Revolution* (Sandpoint, ID, 2012), 48; Dolan, *The Irish Americans*, x, 38-39.

32 *New York Sun*, New York, April 14, 1836.

33 Linn, *Reminiscences of Fifty Years in Texas*, 32.

been similarly applied in regard to the Texas Revolution.[34] The Celtic antecedents and revolutionary traditions of the common people rising up against abusive centralized authority, especially the wars for Scottish independence, was most popularly represented in the collective memory of Scottish nationalist and revolutionary William Wallace (Braveheart), who was one of the first Celtic commoners in Western history to lead a modern national liberation movement, and Rob Roy, who was a Celtic ancestor of Jim Bowie and Jacobite rebel leader.

The glorification and romanticization of traditional Texas heroes and the overall history of the Texas Revolution from 1835-1836 have played a large role in ensuring that the Celtic-Gaelic roots, connections, and influences have gone unrecognized to this day, even though the Texans shared these same distinctive Celtic cultural qualities that applied to the South. For instance, more emphasis has been placed by historians on biased Protestant Texian accounts—both during and after the war—which exaggerated the alleged traitorous roles of Irish Catholics instead of telling the story of their important contributions. This included the mostly Irish and Scotch-Irish soldiers and many recent immigrants who declared the first Declaration of Independence and raised the first banner of independence during the Texas Revolution, "the Irish flag," at Goliad in December 1835. Most importantly, this declaration came months before the official Texas Declaration of Independence in early March 1836.

Although the author himself was of Celtic heritage, Archie P. McDonald's *William Barret Travis*, the first modern biography of the Alamo's most famous commander, made no mention of Travis's Scotch-Irish roots. In truth, this glaring omission has only mirrored the long-existing tradition of American and Texan historians ignoring the most dominant demographic and ethnic group of the Alamo garrison and even its primary leaders in what was the ultimate irony.

The Texas Revolution's participants were distinguished by the thoroughness of their Celtic-Gaelic and Irish composition and their very Irishness in terms of overall contributions at every level in the resistance effort: militarily, economically, and politically. Unlike United States volunteers of Anglo-Saxon descent who benefitted from the most successful democratic experiment in their day, the Ireland-born settlers in Texas were the cultural heirs of a vastly different, contrarian experience that was distinctly un-American. The Celtic people, especially those of Scotland and Ireland, had

34 McWhiney, *Crack Culture*, xiii-271; Webb, *Born Fighting*, 3-184.

long known and experienced a lengthy history of defeats, massacres, conquests, and humiliations at England's imperialistic and often utterly ruthless hands.

With relatively few means upon first migrating to America's shores, the lower class Irish, especially Catholics, journeyed to the meadows, rolling hills, and pine forests of east Texas and the grassy expanse of the Gulf Coastal Plain to escape the injustices of an Old World feudal-like and manorial system that had dominated life in Ireland for generations. Meanwhile, middle-class Irish Protestants, who had witnessed discrimination in their own country, but who were generally less oppressed than Catholics sought to substantially improve their lot in life by gaining a large amount of Texas land.

Ireland-born, particularly Catholic, immigrants who journeyed to Texas hailed from an oppressed, agrarian society dominated by an exploitative system of large, wealthy landowners, who were either British or Anglo-Irish. These native Irish were mostly landless peasants trapped since the establishment of the discriminatory Penal Laws, enduring a thorough exploitation at every level. Here, on Ireland's green fields and valleys of counties such as Kerry, Cork, and Antrim they labored as lowly tenant farmers for large landholders, who lived like feudal lords. In systematic fashion, Ireland's conquerors had earlier stripped the native people of their ancestral lands. This ensured that England grew more prosperous from the massive imports of what this fertile land produced, while the Irish people often went without in times of famine. Blessed by nature but cursed by geography, perhaps Ireland's greatest misfortune was to have been located too close to imperialistic England. Ireland's tragic history was rooted in the longtime cultural and religious differences between the native Irish Catholics and the British Protestant occupiers. Quite unlike the transplanted American settlers who shared a successful revolutionary experience during the American Revolution, the Irish understood more intimately what it meant to be on the losing end of a cultural, social, and revolutionary struggle against a powerful opponent bent on complete subjugation. Consequently, the lessons of Irish history were not forgotten by the Irish, Scotch-Irish, and Celtic-Gaelic descendants of Texas, and remained at the ideological, emotional, and psychological forefront. These lessons now applied seamlessly to political developments in a new land against a new opponent in 1835-1836, when the Irish revolutionary experience was resurrected on Texas soil. These hardy Celtic-Gaelic settlers of Texas had already learned some hard lessons about what was necessary for survival, such as a readiness for conflict against a superior opponent, and that the aggressive transgressions of a foreign power should be met early with sufficient force.

Otherwise, Texas would suffer tragic Ireland's fate of total subjugation, if they did not early take up arms to defend themselves against the threat posed by Mexico.[35]

Born in the same year as the great Irish Revolution of 1798, County Antrim-born John McHenry, who went to sea at age thirteen before settling in New Orleans—which he defended in gunboat service during the War of 1812—was one of the first native Irish warriors in Texas to take up arms in the armed clash of the Texas Revolution at Gonzales, Texas.[36] McHenry's friend, John Joseph Linn, also from County Antrim, early learned the bitter lessons of the Irish revolutionary experience not only from his exiled father but also from other Ireland-born "refugees from British tyranny," including top revolutionary leaders, just before migrating to Texas.[37]

As England had long ago stripped Ireland's native Catholic people of their lands, fortunes, and futures, so General Antonio Lopez de Santa Anna (Perez de Lebron), Mexico's centralist president—who scrapped the liberal 1824 Constitution and emerged as a reactionary conservative with dictatorial power—had embraced an ambitious plan for the reconquest of Texas by late 1835. To some Irish settlers in Texas, Santa Anna's ambitions seemed comparable to the British imperial strategy for Ireland's complete subjugation (1653) at the brutal hands of Cromwell's Puritan holy warriors, who became expert in the merciless art of slaughtering Irish Catholics, because, he said, "this is the righteous judgment of God upon these barbarous wretches." With the sword he spread

35 Fleming, *Washington's Secret War*, 140-142; Murphy, *The Irish in the American Revolution*, 1-103; Haltigan, *The Irish in the American Revolution*, 9-619; Michael J. O'Brien, *A Hidden Phase of American History, Ireland's Part in America's Struggle for Liberty* (New York, NY, 1920), 1-392; Davis, *Land!*, 3-257; McWhiney and Jamieson, *Attack and Die*, 172-190; Bartlett and Jeffery, *A Military History of Ireland*, 1-373; Doyle, *Ireland, Irishmen and Revolutionary America*, xv-151; Phillip Thomas Tucker, *The Important Role of the Irish in the American Revolution* (Bowie, MD, 2009), 9-138; James MacKay, *William Wallace, Braveheart* (Edinburgh, Scotland, 1995), 9-268; Arthur Herman, *How the Scots Saved the Modern World* (New York, NY, 2001), 15-319; Webb, *Born Fighting*, 42-54, 67-101; Archie P. McDonald, *William Barret Travis, A Biography* (Austin, TX, 1995), 21-26; Kennedy, *Scots-Irish in the Hills of Tennessee*, 19-26; Clifford Hopewell, *James Bowie, Texas Fighting Man* (Austin, TX, 1994), 1; Hardin, *Texian Illiad*, 45; Groneman, *Alamo Defenders*, 3-123; Moore, *Eighteen Minutes*, 435-462; *New York Times*, January 27, 1895; "The Alamo: The Irish Heroes of the Alamo," *IC*, internet; Foster, ed., *The Oxford History of Ireland*, 153; McWhiney, *Cracker Culture*, xiii-257; Derr, *The Frontiersman*, 37-40.

36 McHenry, John, The Handbook of Texas Online.

37 Linn, *Reminiscences of Fifty Years in Texas*, 9-10, 12.

Protestantism and ethnic cleansing across Ireland, in the form of a bloody Protestant crusade

Like Cromwell's righteous wrath and to regain possession of its fertile northern province, so Santa Anna planned to accomplish much the same in Texas by driving Anglo-Celtic settlers from Texas's borders by early 1836. Then he planned to resettle this bountiful province with Mexican citizens in what was an old imperialistic formula of ethnic cleansing, just as Ireland had experienced.[38]

Therefore, Georgia-born Colonel James Walker Fannin's mostly Anglo-Celtic and Protestant volunteers, especially Scotch-Irish of the Presbyterian faith, took up arms against Mexico in what they considered a "holy crusade against priestly tyranny and military despotism." Such were the words of Captain John Sowers Brooks, one of the few revolutionaries who possessed United States Marine Corps experience. Killed in the Goliad Massacre on Palm Sunday 1836, upon Santa Anna's orders, the promising, red-haired captain from Virginia served as Fannin's trusty aide-de-camp until captured with the entire command, then executed. Indeed, in the war's beginning in October 1835, militant Texian leaders of the Protestant faith rallied the colonists by simplifying the situation in basic terms, portraying a radical Catholic threat, including the "priest-ridden military despots" lusting to destroy "the lives of unoffending but liberty-loving settlers."[39] Before Fannin's men, divided in four groups, were systematically killed on the open prairie outside Goliad, some Anglo-Celtic prisoners, mostly from the South, shouted in typical Celtic defiance when facing the rows of blazing muskets turned so suddenly upon them, "The Republic of Texas forever!," and, "If we have to die, let's die like brave men!"[40]

---

38 Robert L. Scheina, *Santa Anna, A Curse upon Mexico* (Washington, D.C., 2002), 26-31; Webb, *Born Fighting*, 67-184; Maire O'Brien and Conor Cruise O'Brien, *A Concise History of Ireland* (New York. 1972), 32-69; Hardin, *Texian Illiad*, 5-19; Antonia Fraser, *Cromwell, The Lord Protector* (New York, NY, 1973), 326.

39 Walraven and Walraven, *The Magnificent Barbarians, Little Told Tales of the Texas Revolution*, 90-91; Lack, *The Texas Revolutionary Experience*, 208; Stout, *Slaughter at Goliad*, 41-207.

40 Jakie L Pruett and Everett B. Cole, Jr., *Goliad Massacre, A Tragedy of the Texas Revolution* (Austin, TX, 1985), 97-120; Stout, *Slaughter at Goliad*, 41-58, 174-187; McWhiney and Jamieson, *Attack and Die*, 172-178; James Donovan, *The Blood of Heroes, The 13-Day Struggle for the Alamo and the Sacrifice that Forged a Nation* (New York, NY, 2012), 317.

The dual tragedies of the Alamo and Goliad, within a span of only three weeks in the bloodiest March in Texas history, had been earlier predicted by an insightful journalist of a Lynchburg, Texas, newspaper. On September 8, 1835, and even before the Texas Revolution's beginning, the editor warned that Mexico planned to send a mighty army north "to turn out the Protestants and establish the Roman Catholic Religion."[41] Guaranteed to get a quick response, this emotional appeal especially stirred the mostly Presbyterian Scotch-Irish settlers and their descendants across Texas, partly because of an historical anti-Catholic legacy extending back to the French and Indian War, in which British colonists fought French and Canadian Catholics and their Catholicized Indian allies.

Additionally, many Irish who battled on behalf of Texas independence defied Santa Anna's political designs of reuniting his self-destructing mixed-race nation, now ravished by a civil war's horrors because of the backlash from supporters of the liberal 1824 Constitution. Overall, the threat of military despotism from "foreign" troops dispatched to Texas from Mexico City by the "Usurper" caused the Irish, both Protestant and Catholic, to rise up in October 1835 when the Texas Revolution began, just as the threat of British troops had sparked a comparable gathering of rebellious Celtic-Gaelic clans in the thirteen colonies in April 1775.

For the Irish Protestants, the Texas Revolution closely resembled a religious war. This was true, at least in part, because Texas revolutionary leaders thoroughly exploited differences in religion to rally supporters and galvanize people to take up arms. Educated men who knew their audiences well, these men in leadership positions naturally drew upon historic animosities that had existed for centuries, and which had fueled religious passions and wars across much of Europe.

As a result, during the fall of 1835, the Protestant Scotch-Irish settlers rose up in revolt so that they would not be dominated by a military government, as well as an ecclesiastical-based government of a different faith—the much-feared "iron arm of Catholicism," as one alarmed Baptist preacher wrote. After all, their own Scotch-Irish ancestors had departed northern Ireland and migrated to America as "dissenters," who defied the Anglican Church of England, whose branch in Ireland was the Church of Ireland, in order to worship Presbyterianism in the new land as they pleased. By the mid-1830s,

41 Gaddy, *Texas In Revolt*, 14.

Texas had become the adopted homeland of thousands of Irish and Scotch-Irish settlers, who worshiped Catholicism and Protestantism, respectively, in a pristine land far from Mexico City's control.

Chapter 2

The Roles of the Scotch-Irish
Leading up to Revolution

The story of the Irish in Texas, as noted earlier, began long before the arrival of the flood of Scotch-Irish Americans including latecomers like Sam Houston, William Barret Travis, Jim Bowie, and David Crockett. Deep-seated Irish connections, not only to the history of Texas, but also to the Alamo's story, far predated even the arrival of the first United States citizens of Stephen Fuller Austin's Colony in the early 1820s. When residing in San Antonio, Interim Spanish Governor Hugh (or Hugo) O'Connor, an enterprising native Dubliner who masterfully combined judicious skill and strategic insight, ordered the strengthening of the dilapidated mission later known as the Alamo against raiding Indians during the late 1760s and early 1770s. He had been born an Irish Catholic in 1734. In fact, Spanish census records of the late 1700s have revealed a number of Ireland-born Spanish subjects in Nacogdoches on the eastern border next to Louisiana. The transplanted native Irish residents included Philip Nolan, of Belfast, northern Ireland, in 1792, Richard Sims and William Barrin in the following year, and James McNulty "of Munster," the southernmost province in Ireland, in 1797.

As history came full circle, the last man to organize the belated final efforts to strengthen the Alamo's defenses was the garrison's capable chief engineer, whose ancestors came from northern Ireland, Green B. Jameson. A former lawyer from San Felipe de Austin, about halfway between San Antonio and the

Sabine River, the 29-year-old Kentucky-born Jameson, although not a professionally trained engineer, was innovative and imaginative. Jameson worked diligently to strengthen the Alamo's fortifications before it was too late. Reliable and intelligent, he also served as the personal aide to Colonel Bowie, who commanded the volunteers and then shared joint command with Travis, during the siege of the Alamo.[1]

Virginia-born General Sam Houston, overall commander of Texas forces by the time of the 1836 Texas Campaign and known for his hot temper that easily won him enemies, was of Scotch-Irish descent. Houston's ancestors migrated from Hughstown (later corrupted to the family name of Houston), in the central lowlands of Scotland just west of Glasgow, to find a new home just to the south in east County Antrim, Ulster Province, Ireland.

Along with hundreds of other Scotch-Irish Protestant warriors, Houston's Ulster ancestors had defended the high, stone walls of Derry, when besieged by resurgent Catholic Jacobites under James II in 1689. Houston's great-grandfather, a tenant farmer named John who farmed the rich lands of an upper-class landlord, departed the area of Ballybracken, County Antrim, with no regrets in 1735. The Houston family then headed across the Atlantic for the port of Philadelphia to start of a new life, settling in a land known for religious tolerance: Pennsylvania. Later, like many others the Houston family then pushed south, and established permanent roots in Augusta County, Virginia, which became yet another distinctive Scotch-Irish ethnic and cultural enclave in the Shenandoah Valley. Houston was described by one observer as having a "gay disposition," especially as a younger man, which partly reflected his Irish antecedents, lively in spirit and merry in nature.

Lieutenant Colonel James Clinton Neill was the longest-acting Alamo commander and one of the first, after San Antonio was captured by the Texians in December 1835. Neill's ancestors had descended from the legendary O'Neill clan of die-hard Irish revolutionaries and nationalists, who fought valiantly, but in vain, to retain possession of their ancient northeastern Ireland homeland of Ulster. Neill proudly traced his line to "ancient Irish warrior chieftains dating back to the fourth century" and deep into the fabled pages of Irish history. Though largely forgotten, Neill was a key player, providing invaluable leadership in keeping the Alamo garrison together during the difficult winter of

---

1 The Texas Historical Society notes it is uncertain whether Green B. Jameson was born in Kentucky or Tennessee.

1835-1836. Such was the case of many leading Irish and Scotch-Irish roles and contributions that dominated the Alamo's story from beginning to end.[2]

Indeed, and most symbolic in revealing the sterling qualities of the Irish fighting man, the last assignment among the doomed Alamo defenders on the early morning of March 6, 1836 was undertaken by one of the last surviving garrison members, who just happened to be an Irishman, which was most appropriate. Serving as the Alamo's chief ordnance officer, this capable man of considerable promise was Ireland-born Major Robert Evans, aged thirty-six. The blue-eyed, dark-haired Evans was a popular officer of broad personal appeal among the mostly volunteers. His outstanding physical attributes came, in part, from working the farmlands in his native Ireland, and he possessed a typically upbeat and high-spirited Irish personality: winning ways and amiable natures that had evolved among many Emerald Islanders to cope with generations of severe adversity. All in all, such redeeming qualities of the Irish people had long served as effective survival mechanisms of making the "best of a bad situation." Well-known Celtic-Gaelic qualities and characteristics included high-spirits, a lively sense of humor, and "merry" temperament. And in this regard, Evans and his fellow Irish of the Alamo were no exception.

Also exhibiting the sterling qualities of a natural and popular leader, especially during a crisis situation such as in the Alamo's defense, Major Evans's razor-sharp Irish wit and finely honed sense of humor lifted morale during the darkest days of the Alamo's siege. Having migrated to Texas from New York by way of New Orleans, Major Evans's crucial final mission was risky, if not suicidal: when it was determined that all was lost and when the Mexicans poured over the walls, blow up the garrison's powder magazine that was located

2 *Maryland Gazette*, November 12, 1835; *El Mosquito Mexicano*, Mexico City, March 22, 1836; Dolan, *The Irish Americans*, 22; Hopewell, *James Bowie*, 1-2; Davis, *Three Roads to the Alamo*, 194; Davis, *Land!*, 3-257; Groneman, *Alamo Defenders*, 63-64; Donald E. Chipman, *Spanish Texas, 1519-1821* (Austin, TX, 1992), 182, 186, 190; Irish Texans, Texas Almanac, Texas State Historical Association, internet; James L. Haley, *Sam Houston* (Norman, OK, 2002), 5; Marshall DeBruhl, *A Life of Sam Houston* (New York, NY, 1993), 7-11; Walraven and Walraven, *The Magnificent Barbarians*, 91; Kennedy, *Scots-Irish in the Hills of Tennessee*, 19-57, 99-118; James Clinton Neill, Handbook of Texas Online; *New York Times*, January 27, 1895; "The Alamo: The Irish Heroes of the Alamo," *IC*, internet; Flannery, *The Irish Texans*, 18-19; C. Richard King, *James Clinton Neill, Commander of the Alamo* (Austin, TX, 2002), 3-4, 7-8; *New York Times*, January 27, 1895; John Edward Weems with Jane Weems, *Dream of Empire, A History of the Republic of Texas 1836-1846* (New York, NY, 1986), 57; *Farmer's Cabinet*, Ampherst, New Hampshire; McWhiney, *Cracker Culture*, xiii-257; Webb, *Born Fighting*, 123-184; Lack, *The Texas Revolutionary Experience*, 208; Donovan, *The Blood of Heroes*, 69-71, 95-98.

in two rooms of the Alamo chapel.. Like a good Irish soldier to the very end, Evans attempted to fulfill his key assignment that might save the lives of a good many Texian soldiers in the future, because the 1836 Campaign had only begun However, on the early morning of March 6 when the night's cold yet wrapped the Alamo compound in its late winter grip, the never-say-die Irish officer was destined to be cut down before fulfilling his desperate final mission to deny Santa Anna the Alamo's powder reserves.[3]

Compared to Major Evans, who yet spoke with a thick Irish brogue, a grizzled James Clinton Neill—an old Indian fighter of Scotch-Irish heritage who knew the Comanche's wily ways—possessed a higher level of military experience. Besides his popularity, this broad range of military experience partly explained why Neill commanded the Alamo by early 1836. Without Neill's guiding influence and early command decisions, there would have been no final confrontation of the Alamo. He decided to hold his isolated position at the Alamo, west of the east Texas settlements and on the western frontier, instead of evacuating as Houston wisely suggested.[4]

From beginning to end of the Texas Revolution, Lieutenant Colonel Neill was an inspirational and leading revolutionary, mirroring the demographics of the majority of his followers. And, most significant, Neill's early revolutionary activities partly revealed the significant impact of his distinguished Irish revolutionary heritage that extended back to Ulster Province. Bolstering the defiant stand of Gonzales's citizen-soldiers, including County Antrim, Ireland-born John McHenry, and other Texian volunteers against more than a hundred finely uniformed Mexican dragoons dispatched from San Antonio, Neill fired the first defiant artillery shot—an ad hoc mixture of nails and cut-up horseshoes of western frontier improvisation that made for an effective homemade canister—from the little makeshift "Come and Take It" cannon on the morning of October 2, 1835. Mounted on handmade wheels of solid slabs of wood and a makeshift gun carriage, this small iron cannon had been cast in Mexico. As tensions increased, the cannon became a bone of contention between Texian settlers and Mexican troops headquartered in San Antonio, as it

3 Groneman, *Alamo Defenders*, 47-48; Lord, *A Time to Stand*, 165-166; Mary Ann Noonan Guerra, *Heroes of the Alamo and Goliad, Revolutionaries on the Road to San Jacinto and Texas Independence* (San Antonio, TX, 1987), 21; "The Alamo: The Irish Heroes of the Alamo," *IC*, internet; Nutting, Ireland Beautiful, 62; McWhiney, *Cracker Culture*, 24, 41.

4 Hardin, *Texian Illiad*, 12, 78, 110-111, 117; Groneman, *Alamo Defenders*, 3-125.

had long protected Gonzales's settlers against the lightning-strike raids of the Comanche, who had burned the town down in 1827.[5]

Because of Gonzales's predominate Gaelic-Celtic demographics and obsession with preserving the new-found privileges long denied them back in Ireland, an open clash was inevitable, when Colonel Domingo de Ugartechea, the commandant of Bexar, demanded the cannon's return. This "gun was once the property of the King of Spain; and he lost it with the sovereignty of the country [when Mexico won its independence in 1821]. The Federal Republic of Mexico became the owner. The people of Gonzales returned, in substance, that the gun was the property of the Confederation which they acknowledged, and not of the central Government, which they did not, and they would not give it up to any affairs of the central Government."[6]

Hastening to the call to arms, settlers in the east Texas settlements united to assist the colonists of Gonzales on the western frontier. "Yesterday we were about eighteen strong, to day, one hundred and fifty, and forces continually arriving" wrote Captain Albert Martin, a recent arrival to Texas from Providence, Rhode Island, and an enterprising Gonzales merchant.[7] Martin led the Gonzales contingent not only at the battle of Gonzales in early October 1835, but also the Gonzales Ranging Company of Mounted Volunteers into the deathtrap of the Alamo during the siege.

Initiating the battle of Gonzales, Neill fired his tiny field piece and a clump of small projectiles whizzed across the brown waters of the cottonwood-lined Guadalupe—a lazy river flowing southeast about midway between the Colorado Rive, to the east and the San Antonio River to the west—toward the Mexican mounted troops along the west bank. Not surprising, cannon-fire came from the hand of a man of Scotch-Irish descent and a long line of Ulster revolutionary ancestors, and sparked the Texas Revolution just east of San Antonio and the Alamo. As the westernmost Anglo-Celtic settlement in Texas and the only Texian enclave located west of the Colorado River, Gonzales had

---

5   Hardin, *Texian Illiad*, 11-12; *Maryland Gazette*, November 12, 1835; Jane Bradfield, *Rx Take One Cannon, The Gonzales Come & Take It Cannon of October, 1835* (Shiner, TX, 1981), x-xi, 15-25, 101; McHenry, John, The Handbook of Texas Online.

6   *Maryland Gazette*, November 12, 1835; "The Alamo: The Irish Heroes of the Alamo," *IC*, internet; Cos, Martin Perfecto de, The Handbook of Texas Online.

7   *Texas Republican*, Brazoria, Texas, October 10, 1835; Ron Jackson, *Alamo Legacy, Alamo Descendants Remember the Alamo* (Austin, TX, 1997), 120; Donovan, *Blood of Noble Heroes*, 187.

been settled by Ireland-born pioneers such as Andrew Duvalt. Duvalt would later be killed at the Alamo partly in an attempt to save his western frontier community from Santa Anna's wrath.

This dramatic showdown between the rustic volunteers from Gonzales, led by Neill, and the surrounding area staged on the Ezekiel Williams Ranch earned widespread renown as the "Lexington of Texas." Of course, this revolutionary analogy was made in regard to the initial skirmish between New England colonists and British regulars, dispatched from Boston, at Lexington, Massachusetts, on April 19, 1775, which had initiated another armed struggle for a people's self-determination and liberty.

Neill would also later command Houston's artillery of two guns, the "Twin Sisters" donated by the good people of Cincinnati, Ohio, and cast in that port city along the Ohio River, during the final confrontation at San Jacinto on April 21, 1836. Therefore, Neill played leading artillery leadership roles from the first clash at Gonzales to the last at San Jacinto. In the final showdown, he fell wounded when struck in the hip with a grapeshot from a Mexican cannon. In a strange twist of fate, the defiant Scotch-Irish leader, who was most responsible for the ill-fated decision to defend the Alamo, primarily because of his overestimation of the firepower of the large number of available artillery—around 20 guns captured in December 1835 when San Antonio and the Alamo fell to the revolutionaries—was himself cut down by field pieces manned by the Alamo's victors.

Led by Neill, the next most popular Alamo commander, and also beloved by the garrison's defenders (unlike regulars of the nascent Texas Army), was Colonel Bowie. He was an experienced officer who had earned widespread fame across the Southwest for his knife fighting prowess and feats of daring. Bowie's legendary combativeness can at least partly be explained by his thorough Scottish Celtic roots. Appropriately, even his Bowie Knife possessed such heritage, having descended from the popular dirks worn, for generations, by the Scottish warriors, including William Wallace's rebels, while battling for the dream of an independent Scotland. Dirks were still carried on the Texas frontier in 1836, with western modifications such as deer or buffalo horn handles. Even more, Bowie's first name of James continued the Celtic family tradition of preserving and honoring the memory of James II.

James II was the Jacobite leader who nearly conquered Ireland in his determined bid to regain the English crown to restore a Catholic monarchy, until crushed at the battle of the Boyne. The disastrous rout of Irish Catholic forces on the River Boyne, Ireland, in July 1690 changed the course of Irish history. The memory of this most famous battle in Irish history—which determined if Ireland would be ruled by Catholics or Protestants—was alive and well, dwelling in the consciousness of the Bowie family. Bowie was a dynamic, natural leader of the western frontier, proud of his Celtic ancestors who hailed from the picturesque Scottish highlands before they migrated to the rich tobacco country among the gently rolling hills of southern Maryland.

Likewise, Lieutenant Colonel Travis's feisty words of defiance in written letters to solicit assistance from the besieged Alamo partly indicate a typical Celtic–Gaelic fighting spirit and well-known, never-say-die attitude regardless the odds, even when there was no hope in sight. Young Travis, from the little town of Claiborne on the bluffs of the Alabama River in the southwest part of the state, also possessed a fun-loving Celtic-Gaelic personality and other qualities, indicating in part his Scotch-Irish roots. Travis was ambitious and romantic-minded, a frontier cavalier who was raised on Walter Scott's popular tales of the Scottish people's struggle for liberty against the British invader. He became one of the earliest Texas War Party leaders known as the War Dogs. Having left behind his wife in Alabama, the dapper attorney enjoyed good times: drinking, socializing, dancing (especially the popular "pigeon's wing"), and making love—not necessarily in that order—whenever the opportunity arose and especially with the prettiest ladies he could find.[8]

He possessed winning ways with the ladies, white, black, Indian, Mexican, and Tejano, and Travis was as aggressive on the battlefield as in the bedroom, especially after his Alabama divorce from Rosanna who he abandoned, along with their young son. His journey to Texas in 1831 was meant to escape escalating trouble in his personal life, including spiraling debts. As diligently as he studied law, the young man tallied up a rather impressive total of 59 sexual conquests by November 7, 1834, as recorded in his diary in Spanish, touting the

---

8 *New York Times*, January 27, 1895; Davis, *Three Roads to the Alamo*, 35, 189-206, 259-286, 365-387; Moore, *Eighteen Minutes*, 25, 152-153, 264-267; Bradfield, *Rx Take One Cannon*, x-111; Groneman, *Alamo Defenders*, 42, 47-48; James Atkins Shackford, *David Crockett, The Man and the Legend* (Lincoln, NE, 1986) 293; Hopewell, *James Bowie*, 1; King, *James Clinton Neill*, 3-7; Walraven and Walraven, *The Magnificent Barbarians*, 71-72; Donovan, *The Blood of Heroes*, 10-19; Dolan, *The Irish Americans*, 3-4; Webb, *Born Fighting*, 123-184; McWhiney, *Cracker Culture*, xiii-257; Derr, *The Frontiersman*, 37; "The Alamo: The Irish Heroes of the Alamo," *IC*, internet; McWhiney and Jamieson, *Attack and Die*, 172-178; Edmondson, *The Alamo Story*, 85-86; Michael McNally, *Battle of the Boyne 1690, The Irish campaign for the English crown* (Oxford, England, 2005), 7-91; Smithwick, *Evolution of a State*, x; Hardin, *Texian Illiad*, 107, 111, 117; Mary L. Scheer, *Women and the Texas Revolution* (Denton, TX, 2012), 112.

maturation of his seductive skills. His gambling and careless abandon in the bedroom revealed a carefree, libertine lifestyle of the unruly, transient southwest frontier, and which partly exposed a well-known Celtic proclivity of pursuing what was most pleasurable. He was freed of the artificial societal restrictions and burdens of the Deep South's hypocritical moral code, an unhappy marriage, and his evidently unfaithful young wife back in Alabama. In regard to the sexual conquests, the free-spirted Alabamian of fiery Celtic-Gaelic spirit and eloquence was indeed color blind on the Texas frontier.

But Travis possessed another passion besides taking lovers to the bedroom, back alley, or in his law office in San Felipe de Austin, the rustic capital of the Stephen Fuller Austin Colony, only ten years old by 1834. This frontier community became the center of the brewing rebellion against Mexico, and probably no one worked more diligently in bringing about the Texas Revolution than "Buck" or "Bill" Travis. This energetic role as one of the most active and influential War Dogs came naturally to Travis.

As if fated for a grisly end, he was a natural magnet for trouble, domestic or foreign and in regard to both men and women. Travis possessed an adventurous, healthy zest for life, despite seemingly doing all he could to shorten it by so often openly challenging the Mexican military authority. When not in a combative mood toward Mexico's constitutional laws and officials or not railing against Mexico City, Travis freely partook in San Felipe's all-night-long fandangos that were mostly attended by Tejanos, drinking and socializing, as if to wash away the haunting memories of his troubled Alabama past, failed marriage, and personal demons that yet haunted him on Texas soil.

But Travis became best known for demonstrating typically Celtic-Gaelic defiance in employing a well-known Irish gift for eloquence and deft mastery of language during the Alamo siege. He most famously exhibited this dramatic flair in his February 24, 1836 letter when besieged at the Alamo. In the spirit of the romantic Scott novels he had early devoured, Travis wrote, "I shall never surrender or retreat," during his plea for assistance, and his "Victory or Death" missive to "The People of Texas & All Americans in the World" on that late winter day was one of the most memorable patriotic appeals of not only Texas history, but also American history.[9]

9   Davis, *Three Roads to the Alamo*, 189-206, 259-286, 365-387, 445-470, 540-541; Walraven and Walraven, *The Magnificent Barbarians*, 60; McWhiney, *Cracker Culture*, xiii-257; Huffines, *Blood of*

While Crockett's Scotch-Irish roots from Ulster Province, northern Ireland, have been occasionally recognized by historians, the Crockett family's earliest antecedents were in fact from Ireland's Munster Province to the south. Crockett was also proud of his Irish background on his father's side: his great, great, great grandfather, Antoine de Crocetagne, took a sailing ship north from France to the south of Ireland. As a French Huguenot, Antoine had been forced to flee the sunny south of Catholic France because his Protestantism went against the established Church. He relocated in the commercial port of Bantry because of its commercial and shipping connections to France (Antoine had worked as a commercial agent for French mercantile firms), and because the picturesque region of County Cork was Ireland's warmest region thanks to the Gulf Stream. This quaint seaport and fishing village was nestled between two lengthy rocky peninsulas of almost solid rock that majestically stretched out into the Atlantic's blue waters like the giant fingers of the ancient Roman God Neptune.

Here, in the predominately Catholic area of Munster Province, west of the larger port city of Cork, the ambitious Protestant refugee from France shortened his name to Crockett, making it less Gallic (French) for easier assimilation in a new Celtic-Gaelic land. The wandering life of this free-thinking political refugee, who had been forced to flee his intolerant homeland in the hope of finding a better place for himself and family, was mirrored more than two hundred years later by David Crockett's ill-fated ride from his home in west Tennessee toward the setting sun and an uncertain fate, but seemingly promising future, in Texas. The Crockett family witnessed "hard times, and plenty of them" in Crockett's words about his own life, and he was more than ready for a fresh start in a new land. He described the virgin Red River country of east Texas in a letter written on January 9, 1836—barely two months before his Alamo death—as "the garden spot of the world."

As a young man raised amid the hardwood forests of the east Tennessee frontier, Crockett heard stories of his family's colorful Irish immigrant history. The picturesque Bantry Bay was Ireland's "Bay of Destiny" for its repeated key roles, especially in regard to an ill-fated French invasion in 1796 that the French Revolutionary government hoped would spark an Irish revolt against the British. Here on the southwest coast, the gulf stream from the Caribbean

---

Noble Men, 2; Edmondson, *The Alamo Story*, 182-183; Donovan, *The Blood of Heroes*, 10-12, 18; Smithwick, *Evolution of a State*, 98.

warmed the land, causing wild flowers to grow even in January. Shaped like a dagger, the long rocky peninsula of the bay's southern edge ended at an imposing rocky elevation known locally as Sheep's Head Point, which was one of the most awe-inspiring scenic vantage points in Ireland.

Later, the Crockett family relocated to the island's opposite end—Protestant Ulster Province in northern Ireland—with business more profitable for an enterprising Protestant merchant, compared to the less thriving Catholic south Ireland. Another reason for Crockett to depart south Ireland was because of ant-French sentiment. This growing hostility resulted from the Jacobite invasion of James II, who also commanded thousands of French troops, ending in a crushing defeat in the battle of the Boyne (July 1690), where Irish pikemen proved no match for blazing English cannon, and the earlier battle of Bantry Bay between the French and English fleets in May 1689.

Despite the turbulent ebbs and flows of Irish history, the Crockett family had called Ireland home for many generations. Crockett's own father, John, was either born in Ireland, or came into life aboard a sailing ship during the long journey to America from the Emerald Isle. However, in the creation of an iconic American hero in the popular memory and national consciousness, Crockett's Irish roots have been obscured in the historical record in part for the creation of the mythical all-American frontier hero—as if he were solely the native son of the untamed east Tennessee frontier who had suddenly emerged from the primeval wilderness without such history. After all, according to the romantic myth, an authentic American hero was born of the frontier experience in a Frederick Jackson Turner-like tradition of regeneration with a righteous desire to fight against injustice and oppression, and without acknowledging the importance of the Irish experience.

While Crockett's origins may have been overlooked by American and even Irish historians because of the creation of the Crockett myth, the Tennessean's winning ways, boundless gift of gab (or blarney), and lively personality revealed his thoroughly Irish side, however. He also possessed well-known Irish characteristics of compassion for impoverished and oppressed people because of a shared experience of suffering that could never be fully understood by the privileged, upper-class elite sheltered so securely from troubled times. Crockett's own wife, Mary Finley, who he affectionately called Polly, was the daughter of "an old Irish woman," in the Tennessean's words. Revealing her Celtic-Gaelic antecedents and heritage, her distinctly Irish name was Jean Kennedy Finley.

By the time of the showdown at the Alamo, Crockett possessed only limited military experience, and served under Scotch-Irish General Andrew Jackson as little more than a scout and hunter in the Tennessee Volunteer Mounted Riflemen; proud of their common Irish heritage. Jackson's northern Irish family hailed from Belfast, and he was an uncompromising Irish Presbyterian holy warrior second to none. Crockett's served under Jackson during the Creek (or Red Stick) War of 1813-1814— a bitterly fought affair that proved a disaster for the Creek people. Overcoming the fact that his grandparents had been killed by the Cherokee in East Tennessee, Crockett developed a rare compassion for the suffering of the local native Muscogee, who were crushed by superior firepower and slaughtered across southern Alabama defending their ancestral homeland.

The tragic fate of the Creek Indians was the simple fact that their nation lay in the path of harm's way, a relentless American westward expansionism they were wholly unequipped to deal with or stop. These types of migrations were common throughout history around the globe, and now it was playing out on the American continent. Ironically, Crockett fought beside Creek allies in what was essentially a bitter Creek civil war, learning to admire Indian culture and ways, especially a warrior ethos. Just as Crockett perceived, a rapidly growing and expanding America was practicing its own frontier brand of ethnic cleansing to gain a vast expanse of virgin fertile lands. While serving as a popular Tennessee congressman during the early 1830s, Crockett rather audaciously stood up for his personal beliefs and opposed the Indian Removal Bill proposed by now-President Jackson, idol of the common man and his old commander. Crockett's bold, but unpopular, stance led to his loss of a Congressional seat, as his west Tennessee constituents possessed no love for Indians. It was an example of a true profile in courage, especially in moral terms, to exceed anything that he accomplished during this brief stay at the Alamo, including its much-celebrated defense.

With an acute sense of fair play, Crockett also advocated for squatter rights, because lower class settlers were unable to afford to purchase the land they had homesteaded. As well, Crockett grew to detest slavery, a rarity among Anglo-Celts on the western frontier in early 1830s Texas, lamenting its injustices. Even in Washington D.C., where slaves were bought and sold practically under the shadow capitol's dome, Crockett noted how the powerful slave interests of the Deep South advanced self-serving political agendas that shaped the nation's course and maximized profits, a betrayal of America's fundamental egalitarian principles of the American Revolution. As a Tennessee Congressman, he

This rare photograph shows the front of Our Lady of Loreto Church, Presidio la Bahia, in Goliad, Texas. Here, on December 20, 1835, garrison members who were largely Irish, including a good many immigrants from the Emerald Isle, signed the first Texas Declaration of Independence. *Marketplace Museum Collection, Goliad County Library, Goliad, Texas*

opposed bills to repeal redemption laws in regard to slavery, and voted funds "for the relief of Mathias, a free man of color."[10]

Clearly, Crockett related to the suffering of such unfortunate people, regardless of race, because of not only his own personal struggles with poverty, but also from his family's own legacy of Irish experiences and an Irish tradition of benevolence. Therefore, Crockett remained very much of an outsider, especially among the socialites, career politicians, and crass opportunists of Washington, D.C. Besides compassion for his fellow man, Crockett, the homespun "gentleman from the cane," was most famous for those genuine qualities that were typical Irish: a love for storytelling and a keen sense of humor distinguished by cutting wit, ribaldry, parody, lampooning sarcasm, and an

10 *New York Times*, December 15, 1907; Shackford, *David Crockett*, 3-118, 293; Michael J. Carroll, *A Bay of Destiny, A History of Bantry Bay and Bantry* (Bantry, Ireland, 1996), 203-252; Groneman, *Alamo Defenders*, 133; Davis, *Three Roads to the Alamo*, 9-34, 63-90, 113-141, 165-187, 194; McWhiney, *Cracker Culture*, 3-8; Derr, *The Frontiersman*, 11-269; Edmondson, *The Alamo Story*, 262; Levy, *American Legend*, 29-179; Boylston and Wiener, *David Crockett in Congress*, 8-22, 65-73, 187; Dolan, *The Irish Americans*, 3-4.

uncanny ability to "exact fun from the dreariest [of] subjects" or situations. Such enduring typically Irish traits were part of Crockett's personal appeal and popularity among the common people.[11]

While Texas historians (including an Ireland-born author) have focused primarily on the romantic Crockett of Alamo fame without a hint of Irish roots, the real man, who was far more complex than the one-dimensional, coonskin-cap stereotype, was nearly the antithesis of the much-embellished backwoods warrior, who allegedly slew scores of Mexican attackers at the Alamo. Instead, he was an active and firm supporter of the poor of the West, which consisted primarily of Celtic-Gaelic people like his own family, attempting to scratch out a living on the frontier as best they could under challenging circumstances—the prevalent demographic of the hopeful men and women who settled Texas. Crockett's heartfelt devotion to the lowest segment of American society never ended, because he was one of them. Long before facing the Napoleonic-like formations of advancing soldados on the early morning of March 6, 1836 at the Alamo, Crockett had already fought long and hard against social injustice and odds that he could not possibly overcome.[12]

At considerable professional, personal, and political cost, Crockett bravely upheld his "lonely, unpopular defense of Indians [which] stands out in an era dominated by racism, greed, and injustice."[13] In fact, one insightful Irish historian emphasized that Crockett, who was sensitive and sincere, was also essentially a "socialist" in regard to his deep concern and passionate support for the downtrodden of the lower classes. These were mostly poor farmers, including even African Americans, both slave and free—a rare empathy that was derived in no small part from social values stemming from his own Irish background and his familiarity with the Irish experience, while also reflecting his own often impoverished and lower middle-class status.[14]

---

11 Shackford, *David Crockett*, 3-118, 293; Kennedy, *Scots-Irish in the Hills of Tennessee*, 103-104; *New York Times*, December 15, 1907; Peter Haining, editor, *Great Irish Humor* (New York, NY, 1995), 13-16; Nutting, *Ireland Beautiful*, 61-62; McWhiney, *Cracker Culture*, xxxii.

12 James R. Boylston and Allen J. Wiener, *David Crockett in Congress, The Rise and Fall of the Poor Man's Friend* (Houston, TX, 2009), 7-9, 16, 21; McWhiney, *Cracker Culture*, xiii-267; Webb, *Born Fighting*, 3-184; Krystyna M. Libura, Luis Gerardo Morales Moreno, and Jesus Velasco Marquez, *Echoes of the Mexican-American War* (Berkeley, CA, 2004), 24-25.

13 Boylston and Wiener, *David Crockett in Congress*, 73.

14 Kennedy, *Scots-Irish in the Hills of Tennessee*, 104; Boylston and Wiener, *David Crockett in Congress*, 16, 19, 21-22.

The inside of Our Lady of Loreto Church, Presidio la Bahia, in Goliad, Texas, where Irish garrison members signed the first Texas Declaration of Independence on December 20, 1835. *Marketplace Museum Collection, Goliad County Library, Goliad, Texas*

In consequence, Crockett not only admired but also loved "my people" of the lowest origins. He described how "these people, though poor, are of inestimable value in a free republic [and] they are the bone and sinew of the land."[15] Unable to conceal his respect for the silent endurance and stoic suffering of common people in a remote region, he also explained how among the lowly residents of west Tennessee, "None of them are rich, but they are an honest, industrious, hardy, persevering kind-hearted people [as] I know them" well.[16]

Crockett's absolute disgust with the excessive privileges and abuses of America's corrupt and wealthy ruling elite, including slave-owning powers, was one fundamental reason why he left the United States, journeyed to the southwestern frontier of Texas, and ended up meeting his tragic fate at the Alamo. He revealed the extent of his disillusionment in an August 10, 1835

15 Boylston and Wiener, *David Crockett in Congress*, 311.

16 Ibid., 312.

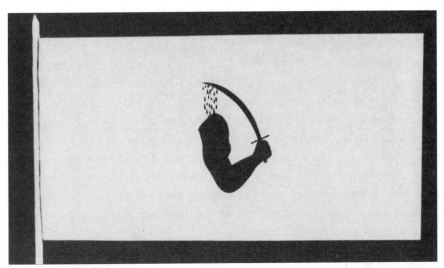

This little-known Irish flag, distinguished by a historic design with Northern Ireland revolutionary antecedents, was raised at the Presidio la Bahia on December 22, 1835, during the celebration of the signing of the first Texas Declaration of Independence. *Author's Collection*

letter: "I do believe Santa Anna's kingdom [Texas] will be a paradise, compared with this, in a few years."[17] And in the words of a journalist of the *Vermont Gazette*, "Davy has become disgusted with this country since his defeat, and has determined to move to Texas, stock, lock, and barrel."[18]

Clearly Crockett had enough of not only politics, but also Washington D.C. and overall life in the United States, where far too many of the common people were dominated like pawns by the ruling class elite and the rich. In a letter written on Christmas Day 1834, it indicated his desire to make a fresh start in a new land far away not only from Washington, D.C., but also Tennessee: "I have almost given up the Ship at last [and] if Martin Van Buren [pro-big business, anti-abolitionist, pro-Southern interests, and part of the aristocratic political establishment] is elected [then] I will leave the United States for I never will live under his Kingdom […] before I will submit to his government I will go to the wildes [sic] of Texas."[19]

17 Ibid., 122, 282.

18 *Vermont Gazette*, Bennington, Vermont, October 6, 1835.

19 *New York Times*, December 15, 1907; McWhiney, *Cracker Culture*, 1-8; Boylston and Wiener, *David Crockett in Congress*, 7-9.

Crockett, however, had no intention or desire to engage in a war of any kind in Texas when he journeyed by horseback on what was nothing more than a scouting and hunting trip. Crockett described in a October 31, 1835 letter how, "I am on the eve of Starting to the Texes [as] I want to explore the Texes well before I return" to Tennessee.[20] Ironically, he seemed more intent on leaving family responsibilities behind rather than engaging in a glorious struggle for liberty. During the trek to Texas and after crossing the Mississippi, when an inquisitive woman asked about what arrangements he had made for his family back in west Tennessee, Crockett merely answered with some relief sprinkled with his trademark humor more oriented toward a male audience than this curious, outspoken Arkansas woman: "I have set them free—set them free—they must shift for themselves."[21]

Crockett's sharp facial features were classically Scotch-Irish and as much a part of Ulster Province as the land's fertility and natural beauty. His sense of humor reflected Irish roots in which Celtic-Gaelic society placed a high premium on entertaining, and practical jokes. In the 1834 words of a northeast journalist, Crockett possessed "rather sharp features, with an extremely pleasing cast of countenance, in which humour [was] strongly portrayed."[22] Crockett also seems to have shared a legacy of Ireland's revolutionary past, along with so many other Scotch-Irish, including Andrew Jackson, whose grandfather went down fighting on Irish soil for what he believed was right.[23]

Meanwhile, other officers of Irish descent served as primary leaders of the Alamo garrison during the siege besides Crockett, Travis, Bowie,, Neill, and Chief Engineer Green Benjamin Jameson. Captain William R. Carey, who was born in Ireland, commanded a company of high-spirited artillerymen at the Alamo. Carey and his men were heady over their December 1835 success in forcing the surrender of San Antonio's Mexican garrison under the leadership of Vera Cruz-born General Martín Perfecto de Cos, the promising son of an attorney and Santa Anna's nephew. When trapped inside the Alamo. Carey played an inspiring leadership role: he suffered a scalp wound from a Mexican bullet, but continued to lead his gunners by daring example.

---

20 Boylston and Wiener, *David Crockett in Congress*, 285.

21 *Arkansas Gazette*, Little Rock, Arkansas, May 10, 1836.

22 *The Portsmouth Journal and Rockingham Gazette*, New Hampshire, May 10, 1834.

23 McWhiney, Cracker Culture, 35.

At the Alamo, Carey commanded 56 cannoneers known as the "Invincibles." Only age 30, the Virginia-born Carey hailed from the busy port of Baltimore, Maryland, where his family had migrated from Ireland. Most appropriately, a little port town named Baltimore lay at Ireland's southern tip in County Cork. The optimistic bachelor son of Moses Carey and mature beyond his years, Carey had migrated to Texas in the summer of 1835. Here, he settled at Washington-on-the-Brazos, but soon found himself stuck in the death-trap of the Alamo. Nevertheless, as written in a letter, Carey was determined "to discharge the duty of a soldier when called on." Indeed, he and his "Invincibles" served as the Alamo garrison's dependable "trouble shooters," under Carey's inspired leadership, after having early gained a reputation for accomplishing tough missions. With pride and as penned on February 25, 1836, Travis praised young Captain Carey, who "rendered essential services" in the Alamo's spirited defense against the odds, after Santa Anna's Army descended upon San Antonio on February 23.[24]Mirroring the demographics of America's general westward expansion, the Irish, Scotch-Irish, and their descendants made up the largest percentage of those men who served not only at the Alamo but also those soldiers who struggled to win Texas independence in both 1835 and 1836. This was appropriate because the leading and disproportionate roles played by the Irish in defending the Alamo reflected their overall demographics and distinctive contributions in Texas' early settlement.[25]

Many reasons explain why the Irish have been mostly forgotten as key players in the colorful story of Texas besides Catholicism, western European and Celtic-Gaelic backgrounds, and lowly, impoverished status. Without education, political connections, monetary means, or the ability to write about their Texas revolutionary experiences because of widespread illiteracy, the story of these Celtic-Gaelic settlers, especially Catholics, influencing Texas history has been left largely unrecorded. This is thanks, in part, to long-existing English

24 Linn, *Reminiscences of Fifty Years in Texas*, 29; Groneman, *Alamo Defenders*, 22-23, 134-138; Hopewell, *James Bowie*, 1-2; Davis, *Three Roads to the Alamo*, 9-10; Cos, Martin Perfecto de, The Handbook of Texas Online; Ron Jackson, *Alamo Legacy, Alamo Descendants Remember the Alamo*, (Austin, TX,1997), 27-28; Todd Hansen, editor, *The Alamo Reader, A Study in History* (Mechanicsburg, PA, 2003), 78; King, *James Clinton Neill*, 3-4; *New York Times*, January 27, 1895; *Nashville Banner and Nashville Whig*, Nashville, Tennessee, April 1, 1836.

25 Groneman, *Alamo Defenders*, 4-123; Moore, *Eighteen Minutes*, 435-462; Fehrenbach, *Lone Star*, 81-92; Graham, *Land!*, 3-257; "The Alamo: Irish Heroes of the Alamo," *IC*, internet; McWhiney, *Cracker Culture*, xxi-257; Webb, *Born Fighting*, 123-184.

Penal Laws that denied Irish Catholics an education, and because of the fact that the Irish people relied primarily upon a vibrant oral, over written, tradition.

Unfortunately, therefore, Texas's past has long been written by historians without an adequate understanding or full appreciation of ethnic contributions and the central importance of the Celtic-Gaelic role in the conflict. Such developments guaranteed that the Irish and the Scotch-Irish have been the forgotten players of not only the Alamo but also the Texas Revolution— ironically much like the fate of the disproportionate percentage of Irish who faithfully served in Washington's Army from 1775 to 1783.

Further explaining why a distinguished Irish role in the annals of Texas history has been long-overlooked was because the Texas Revolution and the Alamo have been viewed by Americans as mostly part of America's overall course of western history and expansion as romanticized within the overall context of an Anglo-Saxon-based Manifest Destiny. Consequently, even the mere presence of sizeable number of Irish immigrants seemed to have been incongruent and even illogical, if not entirely out-of-place, with the mainstream of Texas history, especially the Texas Revolution and most definitely the Alamo's story, from the perspectives of the vast majority of American and traditional Texas historians. In addition, the dramatic story of Texas, one of the most fascinating chapters in American history, has been described by the winners almost exclusively in terms of a great Anglo-Saxon Protestant epic, where the alleged enlightened and superior virtues of Anglo civilization triumphed over a corrupt Old World-like and Catholic nation in the end. Therefore, Anglo heroes—especially Travis, Crockett, and Bowie—were long celebrated without even a mention of their Celtic and Celtic-Gaelic backgrounds and heritage, and the important part these factors played in their lives.

In truth, no people from Europe played a more important role in the settlement of Texas and in the Texas Revolution than the Irish, the Scotch-Irish, and those of Scotch-Irish descent. And even more, no group in all Texas paid a higher or more fearful price for their enthusiastic adherence to the cause of Texas independence than the Irish, especially those of the Irish colonies of San Patricio and Refugio located west of the Guadalupe River. However, the dominance of the traditional, or Anglo-Saxon, interpretation of Texas history has excluded the Irish story and its supreme importance, especially in regard to the Texas Revolution. This development has been most ironic. After all, the Anglo-Celtic settlers, beginning with the Stephen Fuller Austin's Colony in 1821, in the Brazos River country of east Texas, were themselves all immigrants, like the Celtic, Scotch-Irish, and Celtic-Gaelic forefathers of the famed triumvirate of the Alamo, Crockett, Bowie, and Travis.[26]

Latecomers compared to their Tejano neighbors who were longtime settlers of Mexico's unruly northern frontier—the old Spanish borderlands—the first organized group of Anglo-Celts settled in Texas beginning in Stephen Fuller Austin's Colony in the early 1820s. Here, in the well-watered region of east Texas that was much like western Louisiana in terms of geography, climate, soil, and vegetation, they took full advantage of liberal colonization policies of the Mexican government (first established by the Spanish). Both Spain and Mexico had long hoped to transform this untamed wilderness area, long handicapped by Indian raids, into a productive region to bolster weak economies. But that much-anticipated prosperity never developed, a situation that caused Mexico to turn to Anglo-Celtic settlement as a long-sought solution, ensuring that America's westward expansion met the northward expansion of Mexico on Texas soil and setting the stage for the clash of two cultures.

Besides successful colonization providing economic benefits, well-armed migrants from the United States, especially the ever-pugnacious settlers of Scotch-Irish descent, would neutralize the Indian threat, mostly notably from the fierce Comanche, or so it was hoped at first by the Spanish, then Mexican, governments. Both nations believed that Texas would serve as an effective buffer to protect Mexico's interior, particularly Mexico City, and keep this remote northern region free from the greedy grasp of strong European powers like imperialistic and commercial-oriented Great Britain.

What has been generally overlooked in Texas history was the fact that those white immigrants who journeyed the greatest distance to Texas—more than 4,000 miles from the Irish coast—were settlers propelled by destiny, fate, history, and circumstances. Therefore, because England had so long denied equal rights and land ownership to its Catholic inhabitants and discriminated against both Scotch-Irish and Irish Catholics, no people who migrated to Texas

---

26 Davis, *Land!*, 3-257; Haltigan, *The Irish in the American Revolution*, 4-618; Davis, *Three Roads to the Alamo*, 9-10, 35-36; Hopewell, *James Bowie*, 1-2; Dolan, *The Irish Americans*, 22; Groneman, *Alamo Defenders*, 4-123; Webb, *Born Fighting*, 177-184; Murphy, *The Irish in the American Revolution*, 1-86; King, *James Clinton Neill*, 3-4; *New York Times*, January 27, 1895; "The Alamo: Irish Heroes of the Alamo," *IC*, internet; McWhiney, *Cracker Culture*, xiii-257; Webb, *Born Fighting*, 123-184; Flannery, *The Irish Texans*, 11; Irish, The Handbook of Texas Online, internet.

trekked farther than the Irish, dreaming lofty egalitarian visions about the promise of their new homes. Clearly, from the beginning, the average Irish immigrant, both Catholic and Protestant, had a large stake in the intoxicating dream of Texas, and the military, political, and economic roles of both Irish Catholics and Protestants in the Texas Revolution clearly indicated as much.

However, in the end, even the Texas Revolution's own peculiar internal dynamics—anything but homegrown primarily because of direct influences from the United States—also helped to ensure that Irish contributions would be forgotten and left out of the history books. From the beginning, the demographic composition of Texas revolutionary forces, consisting mostly of Protestant Scotch-Irish descendants, also obscured the many significant contributions of Irish immigrants, especially Catholics. The Texas Revolution's initial stages, all the way up to San Antonio's capture by the Texians before mid-December 1835, saw victories won over relatively weak Mexican forces by primarily Scotch-Irish colonists from the east Texas settlements, especially the Austin Colony. Mostly native Texians, primarily those of Scotch-Irish descent and Protestants of the "Army of the People," drove the last Mexican troops from Texas soil by the conclusion of 1835, when Cos marched his paroled troops south.

But this unity among the settlers in the defense of Texas shortly evaporated because the Texians almost universally believed that the war was over by the end of 1835, after Cos's vanquished men departed Texas soil. Consequently, in the time-honored democratic and militia tradition of reverting back to civilian status after an immediate threat disappeared, these "Old Texians" simply went back home en masse to families to take care of their east Texas farms, which had been left neglected since early fall 1835. In addition, a good many old settlers and the largest landowners of the most fertile acres, along the Brazos and Colorado Rivers, flowing southeast in the Gulf of Mexico, began to fear that the revolutionary war effort had been taken over by non-Texians—politicians, large numbers of armed United States volunteers, ambitious officers, scheming Wall Street profiteers, unscrupulous land speculators, and slave traders—all focused on driving up prices and all recently from the United States, including Irish immigrants, mostly by way of New Orleans.

Indeed, the exciting news of early Texian victories of 1835 quickly spread across the Sabine to inspire a new generation of young Americans with revolutionary fervor and greed for lush Texas acres. From western Louisiana to the northernmost tip of Maine (a Gaelic name in origin), hundreds of young United States volunteers headed southwest to fight for Texas. By early January

1836, therefore, the overall composition of the diminutive Texas military forces in the field, including the tiny Alamo garrison that protected the remote western frontier, had evolved into something entirely different from what it had been during the recent 1835 Texas Campaign. Quite simply, Texas's defense was no longer in the hands Texas colonists, who had first poured forth to defend homes, farms, ranches, and families during that exciting early fall of 1835, when war fever reached its peak. Therefore, most native Texians remained safely at home and far from the front tending to hogs, goats, sheep, and cattle in the Celtic-Gaelic cultural traditions of an ancient pastoral society, while making routine preparations for the spring planting of crops and getting the lucrative cotton crop ready for export to New Orleans. By the time Santa Anna's Army reached San Antonio by late February 1836, he caught everyone, especially the Alamo garrison, by surprise.

In a strange paradox, most recent volunteers had never seen Texas before 1835, including Captain Albert Martin from the United States who died at the Alamo. Initially, traditional historians long viewed the Alamo garrison as consisting of hardy Texians, who stood firm for the express purpose of defending the beloved adopted homeland they had made productive, in the same manner as the New England yeoman farmers on Lexington Green. In reality, however, a large percentage of the young men and boys who defended the Alamo came from Europe, especially the Green Isle. Such pervasive misconceptions and omissions about the realities and complexities of Alamo ethnic demographics, beyond the romantic myths, have led to the additional obscuring of the vital roles played by so many Irish immigrants on all levels.

Therefore, the popular view in Alamo historiography that mostly native Texians, or long-time residents, garrisoned the Alamo was simply not the case. Clearly, the mythical Alamo has obscured a host of significant ethnic contribution, especially from Ireland. Far more than has been generally recognized by even Texas Revolutionary War historians, the Alamo garrison was amazingly multi-cultural and multi-ethnic to a comfortable degree.

In early 1836, the armed defenders of Texas, more than 900 troops, consisted of well over three-fourths recent United States volunteers, including hundreds of recent immigrants. With the vast majority of "Old Texians" absent from the army's ranks, remaining peacefully by warm fireplaces in cabins and farmhouses in the Brazos and Colorado River country, far more Ireland-born soldiers and the sons of Irish immigrants served at the Alamo and during the Texas revolution's later stages than has been realized. Ironically, most Alamo defenders were not longtime settlers who owned the land, but mostly single men, including Irish volunteers, who had recently entered Texas to fight against Mexico in the hope of acquiring large amounts of lands in exchange for their military service. As throughout the history of America's westward expansion, most Irish immigrants who migrated to Texas were lower class members who hoped for a better life. In general, and unlike the east Texas settlers who were more conservative because they possessed more property and assets, these Sons of Erin were the real radical revolutionaries, who had more to gain and less to lose than the established Texian settlers with bountiful agricultural wealth, especially in cotton and property. These longtime Texians held both extensive numbers of acres and slaves: a considerable disparity and wide class divide that partly explained why garrison members made their ill-advised gamble to defend the vulnerable Alamo, despite the odds. Indeed, the immigrant Irish were not slave-owners like so many old settlers, or like the Scotch-Irish, those settlers who resided in the bustling and prosperous Austin Colony, and whose economy depended upon a vibrant institution of slavery and cotton production.[27]

By the mid-1830s, what also made the Catholic Irish so different from Americans, including Austin's settlers, was their deeply entrenched, anti-centralized government attitudes and inherent pro-revolutionary proclivities, as well as a vibrant Celtic-Gaelic culture, folkways, and distinct way of life that had survived Protestant British domination since Ireland was conquered in the late 1600s. English invaders had imposed their imperialistic will across Ireland by enforcing discriminatory restrictions, especially the infamous Penal Laws, to ensure that the people remained powerless and easy to rule. Forward-thinking English conquers denied education and the teachings of their faith to Irish Catholics, guaranteeing an illiterate peasantry to work the land for English and Anglo-Irish landowners for the sale of foodstuffs back to England in a feudal-like system. As late as 1719, Catholic-hating Anglo-Irish legislators, hoping to stamp out Catholicism, advocated the branding, on the cheeks, of captured priests, and even castrations of outlawed priests.

---

27 *The New York Herald*, New York, March 29, 1836; Fehrenbach, *Lone Star*, 81-92, 152-201; Davis, *Land!*, 2-257; Groneman, *Alamo Defenders*, 4-125; Marshall, *Uniforms of the Alamo and the Texas Revolution*, 13; Lack, *The Texas Revolutionary Experience*, 55-56, 74, 77, 110-155; "The Alamo: The Irish Heroes of the Alamo," *IC*, internet; Moore, *Eighteen Minutes*, 435-462; Foster, ed., *The Oxford History of Ireland*, 153; McWhiney, *Cracker Culture*, xiii-257; Webb, *Born Fighting*, 123-184; John Francis Bannon, *The Spanish Borderland Frontier, 1513-1821* (Albuquerque, NM, 1974), 1-7, 229-235; Donovan, *Blood of Noble Heroes*, 187.

Nevertheless, no actions by the English government could ever completely eliminate the longing for liberty among the Irish people—especially the lower class—and the quest to own their own land.[28]

Therefore, for the Irish, the bountiful, luxurious lands of Texas offered what was unattainable by them in their homeland and an incredible fulfillment of a lifelong, deferred dream: nothing "but smiling prairies invite the plough" and as far as the eye could see.[29] Ireland-born John Joseph Linn, a fighting man of the Texas Revolution, described how upon first sight, "I was delighted by the appearance of the country [especially in spring when] the landscape was rendered charming by the profusion of many-colored wild flowers that greeted the eye on all sides."[30]

Of Scotch-Irish heritage and like so many others, Noah Smithwick was obsessed by the enticing dream of Texas: "I was but a boy in my nineteenth year, and in for adventure [which] had taken complete possession of me, so early in the following year, 1827, I started out from Hopkinsville, Kentucky, with all my worldly possessions . . . and a gun, of course, to seek my fortune in this lazy man's paradise."[31]

Most appropriately, the first night Smithwick spent on Texas soil was with a new-found friend and fellow Scotch-Irishman named McHenry. Thereafter, Smithwick encountered "quite a family of the McNeals," also Scotch-Irish settlers who had made Texas their home. He also ran into Ned Cullen and Joe McCoy, two more fellow Scotch-Irish. On the west side of the Sabine River, Smithwick had entered the environs of a magnificent land of hardy individuals just like himself.[32]

However, Smithwick had not met Irish settlers, such as James Quinn and Patrick Mahan (both who were destined to fight Mexico) of the Martin de Leon Colony, established in 1824 and consisting of mostly Mexican citizens. It sat near Victoria, Texas, on the gulf coastal plain and 30 miles from the Gulf of Mexico. Here, in the town named for Mexico's first president and hero of the War of Independence, General Guadalupe Victoria, Irishman John Joseph

---

28 Foster, ed., *The Oxford History of Ireland*, 43-147; Dolan, *The Irish Americans*, 3-6.

29 Edwin P. Hoyt, *The Alamo, An Illustrated History* (Dallas, TX, 1999), 11.

30 Linn, *Reminiscences of Fifty Years in Texas*, 13.

31 Smithwick, *The Evolution of a State*, xiii, 1.

32 Ibid., xiii, 3, 16, 19.

Linn thrived as an enterprising merchant in no small part because of an historically tragic Irish past. His father John, an esteemed college professor, had been forced to flee Ireland for his life because of his revolutionary role in the great Irish uprising of 1798.

A native of County Antrim, Linn eventually became the alcalde (municipal magistrate) of the colony that was centered at Victoria, and he was known affectionately to Tejanos as "Don Juan." Linn lived around other Irish, like versatile northern Ireland-born John McHenry, and Linn's own parents and younger brother, who he brought to his new-found frontier paradise in 1831, and then his New Orleans bride three years later. Most importantly, Linn was an enthusiastic support of the cause of Texas, serving as a representative at the San Felipe Consultation to determine a response to Santa Anna's rise to dictator.[33]

Unlike the Martin de Leon Colony, the Refugo Colony was almost entirely Irish Catholic. Founded by Irish empresario James Power and James Hewetson, the Refugio Colony became a dream come true for hundreds of immigrant Irish. From blood-stained Wexford County that was the scene of the most severe fighting and vicious British reprisals against the vanquished Irish rebels of 1798, ten-year-old Power witnessed the horrors of one of the greatest revolutions on Irish soil: an enduring revolutionary legacy not lost to him in Texas. The battle of Vinegar Hill in County Wexford was fought on June 21, 1798 near the River Slaney, where Power was born and raised. Here, on the open hillsides of green that shortly became a grim killing field, the poorly-armed Irish rebels, including a division commanded by Father John Murphy and including his brother Pat who was killed, made their defiant last stand in a true Irish Alamo. Father Murphy was a diehard holy warrior, declaring to the bitter end, "I will never advise anyone to surrender," which sounded much like Travis's famous February 24, 1836 words of defiance at the Alamo.

As could be expected in such a mismatch, the decisive battle of Vinegar Hill quickly turned into a slaughter, with the Irish rebels exposed in the open. A good many of the most fiery Irish revolutionaries of 1798 were cut to pieces by rows of British cannon, and then the lengthy lines of British infantry advanced. Spirited Irish counterattacks of desperate men, mostly armed with wooden pikes, surged down Vinegar Hill, but were hurled back by volleys and explosions of cannon-fire, leaving hundreds of Irish dead and dying in the soft

---

33 Linn, John Joseph, The Handbook of Texas Online; Flannery, *The Irish Texans*, 26, 89-90; Linn, *Reminiscences of Fifty Years in Texas*, 12-27.

light of the first day of summer. However, the crushing and bloody defeat at Vinegar Hill (like the battle of the Boyne) earned a revered place in the collective historical memory and consciousness of the Irish people, including those pioneers who settled on Texas soil.

James Hewetson, born in County Kilkenny, Ireland, in 1796, was Power's partner in the Irish colonization venture at Refugio. The sister Irish colony of Refugio that was composed of mostly southeast Ireland residents, and especially County Wexford, San Patricio Colony consisted of Irish from New York City and Philadelphia, where they were recruited, and also in an overall larger area of Ireland, like County Mayo and County Tipperary. San Patricio settlers included those with the names of O'Toole, O'Connor, Quinn, and O'Boyle. Having migrated with the Irish to Texas, the spiritual leader of the San Patricio Colony was Father Henry Doyle, later replaced by Father John Thomas Molloy. San Patricio de Hibernia (St. Patrick of Ireland) was named in honor of the patron saint of Ireland, St. Patrick.

Both Irish colonies situated on the gulf coastal plain, where traditional Irish crops like cabbage and potatoes were grown, had been established just in time to provide for the large numbers of rebels, who possessed different and distinct Irish accents (or brogues). They represented different regions of Ireland, but were recruited to the cause of Texas in 1835-1836, sharing a revolutionary heritage and egalitarian tradition. After all, for the Irish settlers of the two colonies and among isolated settlements and remote log cabins of hundreds of Irish settlers across Texas, "the details of that magnificent stand [on Vinegar Hill] made by the men and women [revolutionaries] of County Wexford were often recounted around evening firesides" across Texas.[34]

Here, the cherished Irish folk tradition of storytelling thrived as vibrantly on the Texas frontier as it had for centuries among the hills and valleys of rural Ireland. Such popular storytelling, a revered part of Irish culture, entertainment, and society for centuries, served as a prominent feature of everyday life on both sides of the Atlantic, including in Texas. After a hard day's work in the fields from sun up to sun down, Irish families gathered around firesides of plain, thatch-roofed cottages in Ireland and roughhewn log cabins on the Texas frontier for long sessions of storytelling about Irish history, Celtic-Gaelic heroes, and folk ways from ancient times. In this way, Irish nationalist and

34 Golway, *For the Cause of Liberty*, 86; Flannery, *The Irish Texans*, 29-30, 32, 35-47.

revolutionary traditions, martial lore, and egalitarian legacies were kept alive generation after generation in the old country and the new.[35]

From the port of Galway, County Connacht, Ireland, Father John Thomas Molloy provided spiritual guidance to the Irish of San Patricio up to the time of the Texas Revolution. He devoted his life to God in 1813. The Irishman journeyed to Lisbon, Portugal, in 1814 to study for the priesthood and became a member of the Dominican Order. His experience in Portugal and bilingual abilities helped make him an ideal priest for his faithful followers of the San Patricio Colony. More importantly, the Irishman was about to become a true revolutionary in the sacred cause of Texas.[36]

---

35 Brian Lalor, editor, *The Encyclopedia of Ireland* (New Haven, CT, 2003), 1022-1023; Flannery, *The Irish Texans*, 29, 49.

36 Irish Father John Thomas Molloy, Servant of God and Texas, O.P., Sons of DeWitt Colony, Texas, internet.

Chapter 3

Enduring Myths and Realities
of the Texas Revolution

As the winners of wars have been bestowed with writing the history of a conflict, so religion also played a role in deciding whose history was ultimately told in the history books, especially in regard to Texas. Another factor which partly ensured that the Irish were long ignored in Texas history books—even the most respected works devoted to the Alamo and the Texas Revolution—was simply because they were Catholic.

After all, Catholicism was the predominate faith of Mexico. Anti-Catholic, anti-Irish, and anti-immigrant sentiment had been pervasive throughout America since the colonial period, and Texas only continued this dark tradition. America's lengthy legacy of anti-Irish hostility and discrimination was part of the Protestant heritage and cultural baggage inherited from the Mother County, which had obsessively feared the rise of "Popery."

The traditional anti-Catholicism of Protestant America, existed since before the nation's founding because Protestants believed that Catholicism's rise had been orchestrated by Rome, and this sentiment was early and solidly implanted in Texas Anglo-Celtic culture. Xenophobic Protestant Anglo-Americans inherited Protestant England's historic fear and disdain of the Roman Church, viewing it as heretical and dangerous. After all, Catholic Spain was an early threat to England, and Catholic France had been the principal enemy of the thirteen colonies during the French and Indian War. Even priests were often viewed by Protestants as the epitome of evil during centuries of religious intolerance.

But of the cultural and religious differences between two distinct groups, the greatest divide that xenophobic Americans and migrants brought with them across the Red and Sabine Rivers was an intense disgust of mixed-race peoples (Mexican or Tejano) and an excessive obsession with racial purity, seen in how mulattos in the United States were looked upon by whites. From the beginning, the Anglo-Celts, believing their culture and society was superior, "despised Mexicans as they despised negroes and Indians" and primarily for the same, fundamental reason: color.

In striking contrast, this almost pathological sense of revulsion felt by most Anglo-Celts toward Mexicans was not shared by the majority of the immigrant Irish who had the same faith as the Mexican and Tejano people.[1] Ireland-born John Joseph Linn admired and respected them, especially their all-consuming devotion to God and Catholic faith. He became fluent in the Spanish language, and loved the smooth flow of "the soft, rhythmic Spanish" distinguished by its "beauty."[2] He was enthralled by the sincerity of the common Tejano's worship, including ever more isolated shepherds and their families who "recite their prayers and sing a hymn . . . some of the fruits that had germinated from the sacred seed sown by the consecrated messengers of the [Catholic] Church in early Texas."[3]

Clearly, unlike the Ireland-born settlers, this irrational, but prevalent, sense of superiority among the Anglo-Celtic revolutionaries reflected a cultural and racial arrogance, and fueled the dangerous notion in early 1836 that "the Mexicans are slow as usual in their invasions." Therefore, they were convinced that sufficient time existed for Texas and the diminutive Alamo garrison to make adequate preparations to meet any offensive threat from Mexico.[4] But a prophetic December 4, 1835 letter written by an astute American, who knew

---

1   McNally, *Battle of the Boyne 1690*, 7-92; Fehrenbach, *Lone Star*, 168; Davis, *Land!*, 15-19, 158, 167. 193-204; McNally, *Battle of the Boyne 1690*, 54-89; Webb, *Born Fighting*, xiii-257; McWhiney, *Cracker Culture*, xiii-257; Sam W. Haynes and Cary D. Wintz, editors, *Major Problems in Texas History* (Boston, MA, 2002), 98-104; Seamas MacAnnaidh, *Irish History* (Bath, England, 1999), 82-129; McCarthy, ed., *Ireland*, 79-148; Craig H. Roell, *Matamoros and the Texas Revolution* (Denton, TX, 2014), 17.

2   Linn, *Reminiscences of Fifty Years in Texas*, 15-16, 27.

3   Ibid., 15-16.

4   *New York Herald*, March 29, 1836; Roell, *Matamoros and the Texas Revolution*, 17.

the Mexican people as well as the Americans, was more accurate about the situation: "I pity the Texians, first because they are wrong, and secondly because they will meet with little mercy," referring to Santa Anna once he descended upon an ill-prepared Texas.[5]

The stereotypical Anglo-Saxon view of the Irish can be seen in the words from a New York City newspaper, that simultaneously carried a story of Santa Anna's impending 1836 push into Texas "with a large force," and denounced "the Irish character" and especially "the brutal part—the savage—the insolent—the impertinent," all combative qualities that made for an ideal Texas revolutionary.[6] But he then emphasized that an "Irish gentleman is every inch a gentleman—but an Irish blackguard can never be anything else than a savage."[7] Perhaps South Carolina-born Noah Smithwick best described the essence of the rough-and-tumble qualities of the Irish by remembering how "'Texian,' Felix McClusky, a wild Irishman" was a tough character.[8]

But the greatest fundamental difference between the Texians and people of Mexico went far deeper than appearances and beyond simply differences in skin color and culture. As John Quincy Adams, the son of President John Adams, outlined as the central cause of the division between the two people: "there [is] hatred enough between the races which compose your Southern population [in the United States] and the population of Mexico, their next neighbor, but you must go back eight hundred or a thousand years, and to another hemisphere, for the foundation of bitterness between you and them. . . . Do not you, an Anglo-Saxon, slave-holding exterminator of Indians, from the bottom of your soul, hate the Mexican Spaniard Indian emancipator of slaves and abolisher of slavery?"[9]

Indeed, the Republic of Mexico had abolished slavery in mid-September 1829, more than a quarter century before the United States.[10] The typical militant and pro-independence Texan view was articulated by a leading War Dog, Virginia-born William H. Wharton. He emphasized in 1836 how "Texas

5   *New York Evening Star*, New York, New York, January 18, 1836.

6   *New York Herald*, March 29, 1836.

7   Ibid.

8   Smithwick, *Evolution of a State*, 116.

9   Benjamin Lundy, *The War in Texas* (Philadelphia, PA, 1836), 4.

10 Tucker, *Exodus from the Alamo*, 11.

was emphatically a land of agriculture—the land of cotton and of sugar cane," and this meant large numbers of slaves were needed.[11] At the time, Wharton was only able to articulate his fiery stance against Mexico and, of course, "liberty-hating priests" because the fire-eating Wharton had been rescued from a Matamoros, Mexico, jail by Irishman Father Miguel Muldoon.[12]

As in much of the United States, the issue of race also became an obsession among Texians. Thanks to their Protestant culture and heritage and in keeping with the pervasive values of the day, relatively few Anglo-Celts in Texas looked beyond the superficial outward appearances of skin pigmentation and human characteristics. William Fairfax Gray, a 50-year-old opportunistic Texas land agent, retained an open mind that allowed him to be readily tolerant to new cultures and people, including Tejanos. He wrote how the Tejano people of Nacogdoches were a remarkably "quiet, orderly, and cheerful people," the antithesis of so many the unruly, aggressive Anglo-Celts, especially young William Barret Travis and other loudly-barking War Dogs.[13] Such open-minded qualities and traits existed among the Irish such as John Twohig, born in April 1806 in County Cork, who established a mercantile business in San Antonio in 1830. Twohig was one of the early Texian revolutionaries, serving in the siege of San Antonio and the Alamo in 1835. [14]

Just like the Irish Catholics, the disproportionate contributions of Tejano Catholics were dismissed by traditional Protestant historians. Juan Napomuceno Seguin, was the promising son of a respected San Antonio River Valley owner of a 2,000-acre rancho, where "Spanish cattle," hogs, and corn were raised. The sprawling Seguin ranch was christened La Mora (The Moor). Descended from Canary Island immigrants who first settled San Antonio, Juan's father—Juan Jose Maria Erasmo Seguin—served as San Antonio's postmaster, and was a longtime supporter of independence from Spain. Most importantly, the elder Seguin was a good friend of the Texian settlers from the

11 William H. Wharton, *Texas to an Impartial World* (Frankston, TX: Texas National Press, 2005), 11.

12 Ibid., 26; Flannery, *The Irish Texans*, 23.

13 William Fairfax Gray, *Diary of Col. William Fairfax Gray, From Virginia to Texas, 1835-1836* (Houston, TX, 1965), i-viii, 92; Lack, *The Texas Revolutionary Experience*, 200; Weems and Weems, *Dream of Empire*, 5-6.

14 Twohig, John, The Handbook of Texas Online; Roell, *Matamoros and the Texas Revolution*, 17;Nutting, *Ireland Beautiful*, 29, 60-62.

beginning. Farming had not been a traditional way of life in Spain because of geography, infertile soil, and arid climate, and the Tejanos primarily engaged in raising stock and growing maize, or corn, which had been first borrowed from the Indians.

A devout Catholic, Juan Seguin emerged as one of the most respected local Tejano commanders in the struggle for Texas independence. He skillfully led a Tejano company of hard-riding Catholic rancheros in early successes under Bowie—the late December 1835 victory at San Antonio, where as many as 160 Tejanos fought beside the Anglo-Celts, and at San Jacinto. Seguin first received his captain's commission from Stephen Fuller Austin not long after the revolution's beginning, when the feisty Texas revolutionary army was nearly twenty percent Tejano.

These Tejanos, or Mexican citizens born in Texas, were expert riders of the borderland prairies, and came primarily from the San Antonio area. They had long served in ethnically-distinctive ranger companies that protected their isolated frontier communities from Indian raids, and were essentially the earliest Texas Rangers. Wearing sombreros and traditional garb of the Spanish borderlands, the Tejanos early assisted the Texian revolutionaries by providing valuable intelligence gained from stealthy reconnaissance missions and knowledge about their opponent.

Seguin's company of mounted men, who had left behind their pastoral rancherias, reinforced the tiny Alamo garrison before Santa Anna's arrival outside San Antonio on February 23, 1836, ensuring that a handful of Tejanos fell on March 6. Supporters of republican government like their Anglo-Celtic allies, these Tejanos fought against their own countrymen, a "barbarous enemy" in Seguin's words, in what was a tragic Mexican civil war. However, some Tejano soldiers, especially those men who hailed from the Tejano town of San Antonio, avoided the fate of their more unlucky fellow countrymen in the Alamo, when Neill discharged them to assist Tejano families in a hasty evacuation, or later dispatched them as messengers to seek assistance for the besieged garrison.

Seguin escaped the Alamo death-trap on the swift horse of a close friend (Bowie), thanks to one of those courier assignments and because he knew the central plains so well and possessed superior horsemanship skills. No doubt he was wearing a small Catholic crucifix that exemplified the depth of his devout faith inherited from Spain, and even though he left reluctantly—because this meant leaving his beloved Tejanos, whom he described proudly as "Mexican-Texans"—the Captain obeyed orders, which meant riding away. He returned, in early 1837, leading a solemn mounted detail of horsemen to belatedly bury the remains, only "ashes" by this time, of the Alamo's defenders, including seven Tejanos.

Despite his distinguished role in the Texas Revolution, however, one of the leading patriots of Texas independence was eventually dispossessed, disenfranchised, and imprisoned on "trumped-up charges" and false accusations of treason from his political enemies, in no small part because of his Catholicism and race. Largely due to his past successes, he had created personal enemies because they "envied my military position, as held by a Mexican," and he was forced to flee, riding across Rio Grande to Mexico in 1842—his experience being comparable to many other Tejanos and Irish who sacrificed much for Texas independence. After the Texas Revolution, a good many Irish Catholics were forced to defend their rights and possessions, having gained land grants from Mexico by legal means. In the end, they were denied equality in Protestant-dominated Texas, largely because their religious faith superseded their faithful revolutionary service from 1835-1836.[15]

Seguin's tragic fate in Texas was as undeserving as it was unjust, especially for the man who led the detail that buried the remains of the Alamo's defenders. After all, Captain Seguin described with pride how he and his Tejanos played a key role in reaping decisive victory at San Jacinto, achieving early tactical gains that allowed Sam Houston's attack to succeed on the open grassy coastal plain: "My company was in the left wing ... met by a column of infantry, which we drove back briskly. Before engaging that column, we had dispersed an ambuscade that had opened fire against us. The entire enemy line, panic struck, took to flight."[16] Hardly sounding like a "treasonous" Tejano leader, he described how, "On this great and glorious day [at San Jacinto] my company was conspicuous for efficiency and gallantry yet we did not lose one single man,

---

15   *The Telegraph and Texas Register*, January 9, 1836; Jesus F. de la Teja, editor, *A Revolution Remembered, The Memoirs and Selected Correspondence of Juan N. Seguin* (Austin, TX, 2002), vii-122; *New York Herald*, June 25, 1836; Ruben Rendon Lozano, *Viva Tejas, The Story of the Tejanos, the Mexican-born Patriots of the Texas Revolution* (San Antonio, TX, 1985), 34-39, 71; *Houston Telegraph*, Houston, Texas, November 9, 1836; *St. Louis Republic*, St. Louis, Missouri, August 28, 1890; Hardin, *Texian Illiad*, 29, 55, 83, 120, 209, 213; Stephen L. Moore, *Savage Frontier, 1835-1837*, vol. 1 (Austin, TX, 2002), vix, xii; Groneman, *Alamo Defenders*, 97-99, 164; Linn, *Reminiscences of Fifty Years in Texas*, 68; Davis, *Land!*, 103, 198-236; Lack, *The Texas Revolutionary Experience*, 183-197; Haynes and Wintz, eds., *Major Problems in Texas History*, 136; Bannon, *The Spanish Borderlands Frontier*, 233; Edmondson, *The Alamo Story*, 34, 51-53.

16   Teja, ed., *A Revolution Remembered*, 83.

to the surprise of those [Anglo-Celts] who had witnessed our honorable and perilous situation."[17]

Captain Seguin, who early gained an officer's rank from the Texas General Council, was sickened by such ugly racial realities that ruined his reputation, but only after independence had been won and when Tejano support was no longer needed. Disillusioned and heart-sick, he lamented how, "My enemies had accomplished their object; they had killed me politically in Texas [employing] infamous means . . . to accomplish my ruin."[18] Ironically, however, in January 1841, a Texas newspaperman yet applauded Seguin as a "noble hearted soldier [whose] generous courage and patriotism ... distinguished him in the campaign of 1835-36."[19]

And he was not alone. Despite capturing Goliad and commanding the Goliad garrison at the Presidio La Bahia when the first Declaration of Independence was issued during the Texas Revolution in December 1835, even Captain Philip Dimmitt, a "gallant" Jefferson County Kentuckian, was tainted by anti-Tejano and anti-Catholic stereotypes by less open-minded Anglo-Celts. Dimmitt was condemned primarily because he had a Tejano wife, Maria Louisa Lazo, the mother of his children and whom he loved. He had married Maria in an official ceremony, either at the nearest Catholic Church, or by a local priest at his home. One xenophobic Anglo veteran of the Texas Revolution, Noah Smithwick, wrote with some disgust how Captain Dimmitt "had a Mexican wife and was, for all practical purposes, a Mexican."[20]

Situated south of the east Texas settlements, the Irish Catholic colonies of San Patricio de Hibernia and Refugio consisted mostly of recent immigrants from Ireland's shores, and were devastated by the war. Not only did non-Catholic Texians in the 1850s take land from the Irish, including a good many Texas Revolution veterans, but also future profits of the increasingly lucrative cattle industry, which already had been hijacked from the Tejano rancheros to create the American Cowboy. Clearly, this tragedy was an ironic fate for so

---

17 Ibid., 84.

18 Teja, ed., *A Revolution Remembered*, 100; *The Telegraph and Texas Register*, January 9, 1836.

19 *The Telegraph and Texas Register*, January 6, 1841.

20 *The Telegraph and Texas Register*, December 8, 1841; Philip Dimmit Papers, 1833-1904, Briscoe Center for American History, University of Texas, Austin, Texas; Lack, *The Texas Revolutionary Experience*, 190; Groneman, *Alamo Defenders*, 40-41; Edmondson, *The Alamo Story*, 241; Smithwick, *The Evolution of a State*, 18.

many Irish Catholic immigrants, who had served faithfully in the cause of Texas independence. After all, these men had initially migrated to Texas—not to join in a people's revolution on the southwestern frontier—but primarily for an opportunity to own land, which was unavailable to them in Ireland with the establishment of the Penal Laws toward the end of the seventeenth century.[21]

The anti-Catholicism seen in Captain Seguin's unfortunate case encouraged persistent questions about Irish loyalty of the colonies during the Texas Revolution, especially San Patricio de Hibernia (named after Ireland's patron saint, St. Patrick), since it had been established earlier and had closer contacts with Tejano neighbors. Such sentiments also played a role in obscuring the many noteworthy Irish revolutionary contributions from 1835-1836. Indeed, some Irish Catholics were initially prudent, cautious revolutionaries, because they possessed legal Mexican land titles and like so many "Old Texian" colonists, held an "indifference of the people as to the cause of Texas" when war first erupted in early October 1835. After all, for the first time, the Irish immigrants now owned more bountiful acres than at any time in their lives. These fertile acres had been officially bestowed by the Republic of Mexico, and coveted land titles had been only recently confirmed in their favor by the Mexican government.

And, in striking contrast to many prejudiced non-Irish in Texas, such as Noah Smithwick who "looked on the Mexican [Tejanos] as scarce more than apes," the Irish Catholics maintained close relationships with Tejano ranchero neighbors, thanks in part to Catholicism's binding ties, which included worshiping in church together. But what tarnished the overall image and legacy of the Irish Catholics in the annals of Texas Revolutionary historiography was the simple fact that a few of them were early intimidated by a nearby Mexican garrison, including officers like Lieutenant Marcelino Garcia, who was later killed in the Texas Revolution at Fort Lipantitlan, on the west bank of the Nueces River.

As Mexican citizens, they had to obey lawful Mexican dictates and orders. Only a handful of Irishmen were ever pressed into Mexican military service, yet it tainted the widespread and significant contributions of an entire people. By the time of the revolution's beginning, the story of the fort's capture by the Texas revolutionaries demonstrated far more fiery Irish patriotism than disloyalty, including among Irish soldiers who quickly changed sides to the

21 Lozano, *Viva Tejas*, 71-76; Davis, *Land!*, 4-8, 38-71, 103, 198.

Texas cause. As verified by the historic record, the Irish of the San Patricio and Refugio Colonies were among the foremost, leading, and most determined patriots in all of Texas.[22]

The lowly Irish had owned no property in their ancestral homeland, and had been mostly tenant farmers for wealthy Anglo-Irish and British landlords or had been evicted entirely from their properties as farms were turned into pasture for sheep and cattle. Victimized and without a nation of their own, they fled to America at the beginning of the 18th century to escape the oppression of overpopulation, poverty, and shortages of land. The bounty of Texas offered a religious, economic, and political safe-haven, where they could bask in those new-found freedoms, especially landownership, long lost in Ireland.

But throughout much of the Texas Revolution, the Anglo-Celtic settlers of Texas themselves were divided in sentiment. After all, Texas independence was not declared in the autumn or winter of 1835 because the vast majority of native Texians still supported the 1824 Mexican Constitution. Consequently, the official Declaration of Independence only came belatedly on March 2, 1836, a fact never known by the Alamo garrison under siege. In general, in the early 1830s and up to 1835, recent migrants from within the United States, or those of Scotch-Irish descent were more militant revolutionaries in part because they had more to gain, especially Texas land.

In fact, many Irish migrants to Texas considered themselves to be the legitimate heirs of the revolutionary "spirit of '98," because the legacy of the great Irish Rebellion of 1798 was alive and well. Meanwhile, the "Old Texians," (longer-time settlers than the Irish) were far more conservative mostly because they had more to lose—their bountiful land titles guaranteed by Mexico, which faithfully honored its agreements.

Consequently, these long-settled Anglo-Celts were less likely to take up arms against Mexico, especially in early 1836, but also less independence-minded than the more recent migrants from the United States and Ireland: a deep divide that weakened the overall Texas resistance effort, while helping pave the way for the Alamo fiasco. However, this situation was not unlike

22 *The Telegraph and Texas Register*, December 2, 1835; Davis, *Land!*, 103, 121-122, 255-257; Walraven and Walraven, *The Magnificent Barbarians*, 36-39; Lack, *The Texas Revolutionary Experience*, 122-123, 157. 208-237; Teja, ed., *A Revolution Remembered*, vii-viii, 100-102; Flannery, *The Irish Texans*, 63-66; Smithwick, *The Evolution of a State*, 31; Flannery, *The Irish Texans*, 64, 66-67.

during the American Revolution when more than half of American colonists remained loyal or neutral to the Mother County.

While most long-time Texians—conservative landowners with thousands of acres—felt reluctance toward the concept of breaking away from Mexico, such was not the case with the vast majority of the more recently-arrived Irish. In contrast, these men from Ireland thought mostly in terms of Old World, long-term conditions and oppressions as had been imposed on them and their ancestors by an abusive centralized government. They knew that they would have to take a stand against Mexico City's arbitrary dictates and control, and fight to keep their freedom, a lesson learned from London's legendary imperialistic reach in its determined bid to emulate the vast empire of ancient Rome.

While the "Old Texians" became reluctant revolutionaries by early 1836 before Santa Anna's invasion swept into Texas, and were anything but immediate advocates of independence from Mexico, the Irish were far more natural, instinctive revolutionaries in the sense that they were often and early independence-advocates. The fact that the Irish were relatively recent arrivals in Texas made them less conservative, in part, because they had much less to lose than the established Austin Colony settlers, who had prospered in Texas since the 1820s.

But what has been most often overlooked by traditional Texas historians, including leading scholars of the Texas Revolution, was the vibrant revolutionary heritage of Ireland, spanning centuries, that played a key role in inspiring and motivating the Irish to embrace what was already familiar to them and very much a natural, instinctive course of action in 1835-1836—an uprising against a distant, arbitrary, centralized government to fulfill the long-lost dream of independence. Early experience had made these young Irish men more pro-revolutionary in general, than the previous Anglo-Celtic settlers.

In addition, the mostly poor Irish, especially devout Catholics, possessed little interest in owning slaves due to moral and religious reasons, unlike their Anglo-Celtic neighbors, who had created their prosperity with lucrative cotton cultivation largely by slave labor, even if owning only one or two blacks. After all, the Irish people, and particularly Irish Catholics, had long been considered the debased, exploited "white slaves" of Europe; and tens of thousands of these Emerald Islanders had journeyed to America as indentured servants in a form of semi-slavery, before the American Revolution. The concept of servitude was, therefore, not an abstract one to the Irish, and the Alamo's Irish defenders, then, were either immigrant Irish Catholics without a slave-owning tradition

(Ireland's ancient Brehon laws—the "ways of the Irish people"—were anti-slavery), or Scotch-Irish who were more Americanized and therefore possessed a tradition of slave-owning in America.

In contrast, the Mexicans of Santa Anna's Catholic army hailed from a young republic without slavery's moral curse, as it had been eradicated in the republic in mid-September 1829, nearly four decades before the United States. So, while the Texas revolutionaries, including the Alamo defenders, fought in part to defend property rights (protected by the U. S. Constitution and including slaves), Mexico's warriors waged a much more egalitarian-based war on Texas soil that corresponded with the most enlightened and progressive thought the day, especially in Great Britain and the rest of western Europe—the concept of universal emancipation. Therefore, Santa Anna's forces were a liberating army for Texas slaves, contradicting the traditional interpretations, by historians, of the very meaning of the Texas Revolution.

The widespread participation of the more recently-arrived Irish as some of the foremost revolutionaries in all Texas bestows credence on the non-traditional thesis that the Texas Revolution was very much of a "rich's man war, poor man's fight," a realization that kept a good many native Texians of the lower class out of the army as of 1836. Such factors also explain why the contributions of the Irish in the Texas Revolution has been either overlooked or minimized by historians: the fact that it was not the longtime Texas settlers—especially the richest, leading, and largest landowners in Texas—who were the most independence-minded. Nor were they, for the most part, revolutionary advocates and soldiers. Instead the ranks were filled with mostly lower-class, relatively recent immigrants of Catholic and Protestant (mostly Presbyterian) faith from far-away Ireland.

As with the "Anglo-Saxon myth" that has long applied to Texas history and, specifically, the Alamo, the facts challenge the standard interpretation that the people of Texas were all united as one against Mexican oppression and freedom-fighters against an evil dictatorship. Further, only a handful of Texians served in the Alamo garrison, so only a minority of native Texians actually fought in the 1836 Texas Campaign, dispelling the idea that Texians won their struggle entirely on their own. Instead, there were a good many non-Teixans, and especially Irish immigrants, in the army's ranks.

In the beginning of the dispute between Texas and Mexico, many non-Irish Texans viewed their Irish Catholic neighbors from Ireland as natural enemies, thanks largely to a shared religion with Catholic Mexico. Of course, some justification existed for this historic paranoia over the much-exaggerated

Catholic threat, going back to America's earliest settlers, and especially during the French and Indian War. Irish Catholics of the mostly Irish colony of San Patricio, located in southeast Texas and southwest of Refugio, enjoyed good relations with their Tejano neighbors unlike most non-Irish of Texas, especially recent Anglo-Celtic migrants from within the United States.

Relatively, and quite unlike the Irish Protestants, striking similarities existed between Latino culture and Celtic-Gaelic culture of the Irish Catholics. Indeed, English relations with other peoples and races, especially Native Americans and African Americans, were especially noted for their extreme racial intolerance. A historic xenophobic Anglo-Saxon culture (like ancient Roman culture than referred to all non-Romans as "barbarians") possessed a strong distaste for different cultures and peoples, stemming from the legacies of the Protestant Reformation, seemingly endless religious wars in Europe, a strict Calvinist tradition, and the narrow provincialism of English culture fueled by concepts of superiority at all levels. In general, such intolerant qualities were not shared by the genuinely more tolerant and less xenophobic Celtic-Gaelic culture with its easy-going, affable nature; greater respect for the land and different cultures; a heightened sense of humor and vibrant musical tradition; a greater overall sense of humanitarianism; empathy for the underdog and oppressed (a shared status) and; a more people-friendly society based on strong kinship systems. All of these were qualities and characteristics were shared more by the people of Mexico than the English.

For instance, many Irish, especially Indian traders, such as Ireland-born George Groghan, early mixed with Indian people more readily and easily than the English, holding a genuine admiration for Native American ways that was quite rare for the English in colonial America. John Stark, the son of Scotch-Irish immigrants from Ulster Province, became a legendary top officer in Major Robert Rogers's Rangers in the French and Indian War, and one of Washington's hardest fighting generals during the American Revolution, rising to the fore in victories at Trenton, New Jersey, and especially at Bennington, Vermont. Yet he refused to join in Major Rogers's devastating raid upon the Abenaki village of Saint Francis during the French and Indian War, because he had once lived there and loved the people, after having been adopted into the tribe.

Providing another representative example during the colonial period, Ireland-born William Johnson was a famous high-ranking official among those more open-minded and less racist Irish types. He was raised Catholic in a small town just west of Dublin, Ireland. As the Superintendent of Indian Affairs for

England, he was respected by Native Americans, partly because of his thorough embrace of Indian culture and ways, including a pretty Mohawk wife, which was an unthinkable cultural transgression to most English in America. This gifted official from County Meath identified closely with the Indians, who had lost so much of their lands to relentless English encroachment like his own Catholic family had in Ireland. Johnson's relatives had fought at the Battle of the Boyne in July 1690, where the Jacobite Catholic force was crushed by superior Protestant might.

During the process of conquest, westward expansion, and subjugation in America, the English viewed the indigenous peoples in the same negative light as they had the native Catholic people of Ireland.[23] A sense of superiority of an Anglo-Saxon-based culture in east Texas settlements early clashed with Latino culture, xenophobic with its own version of cultural elitism. Yet the Irish Catholics of the San Patricio and Refugio Colonies acclimated to Tejano ways, including raising stock of Spanish cattle (the Texas Longhorn) on the grassy prairies. All in all, Celtic-Gaelic culture and Latino culture blended easily together on the Texas frontier, A shared Catholic faith dissipated preexisting cultural and racial differences between the Tejano and Irish Catholic people in pre-revolution Texas.[24]

However, the historical assumption among far too many Protestants (from the Texian settlers to modern historians) that Irish Catholic settlers were resistant to fighting fellow Catholics of Mexico has no merit, and is one of the great myths of the Texas Revolution. After all, the lesson of Napoleon's

---

23 Foster, ed., *The Oxford History of Ireland*, 90-148; Fintan O'Toole, *White Savage, William Johnson and the Invention of America* (New York, NY, 2005), 1-313; Davis, *Land!*, 154-198; Murphy, *The Irish in the American Revolution*, 22-14; Nutting, *Ireland Beautiful*, 60-62; McWhiney, *Cracker Culture*, 1-22, 35-36; Webb, *Born Fighting*, 81-86; Miller and Wagner, *Out of Ireland*, 10-13, 29, 54; Lack, *The Texas Revolutionary Experience*, 38-155, 208-237; Flannery, *The Irish Texans*, p. 14; Twohig, John, The Handbook of Texas Online; Haynes and Wintz, eds., *Major Problems in Texas History*, 91-145; Nic Fields, *Roman Conquests: North Africa* (Barnsley: Pen and Sword Books Limited, 2010), xvi-xxii; Gleeson, *The Irish of the South*, 16; Randolph B. Campbell, *An Empire for Slavery, The Peculiar Institution in Texas, 1821-1865* (Baton Rouge, LA, 1989), 1-114; Lalor, ed., *The Encyclopedia of Ireland*, pp. 121-122; Ben Z. Rose, *John Stark, Maverick General* (Waverly, MA, 2007), xi-148; Linn, *Reminiscences of Fifty Years in Texas*, 9-10, 42-44; Lundy, *The War in Texas*, 3-56; Linn, John Joseph, The Handbook of Texas Online; Eric Hinderaker and Peter C. Mancall, *At The Edge of Empire, The Backcountry in British North America* (Baltimore, MD, 2003), 92-93; Groneman, *Alamo Defenders*, 3-125; Libura, Moreno an Marquez, *Echoes of the Mexican-American War*, 25.

24 Davis, *Land!*, 17-19, 193-198.

disastrous invasion of the Catholic nation of Spain, beginning in 1808, provides a notable example of the same fallacy. Unfortunately, the shared cultural and religious commonalities with the Tejanos and Mexican enemy instead played a role in tainting the significant Irish contributions to winning the Texas Revolution. As mentioned, a few Irishmen stood beside the Tejano militia, but they were pressed into military service by Mexican leadership, and had no choice. Further fueling the myth of traitorous Irish was an initial reluctance, of some conservative San Patricio Irish colonists, to go to war against their fellow Catholics.

Far more representative of the Irish Catholic role was demonstrated when the Mexicans ordered the return of the cannon, a tiny two-pounder, that had been given to protect the San Patricio setters from Indians. One of the principal founders of the San Patricio Colony, James McGloin, born in County Sligo in northwest Ireland in Connacht Province, flatly refused the cannon's return.

The small fort named Lipantitlan, which had been established for defense against Indian raiders and served as a Mexican customs station, was located on the Nueces River's west bank and just south of the mostly Irish colony of San Patricio. After he captured the key strategic position of Goliad, which was of "vastly more importance in a military point of view" than San Antonio because it cut off General Cos's supply line stretching from San Antonio to Copano Bay, the ambitious Captain Philip Dimmitt laid plans to capture Lipantitlan.

He dispatched two trusty, young Irish lads, John O'Toole and John Williams, to rally San Patricio for assistance, but the couriers were captured and taken prisoner. Dimmitt then ordered Captain Ira J. Westover, who had represented Goliad in the Consultation and was now the leader of the municipal militia of Refugio, to launch a surprise attack and capture the strategic fort. Undertaking their key mission on the last day of October 1835, Westover's band of 30 mounted revolutionaries, including John Joseph Linn from County Antrim, Ireland, and the Ireland-born James Power, who was a primary founder of the Refugio Colony, rode down the dirt road leading to San Patricio. Here the rebels were bolstered by 40 San Patricio soldiers, including volunteers like John Fadden, the nephew of the colony's highly-respected Irish priest, Andrew Michael O'Boyle, Dennis McGowan, and Edward Ryan.

Westover spread his troops out in concealed positions to surround the fort on the outskirts, planning to launch an assault to overwhelm the garrison and gain the release O'Toole and Williams on the cool, but sunny, morning of November 4. However, without firing a shot and on condition of parole, the nearly two dozen Mexican troops quietly surrendered Fort Lipantitlan to the combined force of Anglo-Celts and Refugio and San Patricio Irish. One of the first Texian victories of the war, the fort's capitulation was an early accomplishment thanks partly to the diplomatic efforts of Spanish-speaking Irishman James O'Riley of San Patricio. He had informed the Mexican garrison that they were surrounded and no hope remained for either resistance or reinforcements.

A number of Irish, who had been pressed into Mexican service, promptly joined the Texian revolutionaries, becoming patriots in the cause of Texas. Not long after capturing the fort, the victors were then attacked, but the Mexicans were repulsed in a hot skirmish, the so-called battle of Lipantitlan. A mortally wounded Mexican lieutenant, Marcelino Garcia, was the highest-ranking victim of the hail of rifle-fire delivered from the Texians. His last thoughts might have been of his beautiful Irish fiancée, whose life was shattered forever after Garcia's death. The aggressiveness of Westover's campaign effectively thwarted the Mexican bid to recapture strategically vital Goliad, due mostly to Refugio Irish but also including Ireland-born volunteers like John Joseph Linn. Other Irish soldiers under Westover's command included William Ryan, Michael McDonough, Walter, James, and John Lambert, John Dunn, Nicholas and John Fagan, Patrick and Michael O'Reilly, and brothers Michael John and Patrick Quinn, among others. Clearly, and as it had been for centuries, going to war was very much of a family affair for the clannish Irish. Thomas John O'Brien, Power's nephew, was the youngest Irish soldier at age thirteen.

Unfortunately, because a few Irish Catholics fought against Americans within the Fort Lipantitlan garrison, and a handful of Irish served in Mexican ranks out of coercion, this played a significant role in tainting the overall distinguished effort in the Texas Revolution and painting Irish Catholics as disloyal—even though some of these same soldiers later joined the revolutionaries. More so, anti-Irish, anti-Catholic prejudice placed a dark stain on the accomplishments and sacrifices of the far larger number of Irish patriots from the colony at Refugio, who were, in fact, the leaders of the drive for independence, issuing the first Declaration of Independence at Goliad months before independence was officially declared on March 2, 1836 at Washington-on-the-Brazos. The enduring misconception about suspect Irish loyalty reached new heights in the decades after the Texas Revolution because of an early 1850s lawsuit by the governor, Joseph B. Smith and his nephew. The accusations were based partly on the dubious premise that the Irish Catholics were traitors in the Texas Revolution, but was merely a calculated bid to gain possession of the fertile coastal lands of the Irish settlers.

Yet Refugio Colony sent almost all of its young Irishmen off to war against Mexico from the very beginning, and the entire community (like San Patricio) suffered disproportionately in the war. In truth, a far larger number of non-Irish of Texas—the so-called "Old Texians"—should actually be labeled traitors when considering the San Jacinto Campaign, because they refused to either join Sam Houston's army or support the revolution. Some traitorous non-Irish Texians, who were large landowners with Spanish land grants, supported and openly communicated with Santa Anna.

Complementing extensive military contributions, the Refugio Irish played leading political roles throughout the Texas Revolution. Three principal Irish leaders—Colonel James Power, the head of the Refugio colony born near Ballygarrett, County Wexford, Ireland; John Joseph Linn, and Kentucky-born Major James Kerr, an old Indian fighter of Scotch-Irish descent—were elected delegates to the Consultation government at San Felipe de Austin on the Brazos River. This trio of highly-respected Irish leaders mirrored the key political role played by Irish politiciansm including the Texas Declaration of Independence signers on March 2, 1836, agitated for revolution early on, and led their hardy and highly motivated Irish soldiers from Refugio on Fort Lipantitlan.[25]

Thanks to the anguished historical experience in Ireland, where Protestant conquest and British domination led to an anti-Catholic campaign of repression and cultural domination, Catholicism may have played a role in explaining why some Irish Catholics of Texas were initially reluctant revolutionaries. However, anti-Catholicism in Texas, and America at large, was most responsible for having created one of the most persistent stereotypes and misconceptions of the Texas Revolution, persisting to this day: that the Irish were "traitors" to the cause of Texas Independence. Yet John Joseph Linn had nothing but lavish and well-deserved praise for "the patriotic citizens of 'Saint Patrick,'" and Refugio—for ample good reason.[26]

25 *The Telegraph and Texas Register*, November 14, 1835; Davis, *Land!*, 102-103, 117, 106-153, 255-257; Hardin, *Texian Illiad*, 41-45; *Southern Patriot*, Charleston, South Carolina, November 21, 1835; Barber, *David Kokernot*, pp. 74-79; Westover, Ira J., The Handbook of Texas Online; Flannery, *The Irish Texans*, 70-71; Linn, *Reminiscences of Fifty Years in Texas*, 39-40; 44; Thomas Fleming, *Liberty!, The American Revolution* (New York, NY, 1907), 348; Lawrence H. Leder, editor, *The Colonial Legacy*, vol. 1 (New York, NY, 1971), 1-2; "John (Juan) McMullen, Irish Empresario & Co-founder" Paper, Sons of DeWitt Colony, Texas, internet; Walraven and Walraven, *The Magnificent Barbarians*, 36-39; Flannery, *The Irish Texans*, 29; Teja, ed., *A Revolution Remembered*, 100-102.

26 Davis, *Land!*, 103; Linn, *Reminiscences of Fifty Years in Texas*, 57, 121.

Indeed, the vast majority of the Irish in Texas, including the Catholics who possessed a more lengthy revolutionary experience in Ireland than the Scotch-Irish, wholeheartedly supported the cause of Texas independence, and paid a high price for that support. They served in disproportionate numbers—corresponding with disproportionate contributions and sacrifices throughout the revolutionary struggle—to assist in winning Texas independence. In truth, a good many Irish Catholics were among the earliest and most vocal advocates of proclaiming an independent Texas, long before the majority of their non-Irish fellow Texans embraced this concept, and especially before longtime residents.

Catholic Irish and the Protestant (Presbyterian) Irish were largely identical in regard to having made significant contributions in both the settlement of Texas and the revolutionary struggle. Overall, far more Protestant Irish or those of Scotch-Irish descent fought in the Texas Revolution than Irish Catholics because their numbers were far greater in Texas in 1835-1836. Proportionately, however, Irish Catholic contributions were noteworthy to say the least.

Because of such misconceptions, what has been obscured was the depth of Celtic-Gaelic roots in not only the Alamo's history, but also in the push for independence. As established, the vast majority of Texas Revolutionary soldiers were Irish, Scotch-Irish, or of Scotch Irish descent. The Celtic peoples—Irish, Welsh, and Scots—fought primarily in 1835-1836 so that their Texas lands would not be taken away from them, as they had under British imperialism, and so they could gain additional land in the future. The lessons learned on the other side of the Atlantic fueled their revolutionary proclivities, and was reflected, particularly, in the cultural make-up of men in the Alamo garrison and the Refugio Colony.

Indeed, native Irish represented the highest total of men at the Alamo except for those from Tennessee and Virginia; those of Scotch-Irish ancestry could claim more garrison members than any other distinct ethnic group. As if repeating another revolutionary chapter of Celtic history on Texas soil, the garrison made a defiant last stand against the odds, just like so many Irish ancestors in past battles against English invaders.[27]

27 Davis, *Land!*, 3-240, 255-257; Groneman, *Alamo Defenders*, 4-121; Webb, *Born Fighting*, 67-184; Moore, *Eighteen Minutes*, 435-462; "The Alamo: Irish Heroes of the Alamo," *IC*, internet; Foster, ed., *The Oxford History of Ireland*, 44-153; Webb, *Born Fighting*, 123-184; McWhiney, *Cracker Culture*, xiii-257; Flannery, *The Irish Texans*, 11; Lack, *The Texas Revolutionary Experience*, 121-124.

For those defenders of the Alamo who died, this was not the only tragedy befalling the Celtic-Gaelic peoples. In addition, "no group paid a higher price for Texas independence than did the Irish colonies west of the Guadalupe River. Their men fought and fell at the Alamo, Goliad, San Patricio, Agua Dulce Creek, Coleto Creek, and Refugio. [But also] their homes, land, and livestock were raided and laid waste by Mexican and Texan armies."[28]

Though largely forgotten, another significant episode in the Texas Revolutionary saga took place on a chilly December 20, 1835 at Goliad and exemplifies the widespread extent of the Irish contributions—militarily, economically, and politically—that paved the way for Texas independence. In the stone chapel known as Our Lady of Loreto, located near the main gate at the Presidio La Bahia (Fort on the Bay), candlelight illuminated the dark surroundings and ancient stone walls, revealing one of the most important gathering in the annals of Texas history.

Ira Ingram, Dimmitt's well-educated secretary—who had migrated to Texas in January 1826 and eventually helped to rally resistance in the east Texas settlements after the Alamo's fall—composed "the most complete statement of the independence ideology" and of egalitarian faith in the entire Texas Revolution. This revered document was then placed on the wooden (most likely cedar) altar of the chapel, and one member after another of Captain Dimmitt's Goliad garrison walked forth to sign it.

The egalitarian sentiments contained therein reflected distinct Irish character and influences, and the fight for equality. To the many Catholics from the Refugio Colony who came from southeast Ireland, the fact that this solemn ceremony was held in a small but beautiful Catholic chapel was especially symbolic. In the eerie aura of ceremony, determined Irishmen like Patrick O'Leary, teenager Thomas O'Connor, William Quinn, John James, Charles Malone, Morgan O'Brien, Michael O'Donnell, and other soldiers from the Refugio Colony and the San Patricio Colony signed their names with pride to the Texas Declaration of Independence.

A total of 32 Irish signers at the Presidio La Bahia hailed from the Refugio Colony, including Spirse Dooley, Michael Kelly, Dugald McFarline, Hugh McMinn, and E. B. W. Fitzgerald, along with numbers of Scotch-Irish fighting men. Irish soldiers from San Patricio also signed the document, casting their fates in an independence movement against a formidable opponent. Their

28 Flannery, *The Irish Texans*, 11.

signatures, as part of a revolution that, in their words, was launched for a great "moral renovation," all but their ensured execution at the hands of the Mexicans, if they were captured.[29]

What was signed at Goliad by this zealous group was a most remarkable document that was as historic as it was significant. The extent of its grass roots radicalism is revealed by the sparse, but clear, wording that did not resemble the lofty Age of Enlightenment eloquence of the well-educated Founding Fathers, but instead spoke to lower class influences, especially in regard to class consciousness and past struggles for liberty in Ireland. They proclaimed "a new, invigorating & cherishing policy" for Texas, and one that would be "extending equal, impartial, and indiscriminate protection to all—to the low, as well as the high, the humbly bred, & the well-born—the poor, & the rich; the ignorant, and the educated; the simple, & the shrewd."[30]

Here, on the remote edge of the grassy coastal plain southeast of San Antonio the first declaration of independence in the history of the Texas Revolution was issued. On their own and at great risk to their lives, families, and fortunes, this feisty band of mostly Celtic-Gaelic citizen-soldiers had captured Goliad, chose the dynamic Dimmitt as their leader in true democratic fashion, and then issued their brash Texas declaration.

Ironically as well as symbolically, this bold declaration was issued from the same fortified mission and high walls of Presidio La Bahia, which consisted of sturdy "stone and lime," where Irishman Augustus William Magee, the Celtic-Gaelic leader of the 1812-1813 war of liberation, had raised "the green flag" of Ireland. Here, at Goliad, Magee and his American, Irish, and Tejano troops had established the first republic in Texas history, which was swiftly exterminated by the resurgent Spanish Royalists.

Unlike an isolated San Antonio, which was located on the remote western frontier and so less strategically important in the war, Goliad stood on the main road: the camino real, leading north from the Rio Grande River town of Matamoros, Mexico, and running parallel to the gulf coast's expansive length.

---

29 Linn, *Reminiscences of Fifty Years in Texas*, 57; Davis, *Land!*, 115, 121-123, 151, 255; Walraven and Walraven, *The Magnificent Barbarians*, 46, 48-49; Ingram, Ira, The Handbook of Texas Online; Lack, *The Texas Revolutionary Experience*, 58, 226; Smithwick, *The Evolution of a State*, 40; Philip Dimmitt, The Handbook of Texas Online; Newton Warzecha, Director of the Presidio, Goliad, Texas, to Debra Barker, Curator, Goliad Center for Texas History, Goliad County Library, Goliad Texas, February 2104.

30 Lack, *The Texas Revolutionary Experience*, 58.

The nearby gulf port of El Copano to Goliad's south served as a logistical base against the amateurs in revolution.

On December 22, and before an assembled citizen-soldier force, an impressive ceremony was held on the spacious parade ground of the Presidio La Bahia. Like the gathering of the ancient Celtic clans to confront invaders who had coveted Ireland's rich lands, this gathering of young revolutionaries was most of all distinguished by its fulfillment of the highest revolutionary aspirations of a vibrant grass roots egalitarian ideology, class consciousness, and republican faith.

Contradicting typical Texian revolutionary stereotypes, Spanish-speaking Dimmitt was closely integrated into the mainstream of the Tejano world, including social and cultural norms. Dimmitt married his Tejano wife, Maria Luisa Lazo, in 1828 and became fully acclimated into the vibrancy of Tejano life. Combined with his extensive Tejano connections and deep empathy for Tejanos and Catholics, Dimmitt's relationships confounded and upset less tolerant Anglo-Celts, or Protestants, who possessed no such enlightened racial or cultural views. Most importantly, Dimmitt now commanded a large percentage of Celtic-Gaelic soldiers; his force represented a timely synergy necessary for a successful revolutionary war effort in Texas: the systematic coming together to a multi-cultural Texas and the creation of an integrated "free" nation through a "moral renovation."

While this first declaration of independence was read to Dimmitt's troops, now standing at attention in homespun, coarse wool and cotton civilian clothing (not a uniform was seen), a young man named Nicholas Fagan, the respected Irish political and military leader of these Celtic-Gaelic warriors from Refugio, proudly brought forth "the Irish flag of independence," a bloodied arm holding a saber. Only a short time before, Fagan had cut down a straight sycamore sapling from along the muddy banks of the San Antonio River, which he planted in the center of the grassy plaza of the Presidio La Bahia fortress—a more formidable defensive bastion than the Alamo. Here, in the presidio's sprawling quadrangle, this revolutionary Irish banner, made of cotton cloth and six feet in length, was raised by Fagan in dramatic fashion to the chorus of cheers. The stiff coastal breeze, salty and warm even in December, extended the folds of the flag, which flapped in the sunshine-drenched gulf plain.

For these revolutionary men who had known intimately of British oppression and anti-Irish discrimination in their native homeland, Goliad's December 1835 declaration of independence must have seemed somewhat surreal, accomplishing in a relatively short time what generations of their forefathers had sought to achieve in repeated revolts.[31] It was an act of open defiance toward not only the centralized government in Mexico City but also of the more conservative fledgling Texas government that had yet to embrace the concept of independence—and at a time when most Anglo-Celts in Texas yet supported the liberal Mexican Constitution of 1824.

Here, along the cottonwood-lined banks of the San Antonio River, this distinctive symbol defiantly proclaimed independence, described as an "Irish flag," because of the homogeneousness of its Celtic-Gaelic antecedents and influences, brought to fruition on Texas soil. In striking contrast, the elected delegates of the Consultation of the people of Texas had voted down a declaration of independence by a margin of more than 2-to-1 on November 3, 1835.

Most of the Irish volunteers under arms at Goliad hailed from County Wexford in southeast Ireland. Historically, County Wexford, Leinster Province, was the most revolutionary, anti-British region of all Ireland, and a natural incendiary region where homemade flags of independence—almost always bright emerald green in color—were carried with rebellious zeal and nationalistic pride by Irish revolutionary forces against the British interlopers, especially during the Irish Revolution of 1798. This was not forgotten in Texas.

Envisioning a brighter future for themselves and their families outside of Mexico's arbitrary dictates, these idealistic Irish now supported the cause of independence in Texas as passionately as past generations revolutionaries had pursued their own long-deferred dreams of self-determination. This "first Texas flag of independence" flew over the thick, stone walls of Presidio La Bahia, which had been built by the Spanish in 1749, and was designed by their Scotch-Irish leader, Captain Dimmitt. He had returned to garrison this key strategic position after having served in Austin's people's army during the final attack that had overwhelmed San Antonio in December 1835.[32]

31 *Maryland Gazette*, December 3, 1835; Walraven and Walraven, *The Magnificent Barbarians,* 46-48; Davis, *Land!*, 115, 121-122, 151, 255; Garrett, *Green Flag over Texas*, 149-197; Lack, *The Texas Revolutionary Experience*, 58, 190; Philip Dimmitt, *The Handbook of Texas Online*; Smithwick, *The Evolution of a State*, 18; Gleeson, *The Irish of the South*, 16.

32 *Maryland Gazette*, December 3, 1835; Davis, *Land!*, 45, 72-90, 115, 121-122, 151, 164-165, 255; Walraven and Walraven, *The Magnificent Barbarians*, 46-48; Dickson, *The Wexford Rising in 1798*, 21-183; Foster, *The Oxford History of Ireland*, 153; Lack, *The Texas Revolutionary Experience*, 58; Flannery, *The Irish Texans*, 29, 49.

Of course, the creation of revolutionary flags that proclaimed independence from a menacing centralized power was nothing new, including on America's western frontier. As had their ancestors in Ireland, the transplanted Irish across America had been creating their own independence banners since the American Revolution. Ireland-born John Proctor and his Scotch-Irish and Irish revolutionaries of Westmoreland County, Pennsylvania, had marched under a locally-designed rattlesnake flag, distinguished with the words "DON'T TREAD ON ME." Proctor's independent battalion of Pennsylvania frontier riflemen hailed mostly from Ulster Province. Waging revolutionary war against a monarchy's arbitrary dictates, the soldiers carried this distinctive battle-flag, influenced in part by Ulster Province's blood-stained history and longtime struggle against the same foe.[33]

Perhaps most importantly, the raising of what was essentially an Irish revolutionary banner at Goliad signaled the symbolic death of the popular, but naïve, liberal 1824 Mexican Constitution, which already had been scraped by dictator Santa Anna. Raised in a solemn ceremony this proclaimed independence of the people of Texas was distinguished by the uplifted severed arm holding a bloody saber.

Although the background was not green, the "Irish flag" might well have been. After all, the color green (the nationalistic color of Ireland throughout its history) represented the strongest sentiment of self-determination of the longings of the Irish on the "old sod" for hundreds of years. Symbolizing a long -suffering people and picturesque, emerald-hued island, green had long represented a vibrant sense of Irish self-determination, nationalism, and egalitarian values woven deeply into the very fabric of Celtic-Gaelic culture.

Therefore, in many ways, the dramatic flag-raising at Goliad stood for a utopian-inspired resurrection of the old revolutionary spirit, classless aspirations, and republican ideals of Ireland thousands of miles from where it had first flown to proclaim rebellion against the centralized authority of the monarchy's abusive power. And, most significant, at Goliad, this revolutionary banner had been raised by mostly Irish rebels, who were neither members of Austin's "Army of the People," or even the Texas Regular Army, but free-thinking, humble, and determined citizen-soldiers.

Revealing the depth of Celtic-Gaelic roots, the independence banner of the bloody arm and raised saber was derived from the coat of arms of the ancient

---

33 David Hackett Fischer, *Liberty and Freedom* (Oxford, NY, 2005), 75-77.

O'Neill clan of County Tyrone, Ulster Province, in northern Ireland. Spanning generations, some of Ireland's most renowned revolutionaries had come from the fiery O'Neill clan of diehard rebels, who refused to accept British domination. They won recognition as some of the foremost Irish nationalist leaders and freedom-fighters, especially Hugh O'Neill in the Nine Years' War of 1594-1603. The conflict posed the greatest threat ever to Elizabethan misrule, and fueled the rising tide of Irish nationalism. Hugh O'Neill— hard-fighting earl of County Tyrone—reaped repeated victories over the English and the Protestants during the uprising, sending shock waves reverberating through the ruling class and political elites of London.

By 1595, O'Neill's string of tactical successes "suddenly raised the extraordinary prospect that Elizabethan rule in Ireland might be overthrown." Then, in the Rebellion of 1641 that transformed the green, rolling hills of Ulster Province into a gory battlefield, Owen Roe O'Neill and Sir Phelim O'Neill led the way in attempting to oust the British and Protestants from northern Ireland forever. In much the same way, the Texas revolutionaries of Goliad explained the Irish-inspired symbolism of the declaration of independence flag in simple, but eloquent, terms: "I would rather cut off my arm than bow to the orders of a dictator." Indeed, the traditional family crests of Irish families had long incorporated this distinctive Irish design and symbolism of defiance.[34]

The legacy of the Irish past explained why Irishman like Thomas O'Connor, despite having been granted 4,428 prime acres by the Mexican government in 1834, became a revolutionary soldier, and who signed the Goliad Declaration of Independence. His decision to become a signer may be explained by the fact that he had been born in County Wexford, Ireland, in 1819—where the Irish Revolution of 1798 had reached its peak.[35]

What has been too often overlooked by traditional Texas historians is the fact that this zenith of revolutionary fervor in all Texas occurred at Goliad (and not the Alamo), and stemmed largely from a spontaneous, instinctive impulse of a large number of lower class and common Ireland-born colonists of both Refugio and San Patricio, months before the most revered of Texas heroes, like

---

34 Davis, *Land!*, 45, 72-90, 115, 121-122, 151, 164-165, 255; Walraven and Walraven, *The Magnificent Barbarians*, 46-48; Lalor, ed., *The Encyclopedia of Ireland*, 831-833; Marcus Tanner, *Ireland's Holy Wars, The Struggle for a Nation's Soul, 1500-2000* (New Haven, CT, 2001), 100-103, 142-143; Flannery, *The Irish Texans*, 71-72.

35 O'Connor, Thomas, The Handbook of Texas Online; Golway, *For the Cause of Liberty*, 86.

William Barret Travis, Jim Bowie, and David Crockett, made their ill-fated, last stand at the Alamo.

More important to consider, this first open proclamation of outright independence during the Texas Revolution came at a time when the vast majority of Texian colonists, the Texas revolutionary government, and even many United States volunteers—mostly non-Irish and pro-1824 Constitution supporters who had embarked upon the Matamoros Expedition—possessed little desire to declare independence from Mexico. Indeed, the Celtic-Gaelic experience and anti-centralized authority traditions of Ireland accelerated the process of militant radicalism and participation in open rebellion on Texas soil against Mexico. The Irish were ahead of their time, in regard to independence, especially compared to native Texians.

As so convincingly demonstrated by Captain Dimmitt's citizen-soldiers at Goliad, the Green Islanders possessed pristine republicanism, excessive anti-government and anti-authoritarian belief systems and a desire for an utopian society. They were generally more sensitive to perceived external threats of an autocratic nature, and quicker to react militantly to defend their rights by open revolt and outright declarations of independence than most non-Irish. Quite simply and for good reason, the Irish were the most radicalized and no-compromising fighting men in all of Texas in December 1835. Therefore, besides the signers at Goliad, four Ireland-born signers eventually put their names to the official Declaration of Texas Independence at Washington-on-the-Brazos on March 2, 1836 (when the Alamo was besieged), and months after the Goliad Declaration of Independence.

Ireland-born Nicholas Fagan was one of the best examples of the forgotten leaders of the Texas Revolution. As mentioned, while his comrades cheered, he personally raised the revolutionary "Irish" banner of independence at Goliad for all to see. Fagan was the undisputed leader of these frontier Irish soldiers, a man of strong conviction and a respected member of the Refugio Colony. Fagan had migrated to New York City from Ireland in 1816, perhaps settling in the notorious squalor of Five Points in lower Manhattan, where so many lower-class Irish lived in crowded quarters and misery. Fagan remained in New York City until 1820, when he accumulated enough funds to escape and search for greener pastures.

Like so many others who hoped for a better life far beyond the urban blight of New York City, the Irishman was restless, eager to move on. As usual, the wide, open spaces of the West beckoned Fagan. Consequently, he took his family ever-farther west on an immigrant's odyssey, searching for greater opportunity that always seemed just over the next ridge: first to Philadelphia, Pennsylvania; then to Pittsburgh, Pennsylvania; then to Cincinnati, Ohio, and finally; to St. Louis, Missouri, the former French town on the west bank of the broad Mississippi.

Not liking the Mississippi Valley's biting winter cold and heavy snowfalls, Fagan then led his family south down the Mississippi by flatboat to New Orleans. Here, Fagan lost his wife, and nearly his own life, to the ravages of yellow fever. In 1829, he escaped the swampy, mosquito-infested lowlands along the "Father of Waters" that made New Orleans so unhealthy. Spurred on by the haunting memory of his deep personal loss, he once again headed west, crossing the Sabine's dark waters, searching for a fresh start. He and his family, including an inquisitive, precocious daughter named Annie, settled on the wind-swept coastal plains of Texas—the land of plenty, the Refugio Colony.

Despite purchasing a town lot in Refugio, Fagan was not satisfied. He longed for a life in the country, and here, on the open prairie, he built a sizeable log cabin. A devout worshiper, Fagan transformed the upper story of his home into a frontier chapel, complete with an altar, confessional, and a priest's private room, which was ready for whenever a priest, like Father Miguel Muldoon, paid a visit to the Irish Catholic settlers of Refugio. In this sense, Fagan was a leader in spiritual matters for the Refugio Colony. Most importantly, Fagan's ad hoc chapel was a means of maintaining the revered Irish religious traditions, such as the nightly family rosary and the "Black Fast."

Fagan became a proud owner of his own rancho, known simply as the "Fagan Ranch," and a large number of acres in natural cattle country. He remarried in 1833. Overall, life was good for Fagan and his family along the slow-moving San Antonio River that cut through the fertile soil of the prairies that stretched to the horizon—a sea of tall grass.

By direct contrast, a persistent, strong conservatism existed among the majority of native, or "Old Texians," especially large slave-owners, owning thousands of acres, who remained at home to safeguard their property. This attitude continued to prevail well into 1836 compared to the Celtic-Gaelic militancy and radicalism among so many Irish, and as demonstrated by the raising of the brightly-colored independence banner by the Irish at Goliad.

Helping to pave the way for the fiasco at the Alamo, the strength of non-independence sentiment among volunteers, both Texans and United States citizens, was best represented by the launching of the disastrous Matamoros Expedition, led by Dr. James Grant and Colonel Francis ("Frank") White Johnson in late December 1835, not long after San Antonio's capture by the revolutionaries. The overly-ambitious expedition targeted Matamoros, nestled amid the humid, semi-tropical lowlands on the Rio Grande's south bank just west of the Gulf of Mexico, and was to have led to the establishment of a northern Mexican republic independent of Texas—and after uniting with Mexican federalists to restore the Mexican 1824 Constitution. This was a strategic, geopolitical objective completely contrary to the desire for independence among so many Ireland-born soldiers like diehard Nicholas Fagan and Thomas O'Connor.

Indeed, Captain Dimmitt's Irish eagerly signed their names to the Goliad Declaration of Independence. Ireland-born John Joseph Linn was especially proud of this fact, writing how, "Ira Ingram drew up [the] declaration of independence, at Goliad, which was signed by the members of Captain Dimmitt's company and others. . . . Among the signers were several boys fifteen or sixteen years of age."[36] However, as of early 1836, most military commanders, their troops, and government leaders across Texas yet supported the liberal Constitution of 1824 and certainly not the most radical and revolutionary concept of Texas Independence. Such a notion was considered too extreme by the more conservative Texians.[37]

What has been overlooked by traditional Texas historians—especially those who have cast the Texas Revolution as an Anglo-Saxon heroic epic comparable to the Iliad's showdown between the ancient Greeks and Trojans—was the fact that a large percentage of the Goliad garrison were not only Irish, but also Irish Catholics. By ignoring or minimizing the significant story of the more radical Irish, it has been misunderstood that the banner flown by the Alamo garrison was in fact the 1824 flag that indicated allegiance, not with the radical concept of Texas independence as manifested by the Irish at Goliad, but with the 1824 Mexican Constitution.

The enduring legend of the Alamo—the most mythical of all battles in American history—has obscured the historical significance of not only the first

---

36 Linn, *Reminiscences of Fifty Years in Texas*, 57.

37 Davis, *Land!*, 45, 72-90, 115, 121-122, 151, 164-166, 180, 255; Walraven and Walraven, *The Magnificent Barbarians*, 46-48; Hardin, *Texian Illiad*, 109, 111, 158; Nicholas Fagen, The Handbook of Texas Online; McWhiney, *Cracker Culture*, xiii-257; Dolan, *The Irish Americans*, 22; Webb, *Born Fighting*, 123-184; Murphy, *The Irish in the American Revolution*, 1-103; Lack, *The Texas Revolutionary Experience*, 49-58, 122-124; "The Alamo: Irish Heroes of the Alamo," *IC*, internet; Flannery, *The Irish Texans*, 43, 53; O'Connor, Thomas, *The Handbook of Texas Online*; Anbinder, Tyler, *Five Points, The 19th Century New York Neighborhood That Invented Tap Dance, Stole Elections and Became the World's Most Notorious Slum* (New York, NY, 2002) 7-32.

declaration of Texas independence at Goliad months before, but also its thoroughly Irish influences. Indeed, a good case can be made that no such comparable declaration of independence was made by the Alamo garrison in part because there were less Ireland-born leaders and soldiers in San Antonio than at Goliad. More traditional military men and politicians, representing the conservative views of most "Old Texians" who remained noticeably absent from the Texas Army's ranks in early 1836, loudly disavowed the Goliad Declaration of Independence, because it was considered far too radical, and because they supported the Constitution of 1824.

The generally more conservative group of Texas rebels—Travis, Bowie, Crockett and the Alamo garrison—gained greater recognition than Dimmitt's more-deserving, and principally Celtic-Gaelic, garrison, a thorough overshadowing of the historical record caused by the romance and mystique of the mythical Alamo. The fact that so many Irish citizen-soldiers at Goliad had declared independence in December 1835 unlike the Alamo garrison, even by January, February, or early March 1836, has clearly not only challenged but also overturned some of the Alamo's central myths. Still, because the Irish of Goliad were not slaughtered to become sainted martyrs as were the Alamo's defenders in the most famous last stand in American history, the significance of the declaration of independence has been conveniently overlooked by traditional Texas Revolutionary War historians in what can be described as a silencing of the real story and truths of the revolution.

After all, these Irish Catholic "Texians" had been long falsely and unfairly branded as baseless traitors to Texas, especially when anti-Catholic sentiment reached new heights across Texas after the war, while the Alamo defenders were immortalized. All in all, the fundamental Celtic-Gaelic roots of the Texas Revolution were first Texanized, then thoroughly Americanized, in the decades after the conflict, obscuring the many significant Irish Catholic contributions.

For many of these same reasons, what also has been forgotten is the fact that at the Alamo were more sons, grandsons, and great grandsons of Irish immigrants than at Goliad under Captain Dimmitt. But unlike most Goliad Irish who raised their Irish flag over Presidio La Bahia as if they were the last diehard Irish nationalist freedom-fighters atop Vinegar Hill in County Wexford in June 1798, the Alamo's citizen-soldiers were mostly Irish Protestants of Scotch-Irish descent rather than Irish Catholics. Religion, therefore, was another primary reason that explained why the Irishmen of Goliad, like the homespun Irish leader and rancher Nicholas Fagan, have been overlooked: they were mostly Catholics, while the primary composition of the Alamo garrison consisted of Protestants mostly of Scotch-Irish descent.

Interestingly, religious differences between the volunteer citizen-soldiers of Fort Defiance (the renamed Presidio La Bahia) and the Alamo even reflected Ireland's regional differences. While those of mostly Scotch-Irish descent at the Alamo traced their roots back to Province of Ulster, northern Ireland, and were mostly Presbyterians, the Irish under Captain Dimmitt's command at Goliad consisted of mostly Irish immigrants from the remaining three provinces: Munster, Connacht, and Leinster. These areas were dominated by Catholics.[38]

Feisty Captain Dimmitt, of Scotch-Irish ancestry and a Protestant, had originally been only one of two Anglo-Celts of San Antonio, living in contentment with his pretty Tejano wife from the De Leon Colony. They had made their dreams come true on a sprawling ranch on the outskirts of the town of Guadalupe Victoria, northeast of Goliad, and located on the Guadalupe River. At age 35, Dimmitt made a living as a merchant for himself and family, selling his wares to Tejanos and Anglo-Celts alike.

After moving away from the disease-ridden coastal region and northwest to Bexar, Dimmitt served as a commissary contractor for Mexican troops stationed in San Antonio before the war's outbreak. On Houston's orders, he raised a company of volunteers to reinforce the Alamo in January 1836, and then returned to the Tejano town along the San Antonio River. Described as "this gallant man" years after the Texas Revolution, Dimmitt was one of the earliest and most zealous Texas revolutionaries. His destiny was closely intertwined with the Alamo's fabled story, which has inspired not only generations of Americans, but people around the world.[39]

---

38 Walraven and Walraven, *The Magnificent Barbarians*, 46-48; Davis, *Land!*, 45, 72-90, 103, 121-122, 164-165, 255; Groneman, *Alamo Defenders*, 4-123; Lack, *The Texas Revolutionary Experience*, 58, 121-124; Golway, *For the Cause of Liberty*, 86.

39 The Telegraph and *Texas Register*, December 8, 1841; Philip Dimmitt, Handbook of Texas Online; Walraven and Walraven, *The Magnificent Barbarians*, 47; *The Telegraph and Texas Register*, November 14, 1835 and December 8, 1841.

Chapter 4

Genesis of the Alamo Disaster
and a Rendezvous with Destiny

The great lure of Matamoros, the largest and most prosperous city in northeast Mexico, was simply overpowering to the vast majority of United States volunteers, after San Antonio de Bexar's capture in the second week of December 1835. Few of these homespun victors were immune to the so-called "Matamoros craze" that acted almost like an intoxicant. However, Ireland-born Private James McGee was one who was not affected by this "craze," because he was disabled. He had been severely wounded in the attack on San Antonio de Bexar that led to dramatic victory.

Appealing to the victorious volunteers who had come to Texas from across the United States—and unknown to them at this time—the increasingly popular idea of capturing Matamoros was in reality the most dangerous ambition of the entire Texas Revolution. This idea developed among the young, rambunctious norteamericano volunteers because Matamoros was the golden "El Dorado," the Texas Revolution's most irresistible lure. Cultured and refined to a degree unseen in Texas, Matamoros was the antithesis of the maze of one-story adobe homes, dusty streets, and ad hoc huts of San Antonio de Bexar. Despite Bexar's longtime central importance to Mexico City's administration of Texas, it remained little more than a frontier backwater.

Named in honor of Mexico's revolutionary priest Mariano Matamoros, a revered hero of the long struggle for Independence against Spain, Matamoros (formerly known as Refugio, or refuge) stood like an alluring oasis of green amid an arid plain that seemed to stretch forever. Situated in a distinctive region of serene ox-bow lakes filled with a waterfowl (especially in winter when flocks of geese and ducks migrated south), and nearly impenetrable sabal palm tree thickets that lined the slow-moving Rio Grande, Matamoros was an enigma: a bastion of civilization and bustling commercial enterprise nestled in a vast region of low-lying plains that spanned nearly 300 miles from the Rio Grande to San Antonio de Bexar. North of the Rio Grande, this land lying in today's south Texas, was harsher and dryer than the region around San Antonio.

The thriving Irish Colonies of San Patricio and Refugio, located south of the San Antonio River, were situated on this generally level plain. With its distinctive civic pride and heritage, Matamoros was situated almost directly south of San Patricio and its Irish colonists. Here, just west of the vast Gulf of Mexico, the winding Rio Grande gave life and richness—both natural and monetary—to this unique geographic region and the picturesque city. The Rio Grande finally reached the sea after its epic journey that began in the San Juan Mountains of southwest Colorado. The fourth longest river in today's United States–it was a true river of destiny.

Matamoros' lucrative commercial connections to New Orleans, Europe, and the rest of Mexico appealed to the covetous Texas rebels. It was wealthy, international, and cosmopolitan—the opposite of isolated, impoverished San Antonio de Bexar. Just as New Orleans had long prospered near where the mighty Mississippi enters the Gulf of Mexico, Matamoros stood near the mouth of another of America's most magnificent rivers (called the Rio Bravo del Norte by Latinos), and similarly reaped a bounty of commercial riches.

Just as the Mississippi was the great "Father of Waters," of the United States, so the Rio Grande was to Mexico, its importance not lost on the Texas revolutionaries with their lofty ambitions in late 1835. In terms of overall importance, the wealthy commercial center of Matamoros ranked behind only the prosperous Gulf ports of Vera Cruz and Tampico. Given its strategic and geographic position, Matamoros, distinguished by its sabal palms, stately houses with their artful wrought iron balconies evoking the look of Old Spain, and the gulf breezes that refreshed the city, earned the name of "The Great Gateway of Mexico."[1]

---

1 Roell, *Matamoros and the Texas Revolution*, 1-10, 14-19, 22-25, 37; McGee, James, The Handbook of Texas Online.

Given Matamoros' overall importance, it was destined to play a key role in determining the course of the Texas Revolution, after San Antonio de Bexar's surrender on December 11, 1835. Quite simply, without the launching of the overly-ambitious Matamoros Expedition in late December 1835, there would have been no disaster at the Alamo. The James Grant-Francis W. "Frank" White Johnson expedition, which departed San Antonio de Bexar with high hopes on December 30, and targeted Matamoros for capture severely crippled the Texian-United States volunteer war effort. It splintered the already weak Texas provisional government into factions of feuding politicians, diffusing the war effort's priorities and objectives, creating deep divisions among the political and military leadership, compromising the overall defense of Texas. These events set the stage for Santa Anna's destruction of the Alamo and its isolated band of defenders. The story of the Matamoros Expedition's bid to capture this golden city on the Rio Grande is important, because without it, there would be no Alamo story as we know it today. Few military efforts have been launched with greater—and misplaced—confidence in an easy success (based on the mistaken conviction that pro-republican Mexicans would assist the norteamericano revolutionaries), the Matamoros Expedition proved a monumental fiasco. It was the mother of all the disasters, including at the Alamo, that eventually befell the Texian and United States volunteers during the star-crossed year of 1836 prior to Sam Houston's miracle victory at San Jacinto on April 21, 1836.[2]

However, the true foundation for the disastrous Matamoros Expedition had been laid in the Texas Revolution's early days. In mid-November 1835, the provisional government of Texas had unwittingly sowed the seeds for the 1836 fiascos in its ill-fated attempt to create a regular army for Texas. At that time barely a month after the Texas Revolution's opening shots at Goliad, the government optimistically passed a provision calling for the formation of a 1,120-man Texas Regular Army with a reliable contingent of soldiers serving under two-year terms of enlistments. It was an attempt to create a stable and dependable fighting force—unlike ever-unpredictable volunteers—for the war's duration. Houston was appointed to head the Texas Regular Army.

To the inexperienced Texas politicians, this effort looked good on paper, but the reality was quite different. At this time, the largest military force in the field consisted of the volunteers who had besieged General Martin Perfecto de

---

2   Roell, *Matamoros and the Texas Revolution*, 4-5, 47-86.

Cos and his forces at San Antonio de Bexar. These rowdy volunteers served under their own popular leaders and not the regular officers appointed by the government. These volunteer soldiers of Texas were not under the jurisdiction or control of the Texas government, unlike the recently-appointed members of the nascent Texas Regular Army that still existed mostly on paper.[3]

Ironically, the string of events that led to so many disasters across Texas in 1836 began to take firmer shape because the Alamo (along with San Antonio de Bexar) had fallen so easily to the revolutionaries. That success gave the United States volunteers and the native Texians possession of the city and all of Texas north of the Rio Grande, once Cos's humiliated troops were paroled and retired south in shame. Therefore, in a classic case of history coming full circle in barely three months, the Alamo's surrender on December 11, 1835 created a dangerous hubris among the already overly-confident victors and led directly to the fall of the Alamo in March 1836.

Unfortunately for Texas, the downward course of events began to take shape in part because the victors at San Antonio de Bexar simply found themselves with time on their hands and nothing much to do; their idleness was the genesis of the overly-ambitious expedition to Matamoros that proved so disastrous to all Texian–United States forces throughout Texas in early 1836, including at the Alamo. After securing their victory, the Texian volunteers of the militia departed San Antonio de Bexar and went back to their homes and families in the east Texas settlements because they believed that the war was over. That proved to be a fatal delusion that was destined to haunt the men who remained at the Alamo.

Indeed, what those Texians left behind at San Antonio de Bexar was a diminutive band of mostly United States volunteers of the ragtag Texas Army, far from home and support. Lusting for additional victories over an opponent who they viewed as vastly inferior in every way, the heady volunteers of the Matamoros Expedition consisted of a very independent-minded force—as the Texas government discovered to its shock. These eager men promptly voted for Johnson as their commander; he had recently gained popularity for leading the assault that paved the way to Cos's surrender.

These feisty United States volunteers also declared that they would take no orders from regular army officers, including General Houston, who the government had appointed to take charge of the chaotic situation at San

3 William C. Binkley, *The Texas Revolution* (Austin, TX, 1952), 85-86.

Antonio de Bexar. Johnson, who had earlier asked the government to strengthen its far-flung outposts (including at San Antonio de Bexar), and Grant received full support for their expedition to Matamoros from their enthusiastic United States volunteers, who were eager for adventure. These young men from across "the States" were more than ready for action, especially for the chance to win glory along the Rio Grande far to the south.

A proud and charismatic Celtic chieftain with leadership ability who hailed from Killearnan Parish, Ross-shire (Siorrachd Rois in Scottish Gaelic), northern Scotland, Grant had played a key role in capturing San Antonio de Bexar. He and Johnson, who was of Scotch-Irish descent, prepared to embark upon the most ambitious undertaking of the Texas Revolution. The Matamoros Expedition has been long viewed by historians as having been launched for entirely unworthy objective, the capture of a city generally considered to be of little strategic, political, or economic importance.

But that was not the case: in truth, if captured, a wealthy Matamoros promised to change the Texas Revolution's course in a dramatic way. Nevertheless, the bid to capture Matamoros was a risky gamble for the self-styled "Federal Volunteer Army of Texas" that lacked experience but not confidence and bravado. The gamble of these relatively inexperienced volunteers who rode south under Johnson and Grant, left the Alamo and its diminutive garrison far out on a limb on the remote western frontier, and left it ripe for the taking if the Mexican Army suddenly pushed north.[4]

In his definitive and classic work *Three Roads to the Alamo: The Lives and Fortunes of David Crockett, James Bowie, and William Barret Travis*, gifted historian William C. Davis presented the best analysis of the fortunes of the legendary Alamo triumvirate. With his usual award-winning style, Davis presented most poignantly the many twists and turns of fate in life that had placed Bowie, Crockett, and the young Travis simultaneously at the Alamo by March 1836. Indeed, it was almost as if some kind of a strange destiny had drawn Travis, Bowie, and Crockett together at this ramshackle Franciscan mission from which they would never return.

What has mostly been forgotten was the fact that it was the Irish who had come the longest way and taken the most convuluted course on their journey to

---

4   Roell, *Matamoros and the Texas Revolution*, 3-5, 37, 43-50, 53; Johnson, Francis White, The Handbook of Texas Online; Grant, James, The Handbook of Texas Online; Roell, *Matamoros and the Texas Revolution*, 89-90.

the Alamo, traveling some including some 4,000-5,000 miles and across the Atlantic. Their long journey had deep roots in the torturous centuries of Ireland's history. Ironically, if any of the recurrent past Irish revolts had succeeded and Ireland had gotten free of British rule, then these Irish wanderers would not have been in Texas or at the Alamo. The fact that a good many soldiers like Ireland-born Privates James McGee and Joseph M. Hawkins, and inspirational leaders like Travis, Bowie, and Crockett (all of Celtic heritage) came together at the Alamo, seemingly in the middle of nowhere, was neither by design or original intention.

Davis placed the lives of the Alamo's most famous three defenders in the proper historical perspective when he wrote: "Men like Bowie and Crockett were made to bestride continents. As for Travis, the Alamo got in the way of what almost certainly would have been a career leading to the presidency of the [Texas] republic [and] As for Crockett, he was embracing Texas as a new home, and a new base from which to launch perhaps yet another political career . . .In coming together at the Alamo, they signified the combination of all the forces then in mutual contest with the continent."[5]

The dynamic and popular leader with the most far-reaching reputation as the greatest fighter in all Texas, Jim Bowie, had missed the final Texian-United States volunteer assault on San Antonio de Bexar, Instead, he had been at Goliad in December, after departing Edward Burleson's army of mostly United States volunteers who were besieging San Antonio de Bexar. At Goliad, Bowie inspected the small garrison under Captain Philip Dimmitt, whose Irish soldiers had captured the place and now made up most of its garrison—and in December 1835 issued the first Declaration of Independence of the Texas Revolution. Dimmitt was one of the earliest and most forceful voices for launching a bid to capture Matamoros.

Bowie played no role in improving Goliad's defenses, despite its strategic importance. He returned to San Antonio de Bexar, just missing the determined assault that forced Cos to surrender on Thursday December 11. After Burleson left the army on December 15 to return home like other Texians who believed that the war was over and that Texas was now safe after San Antonio de Bexar's capture, Bowie presented his report of Goliad's condition to the new commander, Johnson. The Virginia-born Johnson, Bowie's friend and

---

5   Davis, *Three Roads to the Alamo*, 585-586; Lalor, ed., *The Encyclopedia of Ireland*, 1040; Hawkins, Joseph M., The Handbook of Texas Online; McGee, James, The Handbook of Texas Online.

Houston's enemy, had taken charge of the United States Volunteers after Burleson departed.[6]

Despite his Tejano friends and relatives (his deceased wife's aristocratic family) still living in San Antonio, Bowie felt restless. Perhaps it was his personal demons, perhaps something else, but he was ready to leave even the beloved Catholic community he had once called home. He and a friend rode out on December 17 and headed east toward San Felipe de Austin, where the tempestuous provisional government was engaged in its political infighting fueled by a toxic combination of inflated egos and self-serving agendas.

When he arrived, Bowie learned from Houston—who was angling for an appointment to command all regulars, militia, and volunteers in Texas—that one of his most ambitious friends, the irrepressible Dr. James Grant, was busy planning an expedition to capture Matamoros. Significantly, Grant earlier had called for Houston to be replaced by Johnson. As the Texas Regular Army's commander under the government's directives, Houston had been ordered by Governor Smith on December 16 to lead the Matamoros Expedition in person or appoint a trusted officer to command it; Bowie was finally chosen on Wednesday December 17. Houston's long-term plan was for Bowie to gather troops and prepare the expedition for moving south to the Rio Grande, before personally taking command of the mounted expedition to Matamoros.

With plans to lead his own Matamoros Expedition himself (Grant's and Johnson's expedition of United States volunteers was entirely independent of Houston's expedition manned by regulars and those United States volunteers who might decide to enlist in his budding Texas Regular Army), Houston had ordered Bowie to Goliad. Governor Smith and the provisional government were intoxicated by the idea of capturing the prosperous Rio Grande River city for reasons beyond strategic and political priorities. As William C. Davis emphasized: "The Matamoros idea took on an additional attraction because it would be a means of employing the army now freed by the surrender of Bexar [and the] government had to feed and clothe those volunteers, and might as well have them doing something for their pay."[7]

---

6   Roell, *Matamoros and the Texas Revolution*, 45, 47-48, 54; Davis, *Three Roads to the Alamo*, 486-487; Johnson, Francis White, The Handbook of Texas Online; Binkley, *The Texas Revolution*, 89; Dimmitt, Philip, The Handbook of Texas Online.

7   Davis, *Three Roads to the Alamo*, 487-489; Roell, *Matamoros and the Texas Revolution*, 48-49, 54, 56-57; Binkley, *The Texas Revolution*, 86-87.

Disgusted over such actions and following Houston's order giving him command of the Matamoros Expedition—which had moved south with Grant at its head by the time Bowie reached Goliad on Monday January 11—Bowie had planned to take charge of the expedition at Goliad despite whatever Johnson and Grant desired. Bowie was angered by the situation at Goliad, because the United States volunteers had as usual charted their own independent course. Bowie wrote to Houston, "Some dark scheme has been set on foot to disgrace our noble cause."[8]

Considering Houston's orders valid, Bowie still planned to "put a stop to Grant's movements," almost as if threatening to employ his famous knife to change the mind (or worse) of the hardheaded Scotland-born physician. While Bowie remained feisty, Grant and Johnson continued to defy the flip-flopping government's orders, including the directive that gave James Walker Fannin official command of the Matamoros Expedition.[9]

On Thursday, January 14, Houston joined Bowie at Goliad. Bowie was unable to take charge of the Matamoros Expedition, for the United States volunteers remained firmly behind Grant and Johnson, who simply ignored Houston and Bowie. It was clear that by this time, political divisions and personal animosities ran much too deep for any cooperation. At Goliad, Houston at last turned his fleeting concern to San Antonio de Bexar and its tiny garrison— which was barely able to survive by this time—after receiving an alarming letter from the town's and Alamo's commander, Lieutenant Colonel James Clinton Neill. His concern was almost an afterthought because of the priority given to capturing the alluring prize of Matamoros. Houston had already revealed his true interests as early as mid-November 1835, when he had advocated to the Texas government that the United States volunteers (even then still besieging Cos) should be withdrawn from San Antonio de Bexar and furloughed, because the government's top priority should be the creation of the Texas Regular Army, which he commanded.[10]

But as a thoroughly alarmed Neill reported new intelligence that a large Mexican force, with as many as 3,000 troops, was preparing to move north, Houston now presented a new mission to Bowie, who was eager for a fresh

8   Davis, *Three Roads to the Alamo*, 491-492; Roell, *Matamoros and the Texas Revolution*, 56-57.

9   Ibid., 492.

10 Binkley, *The Texas Revolution*, 87.

challenge, after having missed the final attack that had forced Cos to surrender. That absence was likely a key consideration in Bowie's eventual decision to make a defiant defensive stand at the Alamo. On January 17, Houston conferred with Bowie about his newly assigned mission: to proceed to San Antonio de Bexar with a small force of volunteer cavalrymen. Bowie was told by Houston to tear down the fortifications (to deny future usage by a resurgent Mexican Army) in the hope that Governor Henry Smith would later officially order the remote outpost's evacuation, because a powerful Mexican Army was about to march north. Then, as Houston desired, the garrison, artillery, and supplies of the Alamo were to be transferred east to either Gonzales or all the way to the gulf to Copano.

At Copano, many Irish from New York City had landed on their way to the Refugio Irish Colony, which had been established on the site of an old Spanish mission located only a few miles inland from Copano Bay. In this highly-politicized environment, Bowie served as a loyal officer to the government and to Houston, who had ordered Lt. Col. James Clinton Neill, to "supervise" San Antonio de Bexar and the Alamo. As fate would have it, Bowie, one of the most aggressive and capable Celtic leaders in Texas, was now destined to make his way to the Alamo, after the government declared that Johnson (not Bowie as Houston desired) was now the official leader of the Matamoros Expedition.

Meanwhile, the small lonely band of troops, who had been forgotten amid the excitement of the Matamoros Expedition and remained dangerously exposed on the western frontier, were trying to make their desperate situation known to the government. As Bowie reported to the governor on February 2, 1836:

Whilst at la Bahia [Goliad] Genl Houston received dispatches from Col. Comdt. [James Clinton] Neill informing that good reasons were entertained that an attack would soon be made by a numerous Mexican Army on our important post of Bejar. It was forthwith determined that I should go instantly to Bejar; accordingly I left Genl Houston and with a few very efficient volunteers came to this place about 2 weeks since. I was received by Col. Neill with great cordiality, and the men under my command entered at once into active service [but] great and just dissatisfaction is felt for the want of a little money to pay the small but necessary expenses of our men [and] no other man [than Neill] in the army could have kept men at this post, under the neglect they have experienced."[11]

Like Bowie and seemingly also propelled by the unseen forces of a strange destiny, the young lawyer William Barret Travis also found his way to the Alamo by an odd combination of accident, destiny, and circumstances. Despite literally begging Governor Smith, who had ordered the young officer to report to San Antonio, to "recall the order for me to go on to Bexar in command of so few men" of the regular Texas Cavalry recently enlisted by him, Travis stoically accepted his fate that placed him at the quiet town (but which was seemingly always a magnet for serious trouble—especially of a revolutionary variety).[12]

Travis experienced far greater and more alarming concerns upon his arrival at the Alamo after getting a first-hand view of the garrison's obvious weaknesses. On February 12, he wrote to the governor about their strategic situation: "This being the Frontier Post nearest the Rio Grande, will be the first to be attacked [but] We are illy prepared for their reception as we have not more than 150 men here and they in a very disorganized State . . . Money, Clothing and Provisions are greatly needed at this Post for the use of the Soldiers."[13]

These crucial shortages were only recently made far more severe by the systematic seizure of invaluable supplies by the men of the Matamoros Expedition, who departed San Antonio de Bexar at the end of December, leaving "Neill in danger of starving."[14] Indeed, with no concern for the garrison's vulnerability and potential fate, Johnson's mounted soldiers "had appropriated the entire stock of movable supplies and equipment"of the garrison.[15]

While the Alamo garrison grew weaker with each passing day during this agonizing winter with its ever-rising tide of discontent and confusion, the threat from below the Rio Grande was growing stronger. In a second desperate letter from the Alamo on the following day, Travis informed the government of

11 Copano, Tx, The Handbook of Texas Online; Hansen, ed., *The Alamo Reader*, 19; Davis, *Three Roads to the Alamo*, 489-493; Lalor, ed., *The Encyclopedia of Ireland*, 1040; Roell, *Matamoros and the Texas Revolution*, 48-49; Tucker, *Exodus from the Alamo*, 57.

12 Hansen, ed., *The Alamo Reader*, 18.

13 Ibid., 21.

14 Roell, *Matamoros and the Texas Revolution*, 54; Davis, *Three Roads to the Alamo*, 491.

15 Binkley, *The Texas Revolution*, 91.

shocking news based upon recent intelligence: "Our [Tejano] spies [mounted scouts] have just returned from the Rio Grande—The enemy is there one thousand strong & is making every preparation to invade us. By the 15th of March I think Texas will be invaded."[16]

Of the famed triumvirate of the Alamo, Crockett was last to arrive, on Monday February 8. John S. Sutherland described how, "Col. David Crockett arrived a few days later, with twelve others, direct from Tennessee. Crockett was immediately offered a command by Col. Travis, and called upon by the crowd for a speech. The former honor he would not accept, but mounted a goods-box on the civil plaza, amid prolonged cheers of the people [and he spoke the following words:] 'And, fellow citizens, I am among you. I have come to your country, though not I hope, through any selfish motive whatever. I have come to aid you all that I can in your noble cause. I shall identify myself with your interests, and all the honor that I desire is that of defending, as a high private, in common with my fellow-citizens, the liberties of our common country'."[17]

Like Travis, Sutherland was shocked by what he saw around him because "the force then [at San Antonio de Bexar was] in a manner destitute. Grant and Johnson had left but a short time previous with their companies—taking with them almost every[thing and] The Government of course, at that day were not able to meet their demands [and after] the consumption of the[ir supplies] at Bexar, had been so rapid for some months past that both [beef and corn bread] were becoming scarce, and not easy to be obtained. They were also out of money. They were all volunteers, and [the] resources upon which they had relied most of the time, even now exhausted. There being no treasury they, of course, had not received anything in the share of pay [and worst of all] The strength of the Texicans at Bexar now consisted of one hundred and fifty-two men. Eighty of those were a part of the original garrison, who had not caught the Matamoros fever; twenty-five had returned with Col. Bowie from Goliad. Col. Travis had brought with him about twenty. Col. Crockett twelve. Capt. [William Hester] Patten [Patton]. These detachments, with their respective commanders, make the number. A few days after their concentration, some

16 Hansen, ed., *The Alamo Reader*, 23.

17 John S. Sutherland Narrative, John Salmon Ford Papers, Briscoe Center for American History, University of Texas, Austin, Texas.

twenty Mexicans [Tejanos] of the City joined them, increasing the number to one hundred and seventy-two."[18]

No one, not even Houston or the dysfunctional Texas government, was now doing anything to reinforce the forlorn men at the Alamo; it was as if Houston had reverted back to his mid-November 1835 argument to the government about not garrisoning San Antonio de Bexar and furloughing the United States volunteers. In fact, he was even going out of his way to discourage assistance and reinforcements to the Alamo. Before riding to the Alamo, Sutherland described how at San Felipe de Austin as early as December 14, Houston already had made up his mind about what he truly thought—as opposed to what Houston later wrote to justify his self-serving actions that paved the way to disaster—in overall strategic terms about San Antonio de Bexar, the Alamo, and its small garrison: "Genl Houston informed me he had just ordered the army there to fall back to the white settlement [of east Texas], and that we need not go to San Antonio, as the Army would have left before we reached that point. The Army, however did not leave as ordered, and a call for volunteers was made by those Commanding [Neill and Bowie] at San Antonio to Keep possession of the place, until [Texas] regulars could be had to defend the country." But the Texas Regular Army existed primarily on paper, and, therefore, it could not come (except only Travis and his handful of regular cavalrymen) to the aid of the Alamo garrison.[19]

Houston had also played a key role in sabotaging the Matamoros Expedition. Like the savvy politician (a former governor of Tennessee with ample experience in backdoor maneuvering) he was, he launched into a vigorous speech-making campaign to dissuade Johnson's men from continuing south to Matamoros. Houston needed them to enlist in the regular army to strengthen his hand as commander. In the end, after considerable effort, he "managed to persuade most of Johnson's men to give up the enterprise."[20]

Meanwhile, the perilous situation in San Antonio de Bexar and the Alamo continued to plummet to new lows with each passing day. In one of his last reports to Governor Smith, Bowie pleaded with renewed desperation: "again we call aloud for relief; the weakness of our post will at least bring the enemy on,

---

18 Ibid.

19 Ibid; Binkley, *The Texas Revolution*, 87.

20 Binkley, *The Texas Revolution*, 89, 92.

some volunteers are expected: Capt. [William] Patton with 5 or 6 has come in. But a large reinforcement with provisions is what we need." The increasingly-frustrated Travis said it best in his February 12, 1836 letter to Governor Smith: "For Gods sake . . . send us reinforcements."[21]

But it was not to be. The Alamo men were now on their own as never before in a small forlorn garrison in an environment that was growing increasingly hostile toward them. The Irish of the Alamo, like Edward McCafferty, a former member of the hard-fighting contingent of uniformed volunteers known as the New Orleans Greys, John Mormon, and 24-year-old Stephen Dennison, age 24, who had departed the port of Galway, County Galway, for New Orleans with high hopes, now saw around them an alien arid land on the southwest frontier that was utterly unlike their native Emerald Isle, which was eternally green and lush. Except the picturesque hill country just to the northwest, the area around San Antonio de Bexar was desolate, especially in winter's dark depths, with relatively little green to be seen anywhere except in the underbrush and small trees that lined the San Antonio River. The Sons of Erin in the Alamo garrison were especially aware of the relative scarcity of water in this region. And any revolutionary sons of the County Wexford rebels, whose freedom-loving fathers had fought for liberty in another failed Irish rebellion, now wished to have with them at the Alamo only a fraction of the large numbers of the Irish peasantry, who had so boldly risen up and created a people's army in 1798.

Meanwhile, another development occurred to help seal the Alamo garrison's doom: the Texas government ceased to exist for all practical purposes, because the bitter political in-fighting had swirled out-of-control. Governor Henry Smith got impeached, leaving Lieutenant Colonel James W. Robinson to serve as acting governor. Both factions of angry, feuding politicians refused to recognize their respective rivals. Of course, all these blundering attempts to govern by both groups of amateur politicians led to greater confusion and turmoil among the defenders of Texas, setting the stage for the disasters of March 1836. For a month and a half while the very life of Texas was at stake, her inexperienced fighting men in the field, including those at the Alamo, were on their own without a government to direct and coordinate a defense. This, of course, was a recipe for unprecedented military disaster at the hands of a sizeable and threatening Mexican Army poised to march north.

---

21 Hansen, ed., *The Alamo Reader*, 20.

The provisional government's collapse was mirrored by the slow, steady disintegration of all possibilities for any organized, united resistance effort among the military commands. The stage was now set for the annihilation of the diminutive garrison at the Alamo—which was under-supplied in everything but bravado. The Alamo garrison was now clearly destined to be sacrificed to the last man largely because of the folly of military and government leaders, including Houston who seemed always to look out for his own political and personal interests. Each commander of these widely-separated forces in Texas, including Neill at the Alamo, was "now left to work out his own plans in the face of a new Mexican advance" of overwhelming might.[22]

George Washington's birthday on February 22 was a special day for the Alamo garrison. The revered national anniversary was celebrated with a lively fandango and the usual patriotic fervor by the United States volunteers and a handful of Texians who were truly deep in the heart of Texas. For many this day was a symbolic counterpart to the Irish tradition of the celebration of St. Patrick's Day in honor of Ireland's patron saint, Patrick. who had brought Christianity to Ireland. The special day was faithfully observed by the Irish across America (including Texas), thriving as a cultural tradition in Irish enclaves from New York City to New Orleans. But the Irish of the Alamo were fated never to celebrate St. Patrick's Day on March 17, 1836–the anniversary of St. Patrick's death—because the Alamo fell eleven days before.

On a festive February 22, meanwhile, all thoughts of the impending approach of Santa Anna's sizeable army were forgotten by young garrison members, like Scotch-Irishman Robert McKinney from Tennessee, amid the intoxicating haze of lively music, the usual abundance of hard liquor (of extremely high alcohol content), and the pretty, dark-eyed senoritas of San Antonio de Bexar. Here, at Domingo Bustillo's popular establishment for social gatherings on dusty Soledad Street, the young men and boys, mostly United States volunteers, danced and made love with the Tejano girls far into the night, perhaps sensing that the good times were soon to come to an end. But for this one day, those ominous feelings were forgotten by the men of the Alamo.

As if still back among his Scotch-Irish people in west Tennessee, Crockett's lively fiddling (continuing the rich musical traditions of his Irish ancestors) added to the merriment of a fandango not soon forgotten by garrison members. Although the Irish soldiers could not know the details of the tragic destiny that

22 Binkley, *The Texas Revolution*, 86-93.

lay in store for them at this old mission by the San Antonio River, the garrison's fate had been spelled out in the carefully-laid plans of Santa Anna, the self-styled "Napoleon of the West." and set up by the self-destruction of the Texian-United States volunteers war effort on every possible level.[23]

To this day, no one knows the exact design of the garrison's flag that flew with pride over the Alamo and flapped in the cold winter wind sweeping over the silent prairie where herds of buffalo had grazed when the first Franciscan missionaries arrived. But what is almost certain was that the Irish soldiers, like Ireland-born Jackson J. Rusk and David P. Cummings, at the Alamo would have wished for that flag to have been distinguished by a more familiar and traditional Irish design, one that was close to their Irish hearts and egalitarian aspirations: a revolutionary green banner that incorporated an ancient Irish harp—the most revered nationalist symbol of their homeland—to represent their participation in a new people's revolt on Texas soil, where they sought to create a new republic like the one those Irish revolutionaries fought and died to create during the ill-fated Rebellion of 1798.[24]

But at the doomed mission, some older Irishmen, like the Alamo Chief of Ordnance Robert Evans, born in Ireland in 1800, among the garrison might have recalled the inspiring words of a popular Irish revolutionary song of 1798. If so, these words offered them a measure of solace, as little else now remained to comfort these Emerald Islanders: "Hope shall endure with our faith in God."[25]

But despite their placing faith in a divine deliverance from a cruel fate, not one of these hopeful Irishmen standing fast at the Alamo was destined to see again the green hills and valleys of their beloved Ireland.

23 Tucker, *Exodus from the Alamo*, 154-156; McKinney, Robert, The Handbook of Texas Online; Mike Cronin and Daryl Adair, *The Wearing of the Green, A History of St. Patrick's Day*, New York, NY, 2002), xv-17.

24 Lalor, ed., *The Encyclopedia of Ireland*, 474. 917-918, 1040; Cummings, David P., The Handbook of Texas Online; Rusk, Jackson J., The Handbook of Texas Online.

25 Lalor, ed., *The Encyclopedia of Ireland*, 918; Evans, Robert, The Handbook of Texas Online.

Chapter 5

James Neill's Most Ill-Fated Decision

The encroaching disaster at the Alamo can only be fully understood by viewing the dynamics and decisions among military leadership at San Antonio de Bexar and the Alamo—an ill-fated situation with all of the qualities of a Greek Tragedy. The true story of what led to the wiping out of the Alamo garrison is more complex than the romantic myth that the leaders and men of the Alamo deliberately chose to die to allow Texas to live and to allow Sam Houston time to create an army. As a cruel fate would have it, the Alamo leaders were caught in the midst of a bloody Mexican Civil War between centralism and republicanism, and in this sense the Alamo was merely a pawn in a much larger game.

Colonel James Clinton Neill was the most seasoned leader of the Alamo garrison in 1836, exceeding both Bowie's and Travis's level of experience. Neill also possessed a coveted officer's commission in the fledgling regular Texas Army. Most importantly, he commanded the Alamo longer than any other officer: a fact that has been generally overlooked and ignored by historians, who have instead focused on Jim Bowie and William Barret Travis. However, Neill has seemingly only garnered greater obscurity in the historical record in consequence, lingering in David Crockett's, Bowie's, and Travis's giant historical shadows. Symbolically, this popular Scotch-Irish leader with deep Ulster Province, northern Ireland, roots was not only the first, but also not the last Scotch-Irish commander of the Alamo.

When the last Mexican troops—Perfecto de Cos's paroled men—marched south and out of Texas after their surrender on December 11, 1835, the governing Council appointed Neill to command San Antonio de Bexar and the Alamo. Neill's solid leadership and popularity kept the ragtag band of volunteers together, convincing them not to desert in disgust, with food, morale, and supplies exceedingly low during the early months of 1836. As mentioned, General Sam Houston, who prudently wanted to defend the east Texas settlements closer to their borders, dispatched Colonel James Bowie and a 30-man detachment of volunteers to the Alamo in mid-January 1836 with the order to use his own personal discretion to abandon vulnerable San Antonio de Bexar. A former officer of the United States Army, Houston emphasized to "blow up the Alamo" if Bowie thought necessary.

However, in a united command decision, Neill and Bowie chose instead to defend the Alamo by the last week of January 1836. Despite having reported to the governor on January 14, 1836 "we must become an easy prey to the enemy" if not reinforced, Neill was the most strident voice for making a lonely defensive stand. Neill's persuasive arguments prevailed in the end, ensuring an inevitable dramatic showdown at the Alamo.[1]

Almost as if he'd forgotten he was about to face Santa Anna's Army of more than 5,000 troops, Neill informed the government on January 14: "we will, till reinforced . . . and if drawn within the walls" of the Alamo, "will defend the garrison to the last." Rather than for sound military and political reasons, Neill's decision was based in no small part on the common, race-based Anglo perception that the Mexican soldiers "were in every respect inferior to the hardy, strong and brave Texians."[2]

Clearly, these cocky and confident Texians had a great deal to learn about their opponents, and Santa Anna was determined to teach them some very hard lessons about committing the folly of underestimating their opponent. The men of the Alamo had no idea that the foe who they held in contempt were now united in a holy war against them and other Texas rebels. Mexican Secretary of War Jose Maria Tornel presented an ominous warning in January 1836 that was

---

1   Hardin, *Texian Iliad*, 111, 117; Alwyn Barr, *Texans in Revolt, The Battle for San Antonio, 1835* (Austin, TX, 1990), 45-59; Richard C. King, *James Clinton Neill, The Shadow Commander of the Alamo* (Austin, TX, 2002), 1-4; *The Telegraph and Texas Register*, January 23, 1836.

2   *The Telegraph and Texas Telegraph*, January 23, 1836; *Richmond Enquirer*, Richmond, Virginia, February 27, 1836.

ignored by the Texians: "Our soldiers ever aspire to shed the blood of foreigners who seek to take away from us our rights and menace our independence. This war is righteous, and should be without remorse."[3]

But neither Neill or Bowie (or hardly anyone else for that matter) appreciated the depth of the Mexican national resolve and determination to regain Texas, or the sterling fighting qualities of Santa Anna's soldados. Enjoying an amicable relationship which was a rare quality among the seemingly always feuding Texas military and political leadership, Neill and Bowie, both old Indian fighters, were as determined to stand firm at the Alamo like the ill-fated Creek warriors at Horseshoe Bend. However, the Alamo was located too far west to adequately protect the east Texas settlements; hence, Houston's desire (military, personal, and political) to withdraw the San Antonio garrison eastward to a safer location. In overall tactical terms, Santa Anna's troops, under General José de Urrea—who commanded the army's right wing advancing north from Matamoros and up the coastal road that led up the gulf coastal plain—would out-flank the Alamo located far to the west. Knowing that the Alamo and San Antonio possessed no true strategic value, therefore, Houston wanted a defensive line established farther east at Gonzales (the westernmost Anglo-Celtic settlement) and closer to the east Texas settlements, where vital manpower could be secured.

In many ways, Neill and Bowie's ill-fated decision to hold the Alamo was very much of a typically Celtic one in the "No Surrender" Siege of Derry tradition, and one distinguished by more brash bravado and outright defiance than strategic wisdom. In part, this bold decision to stand firm against the odds was in no small part rooted in a distinctive Celtic-Gaelic combativeness and an ancient warrior ethos reminiscent of the hard-fighting warriors of the O'Neill clan of Ulster Province, northern Ireland.

Like Neill who admired the fighting spirit of his Scotch-Irish ancestors, Bowie was proud of his Celtic-Gaelic heritage, including fiery Jacobite rebels who fought against English invaders of the sacred Scottish homeland in the William Wallace tradition. Appropriately, this popular commander of the Alamo's volunteers (the garrison contained only a relatively few regulars) was Scotch-Irish like so many Alamo defenders who likewise chose to stand firm. Bowie traced his family back to the Celtic warriors of the Scottish Highlands,

---

3 *El Mosquito Mexicano*, Mexico City, Mexico, January 22, 1836.

including freedom fighter Rob Roy, who inspired a popular uprising among the common people, and other fiery rebels.

These Scottish Highlanders were noted for their combat prowess and courage, especially in the headlong charge. After unleashing a fierce Celtic attack that was cut to pieces by superior firepower, the Scottish Jacobites were crushed by English and loyal Scottish forces on Culloden Moor on a bloody April 16, 1746. Then, the victors systematically dispatched wounded Scottish rebels lying helpless in the grassy bog in their bloodlust. After the slaughter at Culloden, Bowie's ancestors were forced to relocate from Scotland to northern Ireland. Here, they became one of the resettled Protestant families who had migrated from the lowlands of Scotland, the Scotch-Irish. The restless Bowie family then migrated across the Atlantic to settle among the gently rolling hills and fertile tobacco lands in the Patuxent River country of southern Maryland.[4]

As an early popular hero of the Texas Revolution, Bowie heaped lavish praise on the Alamo's Scotch-Irish commander, who, at age 46, had been a member (adjutant) of the original Texas Ranger battalion. He wrote to the governor to praise "the conduct & character of Col. Neill too highly . . . ."Clearly, Bowie and Neill were kindred Celtic spirits. However, this strong Celtic bond between the two leaders boded ill for the fate of their men.[5]

Neill possessed strong motivations to stand firm at San Antonio because of the primary bone of contention in this war: the abundance of fertile land. In his own January 14, 1836 words, Neill admitted that he wanted to defend the Alamo because, "I feel . . . a wish to preserve those lands, [Texas] has acquired in the infant stage of her campaign." Meanwhile, a United States newspaper reported the folly among the increasingly apathetic Texian settlers (unlike the United States volunteers), who had made the Alamo garrison more vulnerable with each passing day: "the general supposition in Texas was that there would be no fighting until the summer was far advanced."[6]

---

4 Hopewell, *James Bowie*, 1-2; Stuart Reid, *The Culloden Moor 1746, The death of the Jacobite cause* (Oxford, England, 2002); *New York Times*, January 27, 1895; Hardin, *Texian Illiad*, 109-111, 117; King, *James Clinton Neill*, 1, 2-3, 8; McCarthy, *The Other Irish*, 19-22, 96; Lalor, ed., *The Encyclopedia of Ireland*, 831-833; Edmondson, *The Alamo Story*, 85-86; Robert V. Remini, *Andrew Jackson and His Indian Wars* (New York, NY, 2002), 75-79; Groneman, *Alamo Defenders*, 3-125.

5 *The Telegraph and Texas Register*, November 7, 1835; Hardin, *Texian Illiad*, 111; Hopewell, *James Bowie*, 1-2.

6 *The Telegraph and Texas Register*, January 23, 1836; *Charleston Patriot*, Charleston, South Carolina, March 14, 1836.

In an ironic twist, young Lieutenant Colonel William Barret Travis had no desire to be stationed at the Alamo, especially after early ascertaining to his dismay that the "indolent, and quite contented" Texians had lost interest in the war effort by January 1836. Yet, thanks to his eloquent appeals for help, and subsequent death, the least experienced and least qualified of all the Alamo commanders became its most celebrated in the annals of Texas history. As the commander of the Legion of Cavalry (of Texians and Tejanos, fellow republicans who served together in this newly-created Texas Regular Army unit), who had still to fill the nascent horse command's ranks, the ambitious young man from the Alabama River country wanted to join the Matamoros Expedition, to reap glory and make a name for himself in an invasion of northern Mexico.

In the end, Travis commanded the Alamo for only a few days, while Neill was in charge of the garrison for around two months during a period of the greatest turmoil prior to the arrival of Santa Anna's Army. Neill, the mature Scotch-Irishman possessed far more leadership ability and experience than Travis, the young attorney consumed by ambition like so many other leaders of the Texas Revolution. While Travis was writing his January 29, 1836 letter to Governor Henry Smith "to beg that your Excellency will recall the order for me to go on to Bexar," Neill attempted to create an adequate defense of the Alamo. Much like Philip Dimmitt in defying Stephen Fuller Austin's order for his removal from command at Goliad, so Neill was determined not to abandon the Alamo in a classic case of Celtic defiance, as Houston prudently suggested in his wise discretionary order.[7]

Clearly, these popular Scotch-Irish military leaders, Neill and Dimmitt, were as defiant toward Texas authority as toward Mexican authority. While the 26-year-old Travis, ever-the-cavalier of romantic inclinations and lofty ambitions, would only contribute to greater dissension among the mostly volunteer Alamo garrison, because of his regular army status and inexperience, Neill kept the disgruntled Alamo garrison together week after week under the most appalling conditions. Throughout this period, adequate clothing, pay, support, reinforcements, munitions, and provisions were not forthcoming to the diminutive Alamo garrison from either the provisional Texas government, or the east Texas colonists.

---

7   Hardin, *Texian Illiad*, 110-111, 117; Hansen, ed., *The Alamo Reader*, 15, 18.

However, Neill departed the Alamo before the arrival of Santa Anna's Army because of an emergency family crisis, which has helped to obscure the importance of his influential leadership role in the Alamo's story. Of course, Neill's hasty departure denied him the legendary hero status gained by Travis, Crockett, and Bowie in their alleged deliberate self-sacrifice to save Texas on March 6. The fact that the Alamo's longest time commander was Scotch-Irish and influenced by Irish revolutionary and cultural antecedents has been long overlooked by historians, especially in terms of their impact on his key command decisions. Ironically, Travis incorrectly believed that Neill would be only briefly absent from the Alamo. As he penned in his February 12, 1836 report to Gov. Smith: "In consequence of the sickness of his family, Lt. Col. Neill has left this Post, to visit home for a short time, and has requested me to take the Command of the Post." Neill also departed the Alamo because it seemed that ample time still existed with the winter far from over, before Santa Anna attempted to reclaim Texas by force. Even Houston, as he wrote on February 19, was convinced that "Our Campaign will commence next month [because] Until the grass rises the Mexicans cannot advance, unless it is by sea— the Mexicans only advance on horses or by water."[8]

Clearly, the isolated band of men of the Alamo were in for the nasty surprise because of a thorough underestimation of their resourceful and resurgent opponent, thanks to prevailing racial stereotypes and the relatively easy victories of the 1835 Campaign. After all, as proclaimed in the February 27, 1836 issue of the *Telegraph and Texas Register* to fuel preexisting negative stereotypes, the Mexicans were nothing more than a weak "people one half of whom are the most depraved of the different races of Indians, different in color, pursuits and character."[9]

Meanwhile, this much-maligned opponent possessed a fierce determination, fueled by a righteous indignation, to regain Texas at any cost. On February 17 from his headquarters on the Nueces River, Santa Anna issued a proclamation to his troops that was most ominous for the fate of the tiny Alamo garrison: "Our most sacred duties have conducted us to these plains, and urged us forward to combat with that mob of ungrateful adventurers [who have] appropriated to themselves our territories, and have raised the standard

---

8   *The Telegraph and Texas Register*, January 9, 1836; Hansen, ed., *The Alamo Reader*, 22; *Nashville Banner and Nashville Whig*, Nashville, Tennessee, March 18, 1836.

9   *The Telegraph and Texas Register*, February 27, 1836.

of rebellion in order that this fertile and expanded department [of Texas] may be detached from our republic."[10]

The Alamo garrison was about to regret Neill's sudden departure. Unlike young Travis, Neill possessed solid experience in the Tennessee, Alabama and Texas militia (a mounted ranger company) before the Texas Revolution. Neill served for months during arduous campaigning under Scotch-Irish General Andy Jackson, including at the March 27, 1814 battle of Horseshoe Bend, in today's east central Alabama. Here, at the Muscogee village of Tohopeka, the Red Sticks' "sacred revolt" to retain their homeland had been brutally crushed along the Tallapoosa River. Once the Indians' defensive line was breached by the swarming attackers, including Scotch-Irish Lieutenant Sam Houston who fell wounded with an arrow in the thigh during the charge and then wounds to the arm, a slaughter occurred, when the fighting blood of Jackson's men reached a fever-pitch. More Creeks were killed at Horseshoe Bend than the number of Santa Anna's Mexicans who were slain at San Jacinto: two of the bloodiest battles, which quickly turned into massacres once the defenses (ironically, the Creeks' defenses at Horseshoe Bend were much more formidable than Santa Anna's makeshift works at San Jacinto) were carried by storm, in the annals of American history.[11]

As for so many Scotch-Irish in Texas, Neill's own personal war against the Indians east of the Mississippi had then continued unabated west of the Sabine River, after battling the pro-British Creeks in Alabama. Familiar with no mercy warfare in a Darwinian struggle of survival of the fittest, Neill was a tough frontier warrior, who readily embraced no quarter warfare like so many of Andy Jackson's boys at Horseshoe Bend. And in a bitter war of survival on the frontier, Neill could be utterly ruthless. As the capable adjutant of the original Texas Ranger battalion, Neill intentionally infected one Indian prisoner with the smallpox virus. He then turned the unfortunate man loose to spread deadly disease to his unsuspecting tribe. Ironically, while killing each other on the frontier for possession of this land of plenty, the Irish and Indians in fact shared a host of common cultural traits, including a lively oral tradition, a revered

10 *Richmond Enquirer*, February 17, 1836.

11 *The Telegraph and Texas Register*, January 9, 1836; Moore, *Eighteen Minutes*, 314-364; King, *James Clinton Neill*, 1, 18, 21, 44; McCarthy, *The Other Irish*, 45-50; Joel W. Martin, *Sacred Revolt, The Muskegees' Struggle for a New World* (Boston, MA, 1991), 160-163.

warrior ethos, a powerful spiritual and religious faith, and a social order that was strongly family-oriented and fundamentally conservative.

Experienced in battling the Creeks in the Alabama wilderness or the hard-riding Comanche on the Texas plains, Neill was inspired by a distinguished "family history [that was] filled with accounts of military deeds in fighting for independence in both Ireland and America." Not surprisingly, therefore, he had been one of the first volunteers to join the fight for Texas. Wearing no uniform in the frontier tradition and as mentioned, Neill commanded the little iron cannon of Gonzales during the "Lexington of the Texas" on October 2, 1835. Benefitting from his artillery experience in the Alabama militia during the Creek War and with reliable gunner Almeron Dickinson, a resourceful Gonzales settler of age 35, by his side, Neill unleashed the first cannon shot of the Texas Revolution with spirited Celtic defiance. While the Texians surged forward, Neill's cannonball sailed over the Guadalupe River and toward the Mexican dragoons of the Alamo de Parras Company to spark a people's revolution (as his ancestors in northern Ireland) that altered the future destinies of two nations. The first official deaths of the Texas Revolution were two soldados of the Alamo de Parras Company, which then retired back to their assigned station at the Alamo, where Cos was headquartered.

As the chief artillery commander of the "Army of the People," Neill then played a key role in the siege and assault on San Antonio. Here, Neill won additional distinction and widespread acclaim, while the exceptionally able Dickinson served as one of his top lieutenants. Then, Neill's artillery pieces were utilized as a timely diversion to mask the main infantry attack, pounding the Alamo's walls, defended by Cos' men, to cover the attack of two Texian columns from west of the river.

In January and early February 1836, Neill's accomplished a good deal in preparing the Alamo's defenses for meeting Santa Anna's fast-approaching army by the time Travis took command on February 24 during the siege. One Texas historian correctly emphasized that without the important contributions of this veteran Scotch-Irish commander from the O'Neill clan of Ulster Province, northern Ireland, "there would have been no garrison for Travis to inherit, no fort, no epic battle, and no entry into Texas legend."[12] Indeed, in the

---

12 *Dallas Morning News*, Dallas, Texas, April 14, 1895; Hardin, *Texian Illiad*, 110-111, 117; Davis, *Three Roads to the Alamo*, 190-194; Groneman, *Alamo Defenders*, 114-115; Stephen L. Moore, *Savage Frontier, Rangers, Riflemen, and Indian Wars in Texas, 1835-1837* (2 vols., Plano, TX,

end, Neill was more responsible for deciding to defend the Alamo to the bitter end than any other Texas leader, including Bowie and Travis. Neill's decision was very much in keeping with the defiant spirit of his Ulster Irish ancestors, who left a legacy of spirited resistance that spanned generations. Clearly, Neill was a complex and enigmatic (rather than quixotic) figure, and a man of many contradictions that have continued to baffle historians to this day.[13]

When he decided to defend the Alamo and influenced other leaders, especially a naive Bowie who was easily convinced since San Antonio had been his home before his Tejano wife's disease death, knew little about conventional warfare (especially about defending a conventional fortified position), and next to nothing about the proper usage of artillery, Neill's opinion was accepted primarily because he possessed more artillery experience that anyone else.

Clearly, this old artilleryman from service east of the Mississippi had been seduced by the large number of cannon, around 20 iron and bronze guns, which he utilized to defend the Alamo. In truth, however, he overlooked the more appropriate tactical lessons of the wisdom of relying upon mobility and stealth in warfare that was most often demonstrated by the wide-ranging Comanche (the most effective light cavalry in America), when he served as a hard-riding Texas Ranger and high-ranking officer of the original Texas Ranger battalion. In a strange irony and as fate would have it, Neill now relied upon the alleged wisdom of a static conventional defense as opposed to the distinct advantages of irregular (or guerrilla) warfare to maximize limited manpower and combat capabilities. Regardless of the large number of available artillery pieces and repeatedly demonstrated (most recently by Cos) in the past, any defensive stand at the isolated, vulnerable Alamo compound, which was too large to be defended by so few men when so far from support, was absolute folly.[14]

2002), vol. 1, 22-29; Alwyn Barr, *Texans in Revolt, The Battle of San Antonio, 1835* (Austin, TX, 1990), 45-46; King, *James Clinton Neill*, 44, 58-60; Edmondson, *The Alamo Story*, 208-212; Wallace Nutting, *Ireland Beautiful* (New York, NY, 1975), 60-62; Ben Maddow, *A Sunday Between Wars, The Course of American Life from 1865 to 1917* (New York, 1979), 16-18.

13 Moore, *Savage Frontier*, vol. 1, 29; Hardin, *Texian Illiad.*, 111, 117,119; James Clinton Neill, The Handbook of Texas Online.

14 Moore, *Savage Frontier*, vol. 1, 22-26; Davis, *Three Roads to the Alamo*, 494.

Chapter 6

David Crockett—the Ultimate "Irishman"

As history and the twists of fate came full circle, the last man to organize the belated final efforts to strengthen the Alamo's defenses was the garrison's chief engineer, whose ancestors came from Ulster Province, northern Ireland, Green B. Jameson. Fortunately, Jameson was immensely capable. A former lawyer from San Felipe de Austin, the 29-year-old Kentucky-born Jameson, although not a professionally trained engineer, was innovative, creative, and imaginative. Jameson worked diligently to strengthen the Alamo's fortifications before it was too late. Reliable and intelligent, he also served as the personal aide and advisor to Colonel Bowie, who commanded the volunteers and then shared joint command with Travis, during the siege of the Alamo.

General Sam Houston, overall commander of Texas forces and known for a hot temper that brought him a good many enemies, was of Scotch-Irish descent. Houston's humble ancestors had migrated from Hughstown, in the central lowlands of Scotland near Glasgow, to a new home in east County Antrim, Ulster Province, Ireland.

Along with hundreds of other Scotch-Irish Protestant warriors, Houston's Ulster ancestors, like those of David Crockett, had defended the high stone walls of Derry, when besieged by resurgent Catholic Jacobites under James II in 1689. Houston's great-grandfather, a tenant farmer named John who farmed the rich lands of an upper-class, wealthy landlord, departed the area of

A 19th century engraving of David Crockett, with his signature. As a politician, the former Tennessee Congressman fought valiantly for the rights of the common man and the poor. Crockett descended from Irish immigrants who migrated to America from Ulster Province, Northern Ireland. *Author's Collection*

Ballybracken, County Antrim, Ulster Province, with no regrets in 1735. The Houston family then headed across the Atlantic to start of a new life in Pennsylvania colony known for its religious tolerance. Later, like many other Scotch-Irish, the Houston family pushed south and established roots in Augusta County, Virginia, which became a Scotch-Irish enclave in the fertile Shenandoah Valley. Houston was described by one observer as having a "gay disposition," especially as a younger man, which reflected his Irish antecedents—lively in spirit, and merry in nature.

As noted earlier, Lieutenant Colonel James Clinton Neill was one of the first—and the longest-acting—Alamo commander after San Antonio de Bexar was captured by the resurgent Texians and United States volunteers in December 1835. Neill's ancestors had descended from a legendary clan of diehard Irish revolutionaries and nationalists, who fought valiantly, but in vain, to retain possession of their ancient homeland of Ulster. Neill proudly traced his family line to "ancient Irish warrior chieftains dating back to the fourth century." From the beginning Neill was a key player in both the story of the Alamo and the Texas Revolution, providing the leadership that kept the Alamo garrison together during the difficult winter of 1835-1836.

Crockett's Scotch-Irish roots in Ulster Province, northern Ireland, have been occasionally recognized by historians but practically only as a footnote. The Crockett family's earliest antecedents were in fact from Ireland's Munster Province well to the south. Crockett was proud of his Irish background on his father's side: his great, great, great grandfather, Antoine de Crocketagne, who sailed north from France to the south of Ireland. As a free-thinking French Huguenot (Protestant), Antoine had been forced to flee the south of Catholic France. The family name was anglicized from de Crocketagne (from the Old Norman French of croquet for a distinctive hairstyle with a curl) to Crockett and, having been a commercial agent for French mercantile firms, he then relocated to the commercial port of Bantry, Ireland, because of its close commercial and shipping connections to France. This picturesque region of County Cork was Ireland's warmest region, thanks to the Gulf Stream. A quaint seaport and fishing village, Bantry was nestled between two rocky peninsulas that stretched out into the Atlantic's blue waters like giant fingers of the ancient Roman God Neptune pointing the way for sailing ships out to the open sea.

Here, west of the larger port city of Cork the ambitious Protestant refugee's new name of Crockett eased his assimilation in the predominately Catholic area of Munster Province. The wandering life of this political refugee, who had been forced to flee his intolerant French Catholic homeland was mirrored more than 200 years later by David Crockett's ill-fated move from his modest home in west Tennessee toward the setting sun and an uncertain fate in Texas. The Crockett family witnessed "hard times, and plenty of them" in Crockett's words about his own life, and he was more than ready for a fresh start in a new land. In a letter written on January 9, 1836—barely two months before his Alamo death—he described the virgin Red River country of east Texas as "the garden spot of the world."

Crockett, who had been raised amid the hardwood forests and hills of the east Tennessee frontier, heard stories of his family's colorful Irish immigrant history. Picturesque Bantry Bay was Ireland's "Bay of Destiny" for its key roles in Irish history, especially in an ill-fated French invasion in 1796 that the French Revolutionary government hoped would spark an Irish revolt against British rule. The long rocky peninsula of the bay's southern edge, shaped like a dagger, ended at a high elevation known locally as Sheep's Head Point, which was one of the most awe-inspiring scenic vantage points in Ireland.[1]

---

1 *Maryland Gazette*, November 12, 1835; *El Mosquito Mexicano*, March 22, 1836; Dolan, *The Irish Americans*, 22; Hopewell, *James Bowie*, 1-2; Davis, *Three Roads to the Alamo*, 194; Davis, *Land!*, 3-257; Groneman, *Alamo Defenders*, 63-64; Chipman, *Spanish Texas, 1519-1821*, 182, 186, 190; Irish Texans, Texas Almanac, Texas State Historical Association, internet; Haley, *Sam Houston*, 5; McCarthy, *The Other Irish*, 19-22, 45-46, 56-59; Marshall DeBruhl, *A Life of Sam Houston* (New York, NY, 1993), 7-11; Bill Walraven and Jane Walraven, *The Magnificent Barbarians, Little Told*

The Crockett family next relocated to the island's opposite end, to protestant Ulster Province in northern Ireland, where business was more profitable for an enterprising Protestant merchant than in the less thriving Catholic south Ireland. Another reason for this business-savvy Crockett to depart south Ireland was its anti-French sentiment. By the time of the Jacobite invasion of James II, who commanded thousands of French troops and Irish Catholic patriots, men of the Crockett clan were defending the walls of Derry with its Scotch-Irish people and soldiers during the long siege. James's invasion ended in a crushing defeat in the battle of the Boyne in July 1690, in another bloody showdown when untrained Irish pikemen proved no match for blazing English musketry and cannon. Despite the turbulent ebbs and flows of Irish history, the Crockett family had called Ireland home for generations. Crockett's own father, John, was either born in Ireland, or aboard a ship during the long journey to America. However, as an iconic American frontiersmen of popular memory and national consciousness, Crockett's Irish roots have been obscured in the historical record by the creation of the mythical all-American hero—as if he were solely the native son of the untamed east Tennessee frontier who had suddenly emerged from that primeval wilderness without Irish antecedents or influences. According to the prevailing romantic myth, an authentic American hero was born of the frontier experience with a natural desire to fight against injustice and oppression. Therefore, the romantic and mythical Crockett was created without any significant acknowledgement of his Irish roots. Ironically, without his death at age 49 at the Alamo, Crockett might have been little more than a footnote in American history.

While Crockett's Irish origins may have been overlooked by many American and Irish historians due to the creation of the Crockett myth and romance, the Tennessean's winning ways, boundless gift of gab (known in Ireland as "blarney"), and lively personality revealed his thoroughly Irish side. He also possessed well-known Irish characteristics of a deep compassion for impoverished and oppressed people, thanks to a shared experience of suffering

Tales of the Texas Revolution (Austin, TX, 1993), 91; Billy Kennedy, *Scots-Irish in the Hills of Tennessee* (Greenville, SC, 1995), 19-57, 99-118; James Clinton Neill, Handbook of Texas Online; *New York Times*, January 27, 1895; "The Alamo: The Irish Heroes of the Alamo," *IC*, internet; Flannery, *The Irish Texans*, pp. 18-19; King, *James Clinton Neill*, 3-4, 7-8; *New York Times*, January 27, 1895; John Edward Weems with Jane Weems, *Dream of Empire, A History of the Republic of Texas 1836-1846* (New York, NY, 1986), 57; *Farmer's Cabinet*, Amherst, New Hampshire; McWhiney, *Cracker Culture*, xiii-257; Webb, *Born Fighting*, 123-184; Lack, *The Texas Revolutionary Experience*, 208; Donovan, *The Blood of Heroes*, 69-71, 95-98.

that could never be fully understood by the privileged elites so securely sheltered from life's economic hardships and troubled times. Crockett's wife, Mary Finley, affectionately called Polly, was the daughter of "an old Irish woman," in the Tennessean's words. Revealing her Celtic-Gaelic antecedents, the mother's name was Jean Kennedy Finley. She was the niece of an Irish Quaker named John "Canady" or Kennedy.

By the time of the dramatic showdown at the Alamo—and contrary to the widespread myth— Crockett possessed limited military experience. He had served under General Andrew Jackson, the consummate Celtic warrior, as little more than a scout and hunter in the Tennessee Volunteer Mounted Riflemen. As a poor frontiersman who struggled to provide for his family, Crockett needed the regular pay with his service. Both Private Crockett and General Jackson were equally proud of their common Irish heritage. Jackson's northern Irish family hailed from the area around Belfast, Ulster Province, northern Ireland, and he was an uncompromising Irish Presbyterian holy warrior. Crockett's served under Jackson during the Creek, or Red Stick, War of 1813-1814, which was a disaster for the Creek people. Overcoming the fact that his grandparents had been killed by a Cherokee raiding party in East Tennessee during the American Revolution, Crockett developed a rare compassion for the suffering of the local native people, the proud Muscogee who, in defending their ancestral homeland in southern Alabama, were crushed by superior firepower and Jackson's tactical aggressiveness.

Of course, the Indian people's tragic fate was simply that their nations lay in harm's way, the relentless American westward expansionism, spearheaded by the always land-hungry Scotch-Irish, which could not be stopped. Ironically, Crockett fought besides Creek allies in what was essentially a bitter civil war (like the Texas Revolution that was part of a Mexican Civil War) among the Creek people, learning to admire Indian culture, especially their warrior ethos. As Crockett saw and lamented, a rapidly growing America was practicing its own frontier brand of ethnic cleansing to gain a vast empire of virgin fertile lands. As a popular Tennessee Congressman in the early 1830s, Crockett audaciously stood up for his personal beliefs and opposed the Indian Removal Bill proposed by President Jackson, his old commander and head of a powerful Democratic political machine. Crockett's bold, but unpopular, stance led to the loss of his Congressional seat, as his west Tennessee constituents—like other lower and middle class Americans on the poorly-protected frontier—had no love for Indians. His was a shining example of a true profile in political courage. Blessed with an acute sense of fair play, Crockett also advocated for squatter rights, as many lower class settlers were unable to afford to purchase the land they had homesteaded. As well, Crockett grew to detest slavery, a rare attitude among Anglo-Celts on the western frontier in early 1830s including in Texas, lamenting its injustices and horrors. Even in Washington D.C., where slaves were bought and sold, Crockett noted how the powerful slave interests of the Deep South advanced self-serving political agendas that shaped the nation's course and maximized profits—a tragic betrayal of America's fundamental egalitarian principles of the Revolution. As a Tennessee Congressman, he opposed bills to repeal redemption laws and even voted funds "for the relief of Mathias, a free man of color."[2]

Clearly, Crockett related to the suffering of unfortunate people, regardless of race, not only because of his own struggles with poverty, but his family's legacy of Irish experiences and an Irish tradition of benevolence for oppressed people. Therefore, Crockett remained an outsider, especially among the career politicians, socialites and crass opportunists of Washington, D.C. Crockett, the homespun "gentleman from the cane," was also famous for those qualities that were typically Irish: a love for storytelling and a keen sense of humor distinguished by a cutting wit, ribaldry, and an uncanny ability to "exact fun from the dreariest [of] subjects." Such enduring and admirable traits and were part of the secret of Crockett's personal appeal and popularity among the common people.[3]

While Texas historians (including at least one Ireland-born author) have focused on the mythical Crockett of Alamo fame without a hint of his Irish roots, the real man, who was far more complex than the one-dimensional, coonskin-cap stereotype, was very nearly the antithesis of the much-embellished backwoods warrior and the roughhewn frontiersman, who

---

2   *New York Times*, December 15, 1907; Shackford, *David Crockett*, 3-118, 293; Michael J. Carroll, *A Bay of Destiny, A History of Bantry Bay and Bantry* (Bantry, Ireland, 1996), 203-252; Groneman, *Alamo Defenders*, 133; Davis, *Three Roads to the Alamo*, 9-34, 63-90, 113-141, 165-187, 194; McWhiney, *Cracker Culture*, 3-8; Crockett Family History, Ancestry, internet; "The Crockett's of Brentwood, Brentwood Trivia, internet; History of Crockett Family, internet; Derr, *The Frontiersman*, 11-269; McCarthy, *The Other Irish*, 19-22, 24-59; Bob Thompson, Born on a Mountaintop, *On the Road with Davy Crockett and the Ghosts of the Wild Frontier* (New York, NY, 2012), 35-75; Edmondson, *The Alamo Story*, 262; Buddy Levy, *American Legend, Real-Life Adventures of David Crockett* (New York, NY, 2005), 29-179; Boylston and Wiener, *David Crockett in Congress*, 8-22, 65-73, 187; Dolan, *The Irish Americans*, 3-4.

3   Shackford, *David Crockett*, 3-118, 293; Kennedy, *Scots-Irish in the Hills of Tennessee*, 103-104; *New York Times*, December 15, 1907; Peter Haining, editor, *Great Irish Humor* (New York, NY, 1995), 13-16; Nutting, *Ireland Beautiful*, 61-62; McWhiney, *Cracker Culture*, xxxii.

allegedly slew scores of Mexican attackers on his own at the Alamo. Instead, he was an active supporter of the poor and the underdogs of the West, primarily of Celtic-Gaelic people like his own family, who were attempting to scratch out a meager living on the frontier as best they could under the most challenging circumstances. Crockett's heartfelt devotion to the lowest segment of American society never ended, because he was one of them and identified with their plight. Long before facing the formations of advancing Mexican soldados on the early morning of March 6, 1836 at the Alamo, Crockett had already fought long and hard against social injustices.[4]

At considerable professional, personal, and political cost, Crockett bravely upheld his "lonely, unpopular defense of Indians [which] stands out in an era dominated by racism, greed, and injustice."[5] In fact, one insightful Irish historian, Billy Kennedy, emphasized that Crockett was actually much like an active "socialist" (meant as a compliment) in regard to his deep concern and passionate support for the downtrodden of the lower classes—mostly poor farmers, including even African Americans, both free and slave, on the western frontier.[6]

In consequence, Crockett not only admired but also loved "my people" of the lowest origins. Most importantly, he explained what his people meant to America: "these people, though poor, are of inestimable value in a free republic [and] they are the bone and sinew of the land." Indeed, these were the people who not only made America but also Texas. Referring to the lowly residents of west Tennessee, Crockett said: "None of them are rich, but they are an honest, industrious, hardly, persevering kind-hearted people [as] I know them" well.[7]

Crockett's absolute disgust with the excessive privileges and abuses of America's corrupt and wealthy ruling elite, including slave owners, was one fundamental reason why he left the United States, journeyed to the southwestern frontier of Texas, where he met his tragic fate at the Alamo.[8] In

---

4 Boylston and Wiener, *David Crockett in Congress, The Rise and Fall of the Poor Man's Friend* (Houston, TX, 2009), 7-9, 16, 21; McWhiney, *Cracker Culture*, xiii-267; Webb, *Born Fighting*, 3-184; Libura, Moreno, and Marquez, *Echoes of the Mexican-American War*, 24-25.

5 Boylston and Wiener, *David Crockett in Congress*, 73.

6 Kennedy, *Scots-Irish in the Hills of Tennessee*, 104; Boylston and Wiener, *David Crockett in Congress*, 16, 19, 21-22.

7 Boylston and Wiener, *David Crockett in Congress*, 311, 312.

8 Ibid., 122, 282.

the words of a journalist writing for the *Vermont Gazette*, "Davy has become disgusted with this country since his defeat, and has determined to move to Texas, stock, lock, and barrel."[9]

Clearly Crockett had enough of not only politics, but also Washington D.C. and life in the United States, where far too many of the common people were dominated and manipulated by the ruling class wealthy elites. In a letter written on Christmas Day 1834, Crockett indicated his desire to make a fresh start in a new land far away from Washington, D.C., and Tennessee: "I will go to the wildes [sic] of Texas."[10]

Ironically Crockett had no desire to engage in a war of any kind in Texas, when he journeyed there by horseback on what was nothing more than a scouting and hunting trip. Crockett described in an October 31, 1835 letter how, "I am on the eve of Starting to the Texes [as] I want to explore the Texes well before I return" to Tennessee.[11] He seemed more intent on leaving family responsibilities behind rather than on engaging in a glorious struggle for liberty on Texas soil. During the long trek to Texas, when an inquisitive Arkansas woman asked about what arrangements he had made for his family back in west Tennessee, Crockett merely answered with his trademark humor: "I have set them free—set them free—they must shift for themselves."[12]

Crockett's sense of humor reflected the depth of his distinctive Irish roots in which Celtic-Gaelic society placed a premium on the art of entertaining, a light-hearted playfulness, and practical jokes. In the 1834 words of a northeast journalist, Crockett possessed "rather sharp features, with an extremely pleasing cast of countenance, in which humour [was] strongly portrayed."[13] Most of all, Crockett shared a direct personal legacy, distinguished heritage, and long-overlooked familial connection to Ireland's revolutionary past that was to be resurrected at a place called the Alamo.[14]

9   *Vermont Gazette*, Bennington, Vermont, October 6, 1835.

10 *New York Times*, December 15, 1907; McWhiney, *Cracker Culture*, 1-8; Boylston and Wiener, *David Crockett in Congress*, 7-9.

11 Boylston and Wiener, *David Crockett in Congress*, 285.

12 *Arkansas Gazette*, Little Rock, Arkansas, May 10, 1836.

13 *The Portsmouth Journal and Rockingham Gazette*, New Hampshire, May 10, 1834.

14 McWhiney, *Cracker Culture*, 35; McCarthy, *The Other Irish*, 19-22, 56-59.

Chapter 7

A Bloody Predawn Reckoning at the Alamo

Antonio Lopez de Santa Anna's army surprised the Alamo garrison on February 23, 1836, but the unprepared garrison evacuated San Antonio de Bexar just in time to escape to the safety of the Alamo. Santa Anna ordered the hoisting of the red banner of "no quarter" from the bell tower of San Fernando Church. The men of the Alamo, including many Irish soldiers, then knew what to expect. No doubt, many were reminded of the comparable no-quarter policies of English military leaders throughout the tragic course of Irish history.

Santa Anna established artillery batteries close to the old Franciscan mission and day after day, the Alamo garrison endured the horrors of a siege. Despite dispatching ever more frantic appeals for help from the Alamo, no assistance was forthcoming from the east Texas settlements.

But the faithful Irish of Gonzales, located just east of San Antonio de Bexar, answered the call, rushing to assist their comrades in the early morning darkness of Tuesday March 1, 1836. They were the Alamo's last reinforcements, consisting of 32 men of the Gonzales Ranging Company of Mounted Volunteers led by Lieutenant George C. Kimbell. John W. Smith, of Scotch-Irish descent and with red hair that gave him the nick name of "El Colorado," guided these courageous men into the beleaguered compound. With ample experience from the Campaign of 1835, Almeron Dickinson was a natural leader in this hard-riding Texas Ranger company. Symbolically, among the soldiers who came to the aid of the garrison were Ireland-born Thomas J. Jackson and Andrew Duvalt. Likewise, Jesse McCoy, who most recently had served as the sheriff of Gonzales, rode into the Alamo with his two sons, Prospect and Daniel. The spirited Scotch-Irish McCoy clan was reminiscent of the rising of the ancient Celtic clans against the invaders of their Irish homeland. Nevertheless, the additional volunteers from Gonzales were not adequate to defend the expanse of stone and adobe walls around the nearly three-acre compound.

On the eleventh day of the siege of the Alamo, Santa Anna developed a plan to overwhelm the depleted garrison trapped in the isolated old Spanish mission. He informed his assembled top lieutenants and leading colonels at a hastily-called commanders' conference in the heart of San Antonio de Bexar on the afternoon of Friday March 4 that he proposed to launch a massive assault to overwhelm the diminutive, but stubborn Alamo garrison.

Santa Anna's decision to conduct a commanders' conference was sparked by the arrival of reinforcements that cold morning as the winter sun shone brightly on the shallow valley of the San Antonio River. The sight of the finely-uniformed reinforcements lifted spirits throughout Santa Anna's Army of Operations, after the soldados' long forced march north to Texas. Around 1,400 men of General Antonio Gaona's First Brigade provided the reinforcements to veteran "National Units" (regulars), reaching San Antonio on the morning of March 4. These were prized veteran troops, including the elite Zapadores Battalion that Santa Anna had been awaiting before launching his assault on the Alamo.

Since laying siege to this seemingly ill-fated place, Santa Anna had decided that the First Brigade would be employed "to act decisively" in an offensive operation against the Alamo. With the addition of the First Brigade, Santa Anna's strength was now about 5,000 men. However, his Army included a large number of recently-impressed recruits, whose quality was still very much in doubt. Hence, Santa Anna's eagerness for the arrival of Gaona's more experienced troops to play the leading role in the upcoming assault was understandable.

At the one-story, adobe Yturri house, located at the northwestern corner of the Main Plaza—La Plaza de la Constitution—in the shadow of stately San Fernando Cathedral, Santa Anna explained his detailed and well-conceived plan of attack to his top lieutenants. He advocated an innovative tactical plan to catch the garrison completely by surprise precisely when the long-suffering band of defenders was most vulnerable. But to his surprise, some of his top lieutenants voiced opposition to the idea of launching a frontal assault, fearing high casualties. Showing more tolerance than usual, Santa Anna entertained these dissenting opinions. After the conference ended at 2:00 P.M., Santa Anna sat down in the Yturri house to dictate new orders to his civilian private secretary, Ramon Martinez Caro.[1]

After remaining more than a week and half in a static position at San Antonio de Bexar, whose predominantly Tejano population numbered about 2,500 people, Santa Anna now needed a resounding victory for not only military, but political reasons. Perhaps he recalled the coup attempt in Paris in late 1812, when Santa Anna's idol, Napoleon, campaigned in faraway snowy Russia. Santa Anna desired to bolster his lofty reputation as the "Napoleon of the South," and sought a military success to impress the leading politicians and people of Mexico with his tactical brilliance and leadership skills. Of course, Santa Anna also wanted to cow the Texas revolutionaries of the eastern settlements into submission with a bloody example of his battlefield power and to demonstrate the futility of armed resistance against his authority and the Republic of Mexico's might.

Santa Anna was the consummate politician; his impatience and decision to overwhelm the Alamo by force of arms revealed as much. He had temporarily left the prestigious office of the republic's president in Mexico City for the express purpose of regaining possession of Texas. Now he viewed reaping a sparkling victory in vanquishing the ragtag Alamo garrison as the best means to demonstrate his power to people across Mexico and the United States. Therefore, his political gesture in launching the assault ensured that a frightfully high price would be paid by the Alamo garrison for openly rebelling against Mexico and for defying the self-styled "Napoleon."

Santa Anna was not about to waste any more time awaiting the arrival of his slow-moving, heavy artillery pieces (12-pounders) to batter the garrison into submission. He also decided against waiting until the defenders ran out of supplies, which was now only a matter of time. The strength of the Alamo garrison had steadily diminished during 12 days of siege and Santa Anna was determined to reap a glorious victory regardless of the costs. He would not

---

1 *New York Herald*, June 25, 1836; Roberts and Olson, *A Line in the Sand*, 150-153; Miguel A. Sanchez Lamego, *The Siege and Taking of the Alamo* (Santa Fe: The Press of the Territorian, 1968), 17, 19, 23, 29, 32, 36; Groneman, *Alamo Defenders*, 36-37, 42, 51-52, 63, 70-71, 77; Hardin, *The Alamo 1836*, 35-36; Tucker, *Exodus From the Alamo*, 164-169, 184-185; Gaddy, *Texas in Revolt*, 55.

allow the opportunity to win a dramatic victory slip away after the men of his army had made one of the longest, most grueling marches in the annals of military history. Therefore, Santa Anna now fairly lusted at the thought of achieving a significant political and psychological victory on the battlefield. The generalissimo had recently sharpened his skills in slaughtering hundreds of republican Mexican rebels at Zacatecas.[2]

Irish Catholic garrison members, like Lieutenant Edward McCafferty of the Refugio Colony—one of Bowie's homespun volunteers—who rode into the Alamo in February, had no idea that their fate was in the process of being sealed by what was quietly transpiring at the plain-looking Yturri house in San Antonio de Bexar.

Santa Anna planned to unleash his overpowering might against the Alamo on Sunday, March 6. The pious Irish Catholics trapped inside the Alamo, never feeling so far from their Irish homeland across the sea than when isolated on the remote Texas frontier surrounded by thousands of Mexican soldados, began to think about the welfare of their souls and the afterlife. Inside the haunting gloom of the Alamo while a cold southwest wind howled and rustled the tall prairie grass outside the mission walls, Irish Catholic defenders no doubt fingered cherished small silver crosses and rosary beads, while praying for shelter from the upcoming storm. Even the non-cynics, Protestant and Catholic, among the garrison knew that the end was drawing near for them. Not even the comforting nearby spiritual presence of the Alamo Church, of sturdy limestone, all the prayers in the world and Saint Patrick himself were enough to now save these Sons of Erin.

Ironically, Santa Anna's men viewed the Alamo's Irish Catholic defenders as little more than interloping heretics, grouping them with the predominantly Protestant garrison. Sensing that death was hovering near, the Catholic Sons of Erin might have looked longingly at the San Fernando Cathedral on the San Antonio River's opposite side. This stately stone and adobe Cathedral, had long served as the very soul and sacred center of San Antonio de Bexar, especially when its large brass bells sounded their eagerly awaited calls to worship. First established as a parish church for a humble flock of a handful of New Spain

---

2 Lamego, *The Siege and Taking of the Alamo*, 29; Roberts and Olson, *A Line in the Sand*, 158; Hardin, *The Alamo 1836*, 24-27, 35-36; Alan Palmer, *Napoleon in Russia* (London, England, 1997), 215-216; Tucker, *Exodus from the Alamo*, 61, 71-72.

settlers, this house of worship continues to welcome parishioners of all races today and remains the vibrant center of the city's Catholic community.

As faithful parishioners before the siege, the Irish Catholics of the Alamo would have heard Mass on Sunday March 6—if Santa Anna's Army had not arrived suddenly to catch everyone by surprise on February 23. With Santa Anna's tightening grip on the ever-dwindling garrison, spiritual faith became more important for the surrounded men with each passing day. The Irish, both Protestant and Catholic, prayed that God had not abandoned them to a cruel fate at this alien place that they were now defending with their lives.

But far more Catholics of Santa Anna's Army probably wished to have been worshiping at San Fernando Cathedral instead of risking their lives in a frontal assault on a fortified position that bristled with more than twenty artillery pieces. Situated in the town's heart, the Cathedral had been completed in 1755. Here, Mexican Independence was celebrated with enthusiasm by the republican-minded populace on September 16, 1829. If not now wearing the well-worn uniform of the Republic of Mexico, these young men of the Catholic faith in Santa Anna's enlisted ranks would have been kneeling and praying in peasant garb at the altar of Our Lady of Guadalupe (the patroness of the Mexican people). Instead, on Sunday March 6, hundreds of these soldados of mostly Aztec descent and peasant origins would be unleashed with fixed bayonets in a desperate attack on the Alamo.[3]

Meanwhile, far from San Antonio de Bexar on this Sunday in late winter, large numbers of the Texian colonists would be faithfully attending church in their rustic home communities all across east Texas, as if no war existed and no sizeable Mexican Army was now on Texas soil. Unfortunately, for the Alamo garrison, the Texians had still not organized to meet the powerful threat on the remote western frontier. Like most other Texians who had simply left military service and departed for their homes after San Antonio de Bexar's capture in December 1835, teenage Kindallis "King" Bryan was now living peacefully in Liberty (the third town founded in Anglo-Celtic Texas), which was nestled in the fertile Trinity River country. Bryan shared a revered Irish heritage and

3 Virgilio P. Elizondo and Timothy M. Matovina, *San Fernando Cathedral, Soul of the City* (Maryknoll, CO, 1998), xii, 8, 12, 20, 25, 28; Randy Roberts and James Olson, *A Line in the Sand, The Alamo in Blood and Memory* (New York, NY, 2001) , 150-151; McCafferty, Edward, Handbook of Texas Online; Tucker, *Exodus From the Alamo*, 182-183, 192; Hardin, *The Alamo 1836*, 26.

distinguished Celtic legacy with the majority of Texian settlers from the United States.

The course of Bryan's life has provided a good representative example of the typical Alamo defender of Irish descent, who was generations removed from the Irish immigrant experience. Born amid the swampy lowlands west of New Orleans on Tiger Island, Louisiana, Bryan was named in honor of his grandfather and family patriarch, Christopher Kindallis Bray. Hailing from the ancestral O'Bryan clan of Clare County, located just south of the port of Galway and northwest of the River Shannon in Munster Province, Ireland, Christopher migrated to America in the 1760s with all the ambitions and high hopes of a typical Irish immigrant.

The Gaelic name of Kindallis meant "ruler of the valley." Dropping the "O" from the family's last name, a deliberate strategy and part of the common Americanization process of Irish newcomers to the New World since before the American Revolution, Bryant then became a fiery American patriot like so many other Irish immigrants during the struggle for independence. He served faithfully in a Virginia Continental Regiment during the American Revolution, battling for the common people's dream of liberty. Symbolically, this Irish immigrant patriot who loved America named one of his sons George Washington Bryan in honor of his beloved Virginia-born commander-in-chief.

However, after the Alamo's fall—which would finally awaken Texian settlers to the fact that the wolf from deep inside Mexico was now at their doorstep, "King" Bryan and other Irish of the Bryan clan, including three brothers (Christopher, Thomas, and Luke, Jr.) and his father Luke Bryan, rallied to the cause of Texas, joining the revolutionary army. As if defending their ancient Celtic-Gaelic homeland against the murdering and raping English invaders from across the sea, they turned out to defend this beloved new frontier land with their trusty flintlock muskets and Bowie knives. By this time, however, the galvanizing of Texian resistance from the settlements was too little, too late for the Alamo garrison.[4]

Time and luck were fast running out for the Alamo defenders. Indeed, the element of time was fading away much sooner than Travis' men imagined possible at this ill-fated place that had such a longtime connection to folly and slaughter. Weary and dirt-grimed garrison soldiers had no idea what it meant

---

4 Michael Day Jones, *Lt. Col. King Bryan of Hood's Texas Brigade* (CreateSpace Independent Publishing Platform, 2013), 1-28; Roberts and Olson, *A Line in the Sand*, 184-185.

when the Mexican artillery bombardment on the evening and night of March 5 failed to erupt as usual. The Mexican cannon had been laboriously moved up to within close range of the Alamo's crumbling limestone and adobe walls, but the guns now aligned on favorable ground stood eerily silent. For soldiers who had been under artillery bombardment for more than a week and a half, the lack of artillery fire must have seemed like a Godsend. But this silence caused the most cynical and wary men of the garrison to wonder if Santa Anna—who was known for his Machiavellian cunning— was up to some trick. Emerald Islanders wondered what this strange silence meant. Why had Santa Anna's cannon suddenly ceased to roar?

Like his men, young Travis had no idea about the cause of this strange silence and its mysterious meaning. Perhaps Travis believed that Santa Anna had decided to conserve his limited supply of ammunition, which had been laboriously transported so far north from deep inside Mexico. After all, the Alamo's commander, Travis had been husbanding his own diminishing reserves of black powder out of dire necessity. Instead of seriously questioning what the silence meant, most of the weary defenders were just thankful that the relentless pounding from Santa Anna's guns had finally ceased. By this time, the mounting burden of this obviously vexing question rested solidly on Travis' shoulders, which already carried considerable weight with overall command responsibility.

Only in his mid-twenties, and with a lieutenant colonel's rank in the Texas Regular Army, the South Carolina-born Travis was now in sole command of the Alamo, after Bowie had fallen sick. Bowie may have been stricken with a bacterial infection from the garrison's contaminated water supply, which came from a recently dug well in the open plaza. Most likely Bowie came down with typhoid fever or cholera, diseases that had claimed the lives of so many mission Indians so long ago. The famous knife fighter's condition had gradually worsened as the siege progressed, and conditions inside the Alamo steadily deteriorated with each passing day. The Louisiana-born fighter was bed-ridden in a darkened room of the so-called Low Barracks, situated along the south wall near the main gate. According to many, it was here that Bowie would meet his end, once the Mexicans broke through the walls and overpowered the defending garrison.

Travis ordered his men, under the dark veil of night, to begin to repair the damage caused by the day's bombardment. He was taking advantage of the darkness and the unprecedented lull from the usual cannonade—doing exactly what the clever Santa Anna expected him to do. The already-worn garrison

If Jim Bowie indeed died as legend suggests, this sketch may well offer a realistic depiction of his final moments. "The Death of Bowie," by Louis Betts of *McClure's Magazine* (January 1902), shows the sickly famous knife-fighter of the southwestern frontier in his bed inside a darkened room along the south wall of the "low barracks" not far from the Alamo's main gate. *Author's Collection*

members worked late into the night of March 5 strengthening the battered north wall and other sectors damaged by the seemingly endless barrage of cannonballs. They exhausted themselves even further by laboring long hours and well into the night—never realizing that this was the last work they would ever do.

By this time, the beleaguered soldiers of the tiny garrison were so weary after 12 days of siege and almost constant bombardment that the true meaning of the quiet artillery pieces—an ambush of sorts—was entirely overlooked by Travis and his men. All in all, garrison members, including at least 15 Ireland-born soldiers (most likely even more Sons of Erin were present), had been victimized by cleverly conceived psychological warfare from the siege's beginning: threatening troop movements and sudden feints, bands playing loudly, the red no-quarter flag flying from the bell tower of San Fernando, and, most of all, the constant artillery bombardment.

*   *   *

The Alamo's Emerald Isle-born soldiers represented volunteer companies from the United States, especially the New Orleans Greys, the San Patricio and Refugio Colonies, and other small Texas communities, especially Gonzales: Major Robert Evans; Lieutenant Edward McCafferty, Sergeant William B. Ward, and Privates James McGee, Stephen Dennison of the New Orleans Grays), plus Burke Trammel, Samuel E. Burns, John Spratt, and John Mormon also of the New Orleans Greys; Thomas J. Jackson, Joseph Mark Hawkins, James Nolan, David P. Cummings, Jackson R. Rusk, and teenage Andrew Duvalt, all from Gonzales. In addition, William Daniel Jackson, a sailor of age 29, was evidently Ireland-born. A far larger number of Alamo defenders were the sons, grandsons, or great grandsons of Irish immigrants: defender Christopher Adams Parker, age 22, took pride in the fact that his ancestor, Samuel Sparrow, had played a role in Robert Emmit's 1803 abortive revolt, which led to his flight to America. The Irish revolutionary spirit was alive and well inside the walls of the Alamo.

Meanwhile, the muscles and backs of Travis' men ached from their heavy work in strengthening the battered earthen defenses, laboring "until a late hour" on Saturday March 5. At this time, the predominant thoughts of these exhausted citizen-soldiers were surely just to get some much-needed sleep. As Santa Anna had likely envisioned, the worn-down Alamo men took full advantage of the rare respite from the harassing artillery, and after their assigned work was finally over Travis' men quickly went to sleep in their insulated stone and adobe quarters—especially in the Long Barracks, which had served as the priests' quarters during the mission years.

With his well thought-out tactical plan, Santa Anna had set a masterful trap to lull the already-weary defenders into a deep sleep. After Travis posted a mere handful of guards and pickets, including three soldiers to man the cold ditches outside the walls, to sound the alarm at the first sign of an assault, the Alamo garrison enjoyed its last peaceful rest on the night of March 5-6—the lull before the storm of Santa Anna's wrath descended upon the Alamo.[5] Indeed, for the exhausted garrison members, this rare "silence was like a dream come true [and] Too tired to be suspicious, many of the defenders fell into a deep sleep."[6]

Travis, staying up late as usual after his soldiers had retired, made his customary time-consuming rounds of the sprawling compound to check the defenses amid the numbing cold and haunting stillness of the early morning hours. This late-winter night could not have been more quiet and calm. Nothing stirred on the open prairie outside the Alamo's walls. No hint of Santa Anna's impending attack was detected by any garrison member, inside or outside the Alamo. Travis and his men may also have let their guard down— as earlier reasoned by Santa Anna—because they knew that they faced a Catholic army of holy warriors who faithfully observed Sunday Mass.

Satisfied that all was secure, Travis finally ended his rounds, and retired to his room in the darkened building located along the west wall just before 3:00 A.M. Lying in his cot with the winter wind howling across the prairie outside, Travis perhaps thought back on the bold words he had once written about Texas in revolt: "I have resolved to stand by her [Texas] to the last, and in a word, to sink or swim with her."[7]

Giving way to his own state of utter exhaustion, Travis left Adjutant John Joseph Baugh, age 35, in charge. If Baugh had once felt that he had made a wise decision in not riding south with the Matamoros Expedition, he now thought differently. Baugh was a trustworthy and respected Virginia-born officer, and

---

5 *Commonwealth*, Frankfort, Kentucky, May 25, 1836; Hardin, *The Alamo 1836*, 26, 36; Frank Thompson, *The Alamo, A Cultural History* (Dallas, TX, 2001), 52; Herbert G. Uecker, *The Archaeology of the Alamo* (Bulverde: Monte Comal Publications, 2001), 11, 44, 70; Davis, *Three Roads to the Alamo*, 557; Groneman, *The Alamo Defenders*, 21, 30, 34, 42, 47-48, 58, 63, 76-78, 95-96; Tucker, *Exodus from the Alamo*, 56-59; Brown, *The New Orleans Greys*, 302-303, 306; File of Irish Alamo Defenders, Author's Collection; "The Alamo: The Irish Heroes of the Alamo," *IC*; H. W. Brands, *Lone Star Nation, How A Ragged Army of Volunteers Won the Battle for Texas Independence—And Changed America* (New York, NY, 2004), 351.

6 Thompson, *The Alamo*, 52; Roberts and Olson, *A Line in the Sand*, 152.

7 Davis, *Three Roads to the Alamo*, 558-559; Tucker, *Exodus from the Alamo*, 178.

formerly a member of the crack New Orleans Greys. Therefore, with a sense of relief, Travis left Baugh with the full responsibilities as the "officer of the day" on this early Sunday morning. Travis had finally ended his self-imposed vigilance of peering incessantly into the quiet darkness of the open prairie hour after hour. Travis had complete trust in Baugh, who was one of his top lieutenants. Of Welsh descent, Baugh commanded the Alamo's few remaining members of the New Orleans Greys, including Ireland-born Private James McGee, who because of a nasty wound suffered in the attack on San Antonio de Bexar, had not departed San Antonio on the ill-fated Matamoros Expedition like the more adventurous Greys (who were now part of the volunteer company renamed the San Antonio Greys), who had ridden south in search of glory.[8]

Before falling to sleep in his lonely quarters, Travis might have thought briefly about the ugly realities of what to expect once the Mexicans attacked and came over the walls with long triangular bayonets attached to the end of their Napoleonic smooth-bore muskets. As he had earlier written: "A blood red banner waves from the [bell tower of the] church of Bejar [San Fernando which meant] that the war is one of vengeance against rebels."[9]

At about the same time, just before 3:00 A.M., that Travis retired to his chilly quarters, some 400 resplendently-uniformed troopers of the Mexican cavalry, including veteran lancers and dragoons, saddled their horses. The horses' mouths evidently were muzzled to prevent neighing and snorting that might alert the garrison. Some of Mexico's finest cavalrymen. the elite of the Mexican Army like the Vera Cruz Lancers and the Dolores and Tampico Cavalry Regiments, then rode slowly from their encampment across the grassy prairie to take their designated positions for a special guardian service this Sunday morning. As ordered by Santa Anna, the assignment of these experienced warriors was to ensure that no defenders, if they tried to flee from the main assault, would escape across the open prairie. On this Saturday night dominated by a haunting silence and despite the feeling that the end was approaching like an oncoming "blue norther," no garrison member heard the

---

8   *Commonwealth*, May 25, 1836; McGee, James, The Handbook of Texas Online; Baugh, John J., The Handbook of Texas Online; Tucker, *Exodus From the Alamo*, 57, 59, 206-207; Charles P. Riddle, "Massacred at Goliad—Joseph P. Riddle," *The Alamo Journal, The Official Publication of The Alamo Society* (December 2012), no. 167, 13.

9   Brands, *Lone Star Nation*, 361.

movement of hundreds of cavalrymen or the infantry that had stealthily advanced closer to the Alamo's four walls.[10]

The early morning hours were eerily still, tense, and anxiety-filled for the 1,400 soldados, wrapped only in the quiet cold of the prairie but without coats or blankets as ordered by Santa Anna. They had eased into their advanced positions without making their presence known to the slumbering garrison. The anxious fighting men of Mexico, who were proud of their combat units that had been named in honor of the revered heroes of Mexico's War of Independence against Spain, awaited Santa Anna's signal to attack. In their assigned positions since around 2:00 A.M., the hand-picked dependable veterans remained perfectly silent hour after hour amid the prairie's cold and winds. Looking like fighting men about to go into battle on a European battlefield of a bygone era, Santa Anna's soldados wore Napoleonic Era uniforms of regulation navy blue. A lesser number of peasant soldiers wore uniforms of white cotton and thin wool, as if they were serving in Mexico's sweltering summer heat.

Santa Anna had made sure that his four assault columns were not composed primarily of ill-trained peasant conscripts, who had been impressed into service from small villages and isolated ranchos during the army's lengthy march north. Here, gripping their muskets (known to them as the morena licha), these soldados had been given ample time to contemplate their fates in the imminent attack. Fortunately, they also had been given time to say their most heartfelt Hail Marys.

Cold and stiff from lying for hours on the damp grass of the river bottoms, Santa Anna's advanced troops were ideally poised on the wide expanse of the open prairie to strike all four sides of the Alamo compound at once, ensuring that the relatively few defenders would be unable to simultaneously defend all four sides, especially against a surprise attack in the predawn darkness. Some of these young Mexican fighting men wore silver crucifixes brought from home and military crosses authorized by Santa Anna for service during this ambitious northern campaign so far from Mexico City.

Shivering in a light, but bone-chilling breeze, these fighting men from across Mexico awaited Santa Anna's signal to attack before daylight. Maintaining discipline and obeying their strict orders, the soldados were ready

---

10 Lamego, *The Siege and Taking of the Alamo*, 33, 36; Davis, *Three Roads to the Alamo*, 559; Groneman, *Eyewitness to the Alamo*, 47; Tucker, *Exodus From the Alamo*, 195-196, 292; Hardin, *The Alamo 1836*, 37.

to charge forward with fixed bayonets. These deadly implements were already attached to the .75 caliber East India Pattern "Brown Bess" flintlock muskets purchased from England as war surplus after the June 1815 showdown at Waterloo ended the French emperor's career in disaster. Most of all, the stoic soldados, without proper winter uniforms, were eager to fulfill Santa Anna's well-designed bid to reach the walls before the garrison was aroused from its slumber.

Inside the quiet darkness of the massive Alamo compound, the men and boys of the garrison were sound asleep in the cold hours before daybreak. The sleeping Sons of Erin, perhaps now dreaming of Ireland so far away or the sweet voices of Irish mothers and lovers that they would never see again, were scattered among various units, both infantry and artillery companies. Why the Emerald Islanders of the garrison had not banded together in a separate Irish company in honor of their native homeland is somewhat of a mystery, given their pride in distinctive ethnicity and cultural heritage.

So far in the early morning hours of this fateful Sunday, Santa Anna's clever plan had worked to perfection. Had the men of the Alamo, especially the most devout Irish soldiers, known they were sleeping on a mass grave of hundreds of mission Indians, past victims mostly of epidemics of smallpox and cholera, and especially that around 1,400 soldados with wooden ladders for scaling the walls, were about to be unleashed, they would have been much less comfortable on the last night of their lives.[11] At the same time, the young men and boys from Mexico were surely haunted by nagging fears about what could happen in the upcoming assault against these warlike norteamericanos, whose prowess with the Long Rifle was well-known. Other fears tormented the minds of Santa Anna's men at this time; one concerned Mexican captain penned in his journal how "a rumor has spread that [the garrison] has mined the exterior and interior of the fortress, so that we can all go up together if we attack them."[12]

The Alamo's esteemed Master of Ordnance, Major Robert Evans had no idea that he was fated to be one of the few defenders to die inside the church, on a typical Sunday and so-called day of peace for which this place of worship had

11 Lamego, *The Siege and Taking of the Alamo*, 43; Scheina, *Santa Anna*, 27; Hardin, *The Alamo 1836*, 15-16, 36-37; Uecker, *The Archaeology of the Alamo*, 11-12, 44; Thompson, *The Alamo*, 39; Tucker, *Exodus From the Alamo*, 192-194; Groneman, *Eyewitness to the Alamo*, 47; Roberts and Olson, *A Line in the Sand*, 160-161.

12 Hansen, ed., *The Alamo Reader*, 412.

The interior of the Alamo church, circa 1910. *Author's Collection*

been built for the Tejano people of San Antonio de Bexar. The highest ranking Ireland-born soldier of the garrison at age 36, a man of imposing size and manner, and mature beyond his years, Evans might have been thinking of the traditional Irish Mass he had attended as a young boy with his family while growing up on the Green Isle, where unlike in Texas.[13] there was now no war at this time.

For good reason, the Alamo men had been apprehensive since the siege's beginning, and their nagging sense of impending doom had grown more severe with each passing day; spirits among the depleted garrison were low by March 5, as they knew that no assistance was forthcoming from the east Texas settlements when most urgently needed. That must have seemed a striking paradox for the mostly volunteer soldiers now defending Texas and the Alamo with their lives.

Travis and his citizen-soldiers never knew when and where Santa Anna would strike with overpowering numbers. Sensing the thoughts and feelings of the men in the ranks, Crockett understood the mood of the besieged garrison.

13 *Commonwealth*, Frankfort, Kentucky, May 25, 1836; Evans, Robert, The Handbook of Texas Online; Thompson, *The Alamo*, 9, 27; Tucker, *Exodus from the Alamo*, 57.

With pride in his Irish ancestors and a father who fought with distinction at Kings Mountain in carrying on a cherished revolutionary legacy from both sides of the Atlantic, Crockett had volunteered for the toughest assignment upon reaching the Alamo: "assign me a position, and I and my twelve boys [of the Tennessee Volunteers] will try to defend it." John Sunderland described this vital position as the "picket wall." Here, Crockett provided inspirational leadership at a key defensive position situated along the lengthy wooden palisade that connected the limestone church to the corner of the south wall. As the siege had lengthened, Crockett earlier had remarked, "I don't like to be hemmed up" inside the Alamo.[14]

Unfortunately for the defenders, the Alamo was anything but a mighty fortress as long believed by generations of traditional historians and filmmakers, who have gone to great lengths to bolster this mistaken belief of a powerful defensive bastion—in part to justify their highly-inflated Mexican casualty figures. In a letter that echoed the views of other Mexican senior officers, General Juan Jose de Andrade, an aristocratic Creole born in Mexico City in 1796 who now commanded a brigade of cavalry, was not at all impressed with the Alamo defenses: "It is a large yard with a few rooms badly built to keep the men and horses of the [prewar] Presidial Companies out of the weather, and to save them from sudden attacks by the barbaric Indians of the frontier."[15] Indeed, Santa Anna's well-calculated plan to hit the diminutive garrison from four directions at once would soon verify Crockett's astute frontier wisdom, homespun common sense, and mounting concerns about the Alamo's extensive defensive vulnerabilities.

By this time, Santa Anna and his top officers already were aware of the multi-cultural composition of Texian forces, including Irish fighting men, both Catholic and Protestant, from the early clashes of the 1835 Campaign. But this fact made no difference to Santa Anna, because he now considered all armed men inside the Alamo compound to be enemies of the Republic of Mexico, and therefore doomed to be killed to the last man. The fact that a handful of fellow Catholics, including Tejanos, were part of the Alamo garrison might have

---

14 Uecker, *The Archaeology of the Alamo*, 70; Lord, *A Time to Stand*, 144; Mark Derr, *The Frontiersman, The Real Life and the Many Legends of Davy Crockett* (New York, NY, 1993), 247; Uecker, *The Archaeology of the Alamo*, 49, 52-53, 56; Thompson, *Born on a Mountaintop*, 19-20, 301; Thompson, *The Alamo*, 2.

15 Lamego, *The Siege and Taking of the Alamo*, 17, 32.

caused some consternation—had they known of the fact—among the soldados, who were determined that their country's territorial integrity be kept intact at all costs.

Mexico's interim president since late January 1836, Miguel (Michael) Barragan, of Irish descent, who headed the federal government in Mexico City, concluded with disgust how "all the bums and adventures from the while world have been gathered to revolt against the generous nation which has tolerated their insolence." Barragan was not aware that the Alamo was defended mostly by citizen-soldiers of Scotch-Irish descent, including a good many Ireland-born soldiers, who were recent immigrants.[16]

One of those men, Sergeant William B. Ward, age 30, was positioned on the cold night of March 5-6 in one of the most prominent defensive positions of the Alamo. Ward, the highest ranking noncommissioned officer, was in command at the all-important U-shaped lunette that protected the main gate located at the south wall's center. A well-designed and formidable defensive structure extending beyond the south wall, the expertly-constructed log and earthen lunette guarded a vital, but vulnerable point.

Because this main entry point into the compound was such an important defensive position, Ward and his gunners almost certainly slept in the lunette instead of in the Long Barracks or in the other buildings along the lengthy perimeter. Guarding the main gate was a 24-hour responsibility for the band of artillerymen and for the sharp-eyed riflemen stationed there to protect the gunners. About 75 feet long and 65 feet wide, the sturdy lunette had been created in accordance with the best military engineering science by General Martin Perfecto de Cos' well-educated engineers. Another artilleryman, Private Burke Trammel, born in Ireland in 1810, might well have been on duty beside Sergeant Ward in the lunette, since the ever-clannish Irish often formed tightly knit groups.

Like most garrison members, the jovial Irishman, Ward, liked to drink in social situations, especially at fandangos in San Antonio de Bexar. But he was hardly the raging drunkard that generations of non-Irish writers and historians (especially Protestant) have suggested and even considerably embellished to conform to a long-existing popular negative stereotype of Irish character. To Ward's commanders, this tough sergeant was not known for drunkenness while performing his duties and was trusted by his superiors. Ward certainly would

16 Lamego, *The Siege and Taking of the Alamo*, 14.

not have been assigned to man such a key defensive position as the compound's main gate during the lengthy siege, if he had a serious drinking problem. Ward and his artillerymen were well-sheltered by the lunette. Its thick protective walls consisted of double rows of sturdy cedar logs reinforced by a heavy layer of dirt in between the parallel rows of timber to create a barrier capable to stopping even a Mexican cannonball.

Three light small-caliber artillery pieces, most likely former Spanish naval guns, guarded the lunette and the main gate. They faced in three directions to provide frontal and double enfilade fire to the north and south to sweep the flanks of any attackers who neared the south wall. The guns were mounted on sturdy wooden platforms to provide a solid foundation for the artillery pieces that, with iron barrels, weighed tons.[17] Clearly, this Irish sergeant from the New Orleans Greys was dependable and trustworthy; the "Alamo had only one entrance, which was on the south," in Mexican Sergeant Manuel Loranca's words that underscored the importance of this key defensive position.[18]

Tough noncommissioned Irish officers like Ward perhaps made up for the deficiencies of the inexperienced Lieutenant Colonel Travis, who admitted in a candid letter written in mid-December 1835 that, "I could not be so useful in the artillery" as a hard-riding cavalry officer in the cavalier tradition.[19] Before falling to sleep on this particular winter night that seemed to offer no serious threat, Travis might have reflected on the twisting course of his life and his own strange fate—a dashing young cavalry officer who now commanded a pathetically small garrison of mostly infantry trapped in an old Franciscan mission on the open prairie.

Travis had only wished to lead his small nascent unit (officially known as the Legion of Cavalry) south toward the Rio Grande on the Matamoros Expedition; he had written on December 17, 1835, "I intend to join the expedition" to capture Matamoros. But fate had deemed otherwise. Now in command of a garrison in a no-win situation, he still resented the orders from Governor Henry Smith who had directed him to the Alamo on what would be

17 Ibid., 31; Ward, William B., The Handbook of Texas Online; Lord, *A Time to Stand*, 144; Uecker, *The Archaeology of the Alamo*, 26-29, 38; William B. Ward File, Library of the Daughters of the Republic of Texas, The Alamo, San Antonio, Texas; Trammel, Burke, The Handbook of Texas Online.

18 Hansen, ed., *The Alamo Reader*, 477; Hardin, *The Alamo 1836*, 28.

19 Hansen, ed., *The Alamo Reader*, 15.

his final mission. Those January 1836 orders were in essence a death sentence to Travis and his horse-soldiers. He had implored the governor that only the formation of a regular army "can save us now," but he now commanded a garrison almost exclusively of volunteers.

Travis had naively hoped that his dozen days of defiance in the face of Santa Anna's overwhelming might have bought Houston and Fannin time to organize an army to come to the Alamo's rescue. But that was not the case. The settlers of the east Texas settlements had failed to rise, instead attending to their personal affairs on their small farms, plantations, and ranches. Contrary to the popular mythology of the Alamo's legendary story, the time won by the Alamo garrison in holding firm for so long during the siege amounted to nothing more than wasted valor. Indeed, Houston only seriously set about the task of creating a new army after the Alamo defenders had been killed.[20]

Meanwhile, only "a short distance from the first trenches" held by a handful of Travis' half-frozen pickets, the 1,400 picked troops of Santa Anna's assault columns waited outside the Alamo's walls for what must have seemed like an eternity. March 5 had been unseasonably warm during the day, but the weather had turned sharply colder on the sudden arrival of a cold front from Canada—a "blue norther"—as so often happened during a winter on the Texas plains. Thoroughly-chilled despite now wearing cotton and wool ponchos, these young soldados, long used to Mexico's warm climates shivered in the night's steadily dropping temperatures. By this time, the late winter moon was high in the sky, but its faint yellow light was obscured by the dark clouds of the cold front that had descended so suddenly.

A slight mist hugged the fertile ground of the bottoms along the little river. To Santa Anna's young men, the mist that hugged the ground seemed to screen them from prying Texian eyes and was viewed as a good omen for the success of the upcoming assault—especially among those inexperienced individuals who were about to engage in their first battle. In overall terms, unlike the men of the Alamo, Santa Anna's soldados were in relatively good shape. They were rested and ready for action. After saying "the night's prayers," as specified in Santa Anna's incredibly detailed orders, his tough fighting men had taken restful naps before assembling at midnight into four assault columns. Not surprisingly, Santa Anna's priority of relying upon the saying of Mass to fortify the spiritual faith and resolve among his soldiers before unleashing them in

20 Hansen, ed., *The Alamo Reader*, 17-18,140; Davis, *Three Roads to the Alamo*, 504-512. 555, 558.

frontal assaults would be continued by him against the norteamericano invaders of Mexico during the Mexican-American War.[21]

Clearly, Santa Anna had left nothing to chance, as revealed in his March 5 orders, to enhance his already excellent prospects for success, after determining that it was "necessary to act decisively upon the enemy defending the Alamo." He had chosen his most capable and experienced officers to lead each of the assault columns. Santa Anna's longtime idol Napoleon would have been proud of the overall battle-plan for overpowering the Alamo.[22]

Symbolically, because he had lost the Alamo and surrendered on December 11, 1835 to an undisciplined force of ragtag revolutionaries, General Martin Perfecto de Cos was chosen by Santa Anna to command the 300-man First Column consisting of Aldama Battalion and San Luis Battalion troops. The First Column was ordered to assault the northern end of the west wall, which was the second longest wall (along with the parallel east wall). Having old scores to settle with the Texas rebels, Cos was a good choice for leading this column of attackers.

Leading the "Second Column," which consisted of 400 troops of the Toluca and the San Luis Battalions, Francisco Duque, colonel of the Toluca Battalion, was directed by Santa Anna to attack head-on from the north in a bid to overrun the north wall. Colonel Jose Maria Romero commanded of the 300-soldado, "Third Column," which was composed of Matamoros and Jimenez Battalion troops. Romero was ordered by Santa Anna to circle around to the rear and assault the Alamo from the east. The "Fourth Column" was assigned to the capable Colonel Juan Morales, who commanded the smallest assault column of only around 100 light troops. He was ordered by Santa Anna to strike the south wall (shorter than the east and west walls) in a diversion to mask the main offensive effort against the north wall.[23]

As carefully orchestrated by Santa Anna, with tactical insight, this was a formidable contingent of assault troops. In striking contrast to the Alamo's

21 *New York Herald*, June 27, 1836; Lamego, *The Siege and Taking of the Alamo*, 32-33, 35; Hardin, *The Alamo 1836*, 36-37; Hansen, ed., *The Alamo Reader*, 402, 422; Amy S. Greenberg, *A Wicked War, Polk, Clay, Lincoln, and the 1846 U.S. Invasion of Mexico* (New York, NY, 2012), 158.

22 Lamego, *The Siege and Taking of the Alamo*, 32-33.

23 Ibid., 32-33; Hardin, *The Alamo 1836*, 36-39; McGee, James, The Handbook of Texas Online; Groneman, *Eyewitness to the Alamo*, 47; H. W. Brands, *Lone Star Nation* (New York, NY, 2004), 369; Roberts and Olson, *A Line in the Sand*, 158-159.

homespun band of citizen-soldiers, who lacked sufficient training or military experience, these hand-picked units were "the best Santa Anna had on hand [because they consisted of] disciplined and trained veterans."[24]

Most importantly, Santa Anna also possessed a large and powerful strategic reserve of well-trained regulars consisting of an elite Zapadores Battalion (also known as the "Sapper Battalion") and five grenadier companies that had been held back from three permanent battalions, Matamoros, Aldama, and Jimenez (which were named for the revered heroes of the War of Independence against Spain), and from two active militia battalions of San Luis and Toluca.

A respected leader of the highly-professional officer corps, Engineer Colonel Augustin Amat led the Zapadores, who were considered Santa Anna's finest troops. These elite combat engineers, looking especially smart and professional in dark blue uniforms with black facings and dark red piping, and the standard Napoleonic shako—which was high and stiff to ward off saber blows from attacking enemy cavalrymen. During the French Revolutionary and Napoleonic Wars, the French "sauper", or Sapper, had risen to prominence as a vital part of the Engineer Corps under Napoleon's expert guidance and tutelage. This crack strategic reserve packed a considerable offensive punch and could maneuver with skill and discipline in a battlefield situation. Like Napoleon in sending his prized and much-pampered Imperial Guard troops into battle only in the most serious crisis situation, Santa Anna would decide exactly when and where to unleash this hard-hitting contingent of elite fighting men.

Positioned in the rear at the north wall, the Sappers were to be sent into action to support the initial assault by Duque's column. These elite warriors were under Santa Anna's direct personal supervision serving in a role comparable to that of ancient Rome's Praetorian Guard. Their overall quality was unmatched in the Mexican Army. Upon Santa Anna's order, these reserves would go in last of all, after the first four attack columns simultaneously struck each side of the Alamo.[25]

---

24 Gaddy, *Texas in Revolt*, 58.

25 Gaddy, *Texas in Revolt*, 55, 59; Hardin, *The Alamo 1836*, 15; Lamego, *The Siege and Taking of the Alamo*, 32-33, 37; Philip Haythornthwaite, *Napoleon's Specialist Troops* (London, 1988), 17; Hansen, ed., *The Alamo Reader*, 411; Andrew Uffindell, *Napoleon's Immortals, The Imperial Guard and Its Battles, 1804-1815* (Stroud, England, 2007), 179.

With a good tactical reason in mind, Santa Anna ordered that relatively few rounds be issued to the soldados, despite the availability of ample ammunition: only six rounds to the tough grenadiers and only four cartridges for riflemen. Santa Anna envisioned a stealthy, fast-moving bayonet attack before the first light of dawn at only a few minutes before 7:00 a.m. as specified in his meticulous orders that "All armaments will be in good shape —especially the bayonets."[26]

He meant to catch the garrison asleep and by complete surprise. At the time of this attack, Santa Anna was in an especially vengeful mood because so many fighting men in Texas, including those inside the Alamo, had recently crossed the United States-Mexico (Texas) border—the Sabine and Red Rivers —to join the Texians in their largely Protestant holy war against a Catholic nation: a direct legal violation of the United States' own Neutrality Laws. He hated the norteamericano rebels (even those born in Ireland), who would be shown no mercy on this Sunday and armed his men for still another slaughter at this ill-starred place that seemed to have been created not for God but for bloodshed and evil. In the generalissimo's own words of righteous contempt: "It is the duty of Mexican military men to die defending their country's rights, and for its glory. We are all ready to make such a dear sacrifice rather than allow foreigners, no matter where they came from [in this case the United States], to insult our land and take our territory."[27]

Santa Anna went into even greater detail in his plan of battle, especially in regard to the preparations among his men. In these orders, he emphasized that despite the biting cold of the dark winter night, "These men will not wear cloaks, carry blankets, or anything else which will inhibit them to maneuver quickly. During the day all shako chin-straps [so that headgear did not fall off to make noise] will be correctly worn—these the Commanders will watch closely [and] The troops will wear shoes and sandals."[28]

For his stealthy attack in the early morning darkness, Santa Anna wanted nothing to impede his attackers in their race to reach the Alamo's forbidding walls and in placing the wooden ladders to scale the high walls. With the element of surprise foremost in his mind, he was even concerned about the

26 Lamego, *The Siege and Taking of the Alamo*, 33; Davis, *Three Roads to the Alamo*, 559.

27 Lamego, *The Siege and Taking of the Alamo*, 37.

28 Ibid., 33; Roberts and Olson, *A Line in the Sand*, 159-160.

possibility of soldados crying out in pain upon stepping on rocks or cactus thus alerting the garrison during the frantic rush for the walls, before resistance was organized. Santa Anna ordered that no sandals were to be worn by the attackers. Ironically, a good many Mexicans now wore leather shoes that were made in the United States, and which had been confiscated from San Antonio stores operated by some of the few American merchants of San Antonio de Bexar.[29]

To get into the compound as quickly as possible, the Alamo's 12-foot- high walls had to be breached before the men of garrison were aroused. Therefore, Santa Anna emphasized in orders to his attackers: "The First Column will carry ten scaling ladders, two crowbars and two axes, the same number by the second; six ladders by the third, and two by the fourth [and] The men carrying the ladders will sling their rifles on their backs until the ladders are properly placed."[30]

To Santa Anna, this was no ordinary battle, and as a master motivator of fighting men, he saved his most encouraging words in his last order to inspire his men and officers to do their duty to the utmost. He reminded them what was at stake in this assault to overwhelm the old Franciscan mission: "Take this into consideration: Against the daring foreigners opposing us, the Honor of our Nation and Army is at stake [and] each man [will be expected] to fulfill his duties and to exert himself to give his country a day of glory and satisfaction."[31]

After having set everything in place with great care, Santa Anna was confident of reaping a one-sided success over the ragtag rebels, who he believed did not know how to wage war in a professional manner. In consequence, he already had bragged to a staff officer on March 5 how "he would take his breakfast in the fort the next morning."[32]

The young men and boys of the Mexican Army of Operations were highly motivated on this early morning on the windswept central Texas prairie, as they now faced their supreme tactical challenge. Sergeant Francisco Becerra, a proud member of one of the detached fusilier companies in the assault column under Colonel Romero, who was ordered to attack the Alamo from the east, wrote

29 Hansen, ed., *The Alamo Reader*, 417; Roberts and Olson, *A Line in the Sand*, 160.

30 Lamego, *The Siege and Taking of the Alamo*, 31, 33.

31 Ibid., 33-34.

32 Groneman, *Eyewitness to the Alamo*, 57.

how the "Mexican troops little thought of the terrible ordeal through which they were about to pass."[33]

In a strange way, the impending battle was actually coming down to a simple equation that had relatively little to do with leadership or tactics: which side was the most rested. Santa Anna had made sure that his front-line troops were rested and refreshed before the assault. The exact opposite situation prevailed with the Alamo garrison that was at the end of its tether in terms of physical exhaustion and morale. The soldados now appreciated the fact that they had retired at dusk on March 5 to gain some rest before they stormed all four sides of the Alamo. They had been worn-down from their long march north and the siege's rigors, but not nearly as much as the Alamo men. But now, Santa Anna's troops were ready to spring forth in a well-designed surprise attack.

*   *   *

Santa Anna's signal to attack finally came around 5:00 A.M. Unleashed, hundreds of soldados in four assault columns swiftly converged in silence on all sides of the Alamo. Flowing smoothly through the inky darkness, and with seasoned officers leading the way, the attackers advanced at a fast pace in tight and closed company columns.

Each separate Napoleonic assault column was now flanked by drummer boys and buglers. But while Napoleon himself had long relied upon lively martial music to inspire his assault troops with large numbers of musicians to "beat the charge," Santa Anna's musicians had been ordered to advance silently without playing their instruments in order not to alert the garrison. Instead, to maximize manpower these smooth-faced drummer boys and buglers now carried muskets with long bayonets, having been instructed to serve as regular soldiers in the attack. Santa Anna's entire battle-plan depended upon achieving the supreme tactical advantage of surprising the garrison, before firm resistance could be established.[34]

33 Hansen, ed., *The Alamo Reader*, 456.

34 Lamego, *The Siege and Taking of the Alamo*, 36; Hansen, ed., *The Alamo Reader*, 457; Gaddy, *Texas in Revolt*, 58; Roberts and Olson, *A Line in the Sand*, 160-161; Philip Haythornthwaite, *Napoleon's Guard Infantry* (1) (Oxford, England, 1984), 32.

Slumbering like his comrades, Joseph G. Washington was a Kentucky-born drummer in his late twenties who had been living in Texas only since 1835. He was a member of Captain William B. Harrison's volunteer company, assigned to defend the lengthy wooden palisade—along with Crockett, who served as an unofficial colonel. Washington had no time to beat the long roll to alert the garrison, before nearly 1,500 Mexicans suddenly struck the Alamo walls.[35]

The surprise of the garrison was complete. The nightmare scenario for the defenders now became an ugly reality. As long feared by Travis and his men, the Alamo compound was struck on four sides nearly simultaneously, and Travis simply had too few soldiers to man the exceedingly long walls. Joe, Travis' black servant from Alabama, emphasized the completeness of Santa Anna's surprise that had come so suddenly out of the night: "when the attack was made, which was just before daybreak, sentinels and all were asleep, except the officer [Adjutant Baugh] of the day who was just starting on his round."[36]

Once the assault was launched, Travis was aroused from his warm blankets in his small room located on the west wall when a frantic Baugh suddenly burst into his commander's quarters and yelled "The Mexicans are coming!" Travis grabbed his shotgun as well as his saber (which might have been a War of 1812 relic). Realizing to his horror that his first alarm precaution—the handful of pickets he stationed in the frigid ditches outside the walls—must have met quick deaths and thus failed to give a warning of the attack. Travis found himself facing the greatest challenge of his life. With little time to rally the garrison, he dashed from his headquarters into the black vastness of the open plaza. With his saber by his side, Travis then raced for the north wall—a sprint of around 70 yards north through the noisy and chaotic darkness—to face "the vengeance of a Gothic enemy," in his own words that now carried grim meaning for himself and the men of his garrison.

Once the alarm was finally sounded amid the swirling tumult that now erupted outside the walls, at least 15 Ireland-born soldiers and their comrades who were mostly Scotch-Irish Protestants, burst on the double out of their sleeping quarters. Upon dashing into the plaza's darkness, they encountered a surreal nightmare. (On the first list of the Alamo dead published in a Texas

---

35 Washington, Joseph G., The Handbook of Texas Online; Hansen, ed., *The Alamo Reader*, 78; Thompson, *Born on a Mountaintop*, 301.

36 *Commonwealth*, May 25, 1836; Davis, *Three Roads to the Alamo*, 539.

newspaper, only four men among the Alamo garrison were listed as having been from "Ireland": an early error that helped obscure the disproportionate contribution of the Irish to the Alamo's defense and in the Texas Revolution.[37] In truth, a good many Ireland-born fighters, both artillerymen and infantrymen, poured forth into the plaza, including Samuel E. Burns, Burke Trammel, Robert Evans, Jackson J. Rusk, Stephen Dennison, John Mormon, Edward McCafferty, Joseph M. Hawkins, James Nolan, and other Sons of Erin. Irish soldiers who had served in ranks of the New Orleans Greys, such as James McGee (if fully recovered from his December 1835 wound by this time) and John Spratt, also dashed across the wide plaza to their assigned defensive positions along walls. Additionally, the recently-arrived mounted volunteers from Gonzales, including Ireland-born Andrew Duvalt and Thomas J. Jackson, also rushed forward with rifles and muskets hoping to reach the walls before it was too late.[38]

Meanwhile, the darkness, confusion, and the initial scattered gunfire of the first breathless defenders at the walls caused Cos' column, which was attacking from the west, to veer north to hit the Alamo's northwest corner. Romero's column of Matamoros and Jimenez Battalion troops, attacking from the east, likewise veered north to strike the northeast corner of the expansive compound. These two columns then joined with Duque's column of troops from the San Luis Battalion and the Toluca Battalion—whose battle-flag was the Mexican tri-color (white, red, and with a giant desert eagle in its center—in attacking the north wall. Effectively, all three assault columns began to converge as one on the north wall.

The massive concentration of troops at the north wall occurred even "before the Garrison were aroused to resistance," in the words of one shocked survivor, who explained the defenders' central dilemma for which there was now no solution. Worse, the light cannon that defended the north wall could not be depressed sufficiently by frantic gunners to fire at the mass of Mexicans, who had collected so quickly at the wall's base. At a severe disadvantage when the battle had barely begun, the first handful of defenders who belatedly

---

37 *Commonwealth*, May 25, 1836; Hansen, ed., *The Alamo Reader*, 78-82; Brands, *Lone Star Nation*, 361; Davis, *Three Roads to the Alamo*, 559-560; Roberts and Olson, *A Line in the Sand*, 161-162.

38 Burns, Samuel E.; McCafferty, Edward; Trammel, Burke; McCoy, Jesse; Duvalt, Andrew; McGee, James; Spratt, John; Jackson, Thomas J.; Hawkins, Joseph M; Evans, Robert; Dennison, Stephen; and Rusk, Jackson J. Biographies, *The Handbook of Texas Online*.

reached the north wall finally gained their positions and opened fire. General Duque early went down with a leg wound, but his troops were not discouraged and continued to push through the darkness, determined to overpower the north wall defenders with their bayonets.

Meanwhile, the defenders of the compound's opposite side, at the earth and log lunette, and the south wall held firm against the much lighter pressure of Morales' smaller column—largely because their assault was merely Santa Anna's feint to mask the main effort on the north. To stay clear of the entangled abatis of felled trees (the day's version of barbed wire) lying before the lengthy wooden palisade and to avoid the fire of the three cannon from the small lunette, where Sergeant Ward and his artillerymen manned the gun that protected the main gate, Morales' three companies of cazadores (light troops consisting of riflemen) from the Matamoros, San Luis, and Jimenez Battalions skirted the low, timbered palisade held by Crockett and his Tennessee boys between the southwest corner of the stone church and the east end of the south wall.

Morales' soldados surged forward to attack the compound's southwest corner, where the 18-pounder stood facing San Antonio to the west. Meanwhile, at the timbered palisade, Crockett continued to provide inspired leadership in this crisis. Travis had earlier commended Crockett for "animating the men to do their duty." Now, the Tennessean implored the defenders to stand fast at this key position where the Volunteer State was, at least thus far, proudly represented and holding firm.[39]

A breathless Travis reached the north wall only after large numbers of the soldados already had gained the north wall's base. He galvanized an initial desperate defense among the handful of newly-arrived men with a war cry: "Come on Boys, the Mexicans are upon us, and we'll give them Hell!" He leaned over the top of the north wall to shoot down on the attackers. Travis fired dual blasts from his double-barrel shotgun (weapon of choice for hard-riding frontier cavalrymen) into the surging mass of soldados below, where troops of the Toluca Battalion had concentrated in large numbers.

39 Davis, *Three Roads to the Alamo*, 560, 542, 560-561; Lord, *A Time to Stand*, 160; Ward, William B., The Handbook of Texas Online; Lamego, *The Siege and Taking of the Alamo*, 31; William B. Ward File, Library of the Daughters of the Republic of Texas, The Alamo, San Antonio, Texas; Tucker, *Exodus From the Alamo*, 175-176, 244-245; Groneman, *Eyewitness of the Alamo*, 47; Hansen, ed., *The Alamo Reader*, 74; Thompson, *Born on a Mountaintop*, 301; Hardin, *The Alamo 1836*, 37, 39-40, 80.

By this time, Cos', Romero's, and Duque's columns already had merged into one at the base of the north wall. But firing over the top of the wall was dangerous for Travis and the defenders who had just gained firing positions, requiring full exposure of head and upper body. Defenders began to get hit by Mexicans who fired their Brown Bess muskets almost straight up. And while firing at the milling crowd of soldados at the north wall's base, garrison riflemen began to fall, hit by the Mexican volleys.[40]

Displaying his characteristic impatience for quickly gaining a decisive result, Santa Anna sent in his reserves early, including elite Zapadores under Colonel Amat. This second wave of crack troops charged south toward the unearthly din at the embattled north wall, where exchanges of gunfire illuminated the wall, now obscured by a rising cloud of sulfurous smoke.[41]

As the precision of Santa Anna's attack plan disintegrated in relatively short order, some unexpected problems soon developed for his soldados. Foremost of these problems was the horror of fratricide in the darkness. A crisis erupted for the attackers, as a good many of them fell to fire from the rear, after having been shot hit in the back by their own comrades. Nevertheless, the sheer weight of the massed concentration of troops from Santa Anna's three columns at the north wall's base began to pay off as some daring Mexican leaders took charge of the chaotic situation. Indeed, Mexican leadership rose magnificently to the challenge of overwhelming the north wall. Travis attempted to hold firm there, against the odds, desperately trying to defend the lengthy stretch of the north wall with just a handful of soldiers. Travis, like his followers, now knew what to expect from a determined opponent, "who is fighting us under a blood-red flag." Mexican generals and colonels led the way, scaling the high north wall under fire, inspiring the common soldiers who gamely followed their leaders.

Travis was hit by the crackling musketry from below and fell over a gun-carriage at the battery of smoothbore 8-pounders positioned at the north wall's center. Taking a bullet in the forehead, he went down to rise no more, before he had been able to stem the surging Mexican tide that would soon prove unstoppable. Travis' death was a loss that led to a swift collapse of resistance at the heavily-pressured north wall.

---

40 *Commonwealth*, May 25, 1836; Davis, *Three Roads to the Alamo*, 560; Hardin, *The Alamo 1836*, 40; Roberts and Olson, *A Line in the Sand*, 162; Thompson, *Born on a Mountaintop*, 301.

41 Hardin, *The Alamo 1836*, 41; Roberts and Olson, *A Line in the Sand*, 162-164.

With drawn swords and shouting words of encouragement, Santa Anna's officers, including Cuban-born generals Pedro Ampudia and Juan Valentin Amador, led the way through the sulfurous cloud of battle smoke. Amador was especially motivated and active in encouraging the attackers onward and over the top since he had been recently "suspended" and was not even invited to Santa Anna's March 4 commanders' conference at the Yturri house. That humiliation was a sore point and stain he sought to erase with battlefield heroics. Thankfully for him, the proud general, who was a capable veteran leader, had been reinstated in time for the attack—a wise decision when every inspirational officer was needed for the assault.

With much to prove, the determined Amador was one of the first Mexican officers to scale the north wall. Of course, officers of lower rank also played leading roles, including young Lieutenant Colonel Jose Enrique de la Pena, who was also one of the first to go up and over the top. Colonel Esteban Mora and Lieutenant Colonel Marcial Aguirre also encouraged their soldados over the north wall, where the bodies of dead and wounded defenders were now sprawled. Mora had earlier led the advance on San Antonio de Bexar, and he continued that vanguard role in scaling the Alamo's north wall and urging his fighters onward.

Meanwhile, back at the rear of the charging reserves, Santa Anna ordered his fine brass band to play a martial air to inspire the attackers. All of these respected Mexican officers and many unknown enlisted men displayed inspired leadership in overrunning the elevated battery of three guns located in the north wall's mid-section.[42]

According Joe's account, Colonel Mora might have even delivered a death blow to Travis with his saber. He stated how, "As Travis sat wounded . . . General Mora, in passing, aimed a blow with his sword to dispatch him [and] the body of Travis [was then] was pierced with many bayonet stabs."[43] But despite Mora's better known heroics, the seemingly incensed Amador, who was determined to redeem his tarnished honor, had been the first officer over the

---

42 Davis, *Three Roads to the Alamo*, 560; *New York Herald*, June 25, 1836; Hardin, *The Alamo 1836*, 37, 40-41, 44; Groneman, *Eyewitness to the Alamo*, 48, 59, 76; Hansen, ed., *The Alamo Reader*, 455; Roberts and Olson, *A Line in the Sand*, 150, 162-164; Ampudia, Pedro de, The Handbook of Texas Online; Gary Zaboly, "A New Look at the North and Northeast Walls," *The Alamo Journal*, issue no. 162 (September 2011), 4.

43 *Commonwealth*, May 25, 1836.

north wall and then to drop inside the Alamo compound to confront defenders in the smoky air and noisy confusion.[44]

In his journal, Captain Jose Juan Sanchez-Navarro described the decisive moment of the Mexicans' dramatic breakthrough that doomed the defenders to grisly deaths at the hands of the screaming soldados. "Our commanders, officers, and troops, as if by magic, topped the walls at the same time and rush in" the sprawling Alamo compound.[45] Forty-six-year-old Colonel Romulo Diaz de la Vega, born in Spain, was another "of the first to fight his way up the parapet" and over the top amid the whizzing bullets, leading the soldados by his brave example.[46]

But it was Amador who played a larger role in winning the day, especially after gaining his foothold in the confusing darkness of the open plaza where a savage flurry of close range fighting raged. He took charge, rallying the men who were first to make it over the top, and with the assistance of nearby soldados, opening a small postern to allow a concentrated flood of attackers into the wide plaza—to seal the garrison's fate.[47]

On the plaza's opposite side, the resourceful Morales and his disciplined troops of the "Fourth Column" launched their final offensive effort to overwhelm the Alamo's southwest corner and capture the 18-pounder. After multiple breakthroughs, especially at the north wall which was overwhelmed by so many attackers, the remaining defenders seeing their quandary hurriedly abandoned their doomed defensive positions, leaving the walls unmanned and retiring on the double in the hope of saving their lives before it was too late.[48]

A handful of surviving and increasingly desperate garrison gunners sought to stem the tide. With time rapidly running out for them and the entire garrison, these brave artillerymen, performing like seasoned regulars in a true crisis situation, attempted to turn at least one Alamo cannon of the artillery arsenal toward the north. But nothing could slow the Mexican onslaught.

An elated Amador led his cheering troops deeper into the smoky confusion of the open plaza. Amid the sheer terror of the hand-to-hand combat,

44 Hardin, *The Alamo 1836*, 41, 44.

45 Hansen, ed., *The Alamo Reader*, 412.

46 Lamego, *The Siege and Taking of the Alamo*, 38.

47 Hardin, *The Alamo 1836*, 44.

48 Ibid., 45.

Ireland-born Captain William Ridgeway Carey organized as much last-minute resistance as he could among his cannoneers, including Irish artillerymen Private Samuel E. Burns, and his fast-working gunners of Scotch-Irish descent.

Carey's "Invincibles" gamely fought to the very end. Frantically, they loaded their guns in the hope of getting off an effective blast of homemade canister, knowing they would never again see their homelands if the surging Mexican tide was not somehow beaten back.[49] Sergeant Francisco Becerra, formerly of the Matamoros Battalion, described how, at this time, the "crash of firearms, the shouts of defiance, the cries of the dying and wounded, made a din almost infernal."[50]

The rising crescendo of Mexican victory cheers echoing over the Alamo and the success of the overrunning of the north wall spurred Morales and his men to greater exertions against weakening resistance at nearly every other point along the perimeter walls. At the southwest corner, the resurgent soldados of Morales' diversionary column finally climbed the wall and went over the top with shouts of triumph. They dropped into the still-dark plaza amid flashes of gun-fire, and after pushing aside light resistance captured the Alamo's southwest corner.

With growing numbers of Mexicans swarming into the plaza with fixed bayonets and victory cheers, Sergeant Ward and his small group of artillerymen defending the lunette, courageously held their positions as ordered. They did not stand a chance. Morales' light troops of the Matamoros and Jimenez Battalions swarmed over the 18-pounder at the Alamo's southwest corner, then poured into the plaza. The defiant Irish sergeant remained as ordered at his assigned post beside his three cannon to protect the main gate from an attack from the south. But when the Mexicans swarmed into the rear of the main gate, they cut off the escape route for the outflanked lunette defenders. Ward continued to stand his ground as if defending the sacred soil of his Green Isle homeland against a charging formation of hated redcoats. He "fired a last broadside and fell under an avalanche of bayonet-slashing men."[51] Very likely,

49 Uecker, *The Archaeology of the Alamo*, 38; Carey, William Ridgeway, The Handbook of Texas Online; Burns, Samuel E., The Handbook of Texas Online; Hardin, *The Alamo 1836*, 41, 44-45.

50 Hansen, ed., *The Alamo Reader*, 457.

51 William B. Ward File, LDRT; Lord, *A Time to Stand*, 160; Ward, William B., The Handbook of Texas Online; Lamego, *The Siege and Taking of the Alamo*, 31; Roberts and Olson, *A Line in the Sand*, 165-166.

the final cannon shot of the Alamo's defense was fired by Ward, who was well known for his never-say-die fighting spirit.

Overpowered from multiple directions, the last remaining Alamo defenders continued to flee the walls and dash through the wide plaza. They headed for the shelter of the Long Barracks, which now served as a secondary defensive position. After the Mexicans poured over the walls, Santa Anna's secretary, Ramon Martinez Caro, described after the battle how the "enemy immediately took refuge in the inside rooms of the fortress, the walls of which had been previously bored [into the adobe] to enable them to fire through the holes."[52] And a battle-hardened fusilier serving in Colonel Romero's column, Sergeant Francisco Becerra wrote how, "There was a long room on the ground-floor—it was darkened. Here the fight was bloody."[53]

Meanwhile, large numbers of garrison members fled out of the smoke-filled compound, many by way of the low palisade that offered an easy escape point with Morales' men no longer in their front. Since he was stationed at the palisade—and contrary to traditional accounts—Crockett might have taken flight with the many others who fled the compound over this low palisade. Seeing that it made no sense to sacrifice their lives in a hopeless defense, these desperate men now "attempted in vain" to escape the death-trap by fleeing onto the wide prairie that led to the Gonzales Road, where the first streaks of light had begun to appear on the eastern horizon. Clearly, they believed it was more important to live and fight another day than to be killed for nothing. But on the open ground of the grasslands where they were the most vulnerable, these fleeing soldiers were about to meet grisly deaths from Santa Anna's encircling ring of experienced cavalrymen, including the much-feared Vera Cruz Lancers, who were waiting for them on the open prairie.[54]

The few surviving Irish riflemen were still offering spirited resistance inside the compound. Nevertheless, with the first faint light of dawn making visibility possible despite the drifting palls of choking smoke, some remaining Sons of Erin might well have turned their rifles on one of the most dramatic acts played out in the bloody struggle for the Alamo's possession: the daring attempt of the

---

52 Groneman, *Eyewitness to the Alamo*, 48.

53 Hansen, ed., *The Alamo Reader*, 457.

54 Groneman, *Eyewitness to the Alamo*, 76; *New York Herald*, June 27, 1836; Hardin, *The Alamo 1836*, 45; Tucker, *Exodus From the Alamo*, 272-294; Thompson, *Born on a Mountaintop*, 304.

soldados to capture the garrison's battle flag flying from a flag pole atop the roof of the Long Barracks known as El Cuartel (The Quarters).

In the light of a red dawn that now began to illuminate the ghastly scene inside the compound, the Alamo's flag—its exact appearance remains unknown to this day—was an especially tempting target for the most courageous Mexican soldiers, both officers and enlisted men of the Jimenez Battalion, who hoped to distinguish themselves by capturing it. But in making a bold rush to secure the prized battle-flag, a number of Jimenez fusiliers were cut down by hot fire from the windows of the Long Barracks. The well-trained members of the crack reserves, the Zapadores of the Sapper Battalion, then made a spirited dash to secure the banner that still waved in the smoky half-light of early morning.

Almost immediately, three of the foremost Sappers, color sergeants, were shot down. Undaunted by the sight of dead and dying comrades around him, young Lieutenant Jose Maria Torres retrieved the Mexican flag from a fallen color bearer. Against the odds, he climbed to the rooftop of the Long Barracks amid a hail of bullets. In the hospital located on the Long Barracks's second floor, even "the sick and wounded," perhaps including Ireland-born James McGee in one soldado's astonished words, continued to fight fiercely; they all knew there would be no quarter on this hellish morning. This spirited resistance was concentrated and especially determined at the commanding perch on the second floor. By this time, the plaza was filled with victorious soldados, who believed the day was won until they were suddenly hit by close-range fire from the second story of the Long Barracks. At this point in a desperate situation, exactly how many surviving Irish soldiers now continued to fight for their lives can never be known.

The last defenders, almost certainly including some Irish, who were bent on selling their lives as dearly as possible, continued to rapidly load and fire from the defensive bastion of the Long Barracks. Ironically, the large, old convento building (once the living quarters of Franciscan priests who had devoted their lives to God and bestowing Christianity on the Indians) had been transformed into the true fortress of the Alamo. Here, surviving men blasted away from windows and firing holes. The Long Barracks' defenders thus bought precious time to allow the escape of a good many men, who made a desperate bid to reach the Gonzales Road that led east to safety.

While bullets whizzed by him Lieutenant Torres finally reached the rooftop now bathed in the early morning light. He then lowered the rebel banner that had symbolized so many of the defenders' loftiest dreams and ambitions for a bright future life in Texas. In its place Torres raised his battalion's Mexican tri-color of red, green, and white (called "the colonel's flag" in honor of Sapper Battalion commander Col. Amat who already had risen to the fore in leading his reserves this early morning), a courageous act that symbolized the fall of the Alamo. However, the heroics of capturing the garrison's flag cost Torres his life. The promising lieutenant fell mortally wounded; he might have been to shocked to learn that he might have received his fatal wound from a fellow Catholic who had been born in Ireland.[55]

Meanwhile, Generals Ampudia and Amador, who had played key roles in leading their troops over the north wall and into the midst of the embattled plaza, once again took the initiative. To wipe out the last pockets of resistance in the Long Barracks, especially the rifle fire pouring from the hospital, the officers shouted orders for their men to turn the Alamo cannon upon that ad-hoc defensive bastion that already had cost many Mexican lives. Caro described the killing of some of the few remaining defenders, who battled to the very end: "Generals Amador and Ampudia trained the guns upon the interior of the fort to demolish it as the only means of putting an end to the strife."[56]

In the words of a Mexican officer, who explained how howitzers were brought into the compound and turned on the Long Barracks to fire a barrage of exploding shells: "Ampudia, was commanded to set up the howitzers, and fire four grenades, which made them [then] raise up a white flag."[57]

The survivors' white flag was ignored. To the horror of the dwindling band of defenders who were trapped and without prospects of escape or surrender, even more firepower was then turned against some of the Alamo's last defenders. The Mexicans dragged the captured 18-pounder down the long earthen ramp—that pointed straight toward the Long Barracks. In the last bitter irony of the Alamo's tragic story,[58] the garrison's largest cannon was turned against their former owners. Sergeant Becerra was in charge of the detachment that brought the 18-pounder down the ramp and the Alamo's largest gun "was

55 Lamego, *The Siege and Taking of the Alamo*, 39-39; Davis, *Three Roads to the Alamo*, 540; Groneman, *Eyewitness to the Alamo*, 48; Tucker, *Exodus from the Alamo*, 253-300; Hansen, ed., *The Alamo Reader*, 457; McGee, James, The Handbook of Texas Online; Gaddy, *Texas in Revolt*, 58-59.

56 Groneman, *Eyewitness to the Alamo*, 48; Hansen, ed., *The Alamo Reader*, 457.

57 Hansen, ed., *The Alamo Reader*, 440-441.

58 Hardin, *The Alamo 1836*, 48.

placed near the door of the hospital [Long Barracks], doubly charged with grape and canister. We entered and found the corpses of fifteen Texians."[59]

Indeed, after the close-range cannon fire smashed through the thick wooden doors of the Long Barracks, grim-faced soldados went about the bloody work of finishing off with their bayonets the final surviving defenders whose end had finally come at this ill-fated place. The final flurry of no-quarter combat and ugly deaths was especially vicious in the dark, smoke-filled rooms of the Long Barracks. Colonel Fernando Urriza, who served on Santa Anna's staff, never forgot the lethality of Mexico's aroused fighting men who, like their commander-in-chief, sought revenge during the final stage of this bloody struggle: "Even a cat was shot, as the soldiers [no doubt superstitious peasant warriors of Aztec descent] exclaimed, 'It is not a cat, but an American'."[60]

Some of the last defenders were overpowered and killed inside the old church on this bloody Sunday. Others fought on to the end: Sergeant Becerra later wrote about the spirited defiance by Captain Almeron Dickinson's surviving gunners, who busily worked their cannon on the elevated firing platform at the rear of the church, on "the top of the church building I saw eleven Texians [who] had some pieces of artillery."[61]

Outflanked from multiple directions, Crockett and some of the Tennessee men, who had defended the wooden palisade until it became untenable, already had either retired toward or into the church. One attacker described how the last doomed survivors were trapped after the combat spilled over from the Long Barracks to a new location: "We then found that all the Americans were alive inside the church."[62]

Susanna Dickinson, who had been born during the War of 1812 and lost her artilleryman-husband Captain Almeron Dickinson in the no-quarter struggle inside the church, described the horror of when "three unarmed gunners [of Dickinson's battery on the elevated wooden firing platform at the rear of the church] who abandoned their useless guns [out of ammunition] came into the church where I was, and were shot down by my side. One of them was from Nacogdoches and named [Jacob] Walker [and] I saw four Mexicans

59 Hansen, ed., *The Alamo Reader*, 457.

60 Groneman, *Eyewitness to the Alamo*, 56-57.

61 Hansen, ed., *The Alamo Reader*, 457.

62 Hardin, *The Alamo 1836*, 49; Thompson, *Born on a Mountaintop*, 301, 304; Hansen, ed., *The Alamo Reader*, 481.

CROCKETT'S FIGHT WITH THE MEXICANS.

A fanciful depiction (and one of the earliest) of David Crockett's famous last stand against impossible odds—part of the creation of one of the Alamo's most iconic images. The fighting Tennessean is shown swinging his favorite hunting rifle at horrified Mexican soldiers, who are about to be dropped by Crockett's repeated blows. *Author's Collection*

toss him up in the air (as you would a bundle of fodder) with their bayonets, and then shoot him."[63]

Symbolically, it was now left to the highest ranking Irish-born officer of the garrison, Major Evans, to perform the final heroic act at the Alamo. Evans was the mission's capable and proficient chief of ordnance. Possibly one of the last defenders left alive by this time, he was about to undertake the garrison's final mission and his last act of defiance in the midst of the grisly defeat.

It seems likely that Evans embarked upon his suicidal mission on his own initiative, though some scant and unsubstantiated evidence suggests that Travis had earlier directed the last remaining defenders to blow up the garrison's powder supply. (This evidence is suspect, however, because of the overall romanticizing and glorification of the Alamo's dead commander as a martyr.) It is clear that Evans needed no orders from his commanding officers to take the initiative in such a crisis situation, and to make the attempt to ignite the Alamo's powder supply to kill additional attackers and to deny Santa Anna the tons of extra black powder that might later assist in the crushing of Texian forces to the east. Moreover, during the confusion of the sudden surprise attack and especially with his early death at the battle's beginning, Travis had little, if any,

63 Hanson, ed., *The Alamo Reader*, 46, 60.

The final desperate moments of Tennessee-born Jacob A. Walker, as portrayed by artist Gary Zaboly. Walker was a faithful volunteer fighting with Capt. William Ridgeway Carey's artillery company ("The Invincibles"). Walker was trapped inside the stone church when the Mexicans burst through its wooden doors during the final phase of the battle. The Nacogdoches, Texas, native and father of four was bayoneted to death. *Gary Zaboly*

time to have issued an order to destroy the powder magazine. Indeed, this widely-accepted popular legend has long been promoted by traditional historians to emphasize the sterling qualities of Travis' leadership, regardless of what really happened on that fateful Sunday morning. It seems far more likely that Evans decided on his own to make the desperate attempt to destroy the Alamo's powder magazine. As an intelligent and capable high-ranking officer, he had his own sense of duty and was determined to perform his duty to the best of his ability to the end.

By this late stage of the bloody contest for possession of the Alamo, when the messy work of mopping up the last resistance had all but ended for the soldados, Evans's trusty assistant, Tennessee-born Captain Samuel Blair, a hard-fighting officer of Irish descent from the Refugio Colony and a veteran of San Antonio's capture who had been commended for gallantry by Travis, was most likely dead by this time. If not, then the two last remaining Irishmen of the garrison still alive, might well have embarked together upon this last mission. Despite being badly wounded and with his fellow Ireland-born citizen-soldiers from Refugio, San Patricio, Gonzales, and the United States already cut down, Evans embarked upon the final defiant act at the Alamo as the last, savage flurries of bloody fighting died down inside the smoke-filled church. He surely realized that by destroying the tons of black powder in the magazine, he could at least deny this valuable asset to the invading Mexican Army, and deny its use to Santa Anna in future battles that would be fought to decide the fate of Texas.

But with so many victorious soldados swarming everywhere along the walls, inside the old church, throughout the Long Barracks, and filling the plaza, the wounded Evans had no realistic chance of fulfilling his last mission. Nevertheless, despite blood loss and the pain of previous wounds, he attempted to perform this last desperate act. With his remaining reserves of energy, "Evans—now wounded-grabbed a torch and crawled for the powder room, hoping to blow up the magazine [but] A Mexican bullet [fired] by an officer got him first."[64]

This courageous Irish officer was one of the last, and perhaps the final, defender to die inside the Alamo. Near the powder room—the darkened

---

64 *El Mosquito Mexicano*, April 5, 1836; Lord, *A Time to Stand*, 165-166; Alamo Vertical Fiels, Texas State Library and Archives, Austin, Texas; Groneman, *Defenders of the Alamo*, 14, 22-23, 47-48, 93, 134-138; Hansen, ed., *The Alamo Reader*, 55; *San Antonio Daily Express*, January 5, 1878; Evans, Robert, The Handbook of Texas Online.

confessional room—inside the ancient limestone church now shrouded in a cloud of sulfurous smoke, Evans died at this remote western frontier outpost for what he believed was right. One of the most heroic acts in the Alamo's defense was thus performed by this courageous officer, whose distinctive Irish roots have been overlooked by historians who have long viewed the garrison as homogenous, through a traditional Anglo-Saxon lens. Survivor Susanna Dickinson left the most vivid first-person account of Evans's final mission at the Alamo: "this man named Evans, wounded and spent with weariness, was killed while making his painful way to the powder room."[65]

Finally, with the sun rising in a red-streaked sky on this nightmarish Sunday morning, the struggle for the Alamo sputtered to a gory end after less than one hour of savage fighting. After the last shot was fired in anger, the powder-streaked soldados obeyed Santa Anna's orders and roamed the compound, church, and buildings along the walls, methodically bayoneting the blood-stained lifeless bodies of defenders to make sure that no Texan, Tejano, Irish, or United States volunteer survived to tell the tale of the horror at the Alamo.[66]

Never forgetting the Alamo's slaughter and the garrison's sacrifice on the early morning of March 6, Becerra described how, "Blood and brains covered the earth, and the floors, and had spattered the walls. . . . The victory of the Alamo was dearly bought."[67]

65 Hansen, ed., *The Alamo Reader*, 55; Evans, Robert, The Handbook of Texas Online.

66 Roberts and Olson, *A Line in the Sand*, 168.

67 Hansen, ed., *The Alamo Reader*, 458-459.

Epilogue

One of America's most iconic and unforgettable stories, the bloody struggle for possession of the Alamo, has evolved into a defining moment in American history. The fact the Alamo garrison included a large number of Ireland-born soldiers, and the sons and grandsons of Irish immigrants, has long seemed inconsistent with what generations of Americans, including many leading historians, have understood about this dramatic story at the "cradle of Texas liberty." The struggle in Texas in general, and at the Alamo in particular, has long been viewed as a stirring Anglo-Saxon epic without any alleged "taint" of ethnicity.

The story of the Alamo, however, was as much a Celtic-Gaelic one as anything else. Disproportionately large numbers of determined Texas revolutionaries spoke Gaelic in thick brogues while dreaming of their faraway Emerald Isle. They still cherished their ancient Irish customs and values. Despite extensive scholarship about the Alamo and the Texas Revolution, the important Celtic-Gaelic contributions have been long absent from the traditional historiography and from even the most respected works of historians, including even scholars of Irish descent. This, the true hidden history of the Alamo and the Texas Revolution, has been a glaring omission in the historical record for generations, as the Irish have become the forgotten players in these stirring dramas. It remains a striking paradox given their contributions in the winning of the revolution and the shaping of the heart and soul of Texas.

No ethnic group in Texas played a more important role in sustaining, and ultimately winning the Texas Revolution and in molding the distinctive identity of Texas than the Irish. These Celtic-Gaelic warriors were the most determined and diehard revolutionaries in Texas at a time when most native Texians were far less enthusiastic and devoted to the concept of Texas independence. These key players in the birth of a people's republic and the shaping the identity of Texas have largely been lost in the historical record— a classic demonstration of how some of some of most important aspects of history can be ignored and lost as the generations pass. Indeed, in the historical record, the Irish were transformed into true-blue Texans without any importance being placed on their distinct Irish identity, which they were determined to preserve in a new land.

The disproportionate contributions and sacrifices of Irish Texas patriots were at the core of the remarkable story of the revolutionary birth of Texas and a common people's struggle for liberty against very long odds. The Sons of Erin of Texas became the sons of Texas and America. Hopefully, historians and future generations will remember this each time they think of the dramatic showdown at the Alamo.

Erin go Bragh.

An Interview with the Author

SB: Why did you decide to write your book on this topic?

PTT: When I realized the considerable void about the Irish in the historical record, not only in regard to their role with the Alamo but the entire Texas Revolution, I strongly felt the need to research the topic more deeply and tell the important story of the Irish and their significant contributions.

SB: *You're Irish. Did that influence you?*

PTT: I supposed it did, yes. But there was a large gap in the historical record that needed to be filled. Because of my strong background in Irish history on both sides of the Atlantic and my own Irish roots, it was only natural that I focused on the fascinating story of the Irish at the Alamo. This focus on the Irish represents one of the few, but I think and hope one of the best, remaining untold stories of the Alamo and the Texas Revolution.

SB: Why do you think historians have largely ignored this part of Texas and Irish history?

PTT: First and foremost, the story of the Alamo has been long dominated by romantic myths and outdated traditional views. The struggle at the Alamo has been traditionally viewed as part of America's westward expansion within the overall context of an Anglo-Saxon epic and a national Manifest Destiny.

Therefore, the traditional view has been that the Alamo's defenders were a homogeneous garrison of Anglo-Saxons, when in fact, the majority of garrison members were of Celtic (Irish) heritage, and mostly Scotch-Irish.

SB: So the Alamo garrison can be properly described as an Anglo-Celtic one?

PTT: Yes. The Alamo garrison also included at least fifteen Ireland-born defenders. But a far larger number of garrison members were the sons, grandsons, and great-grandsons of Irish immigrants, both Catholic and Protestant. Other Alamo defenders proudly pointed to their Irish immigrant ancestors going all the way back to the colonial period before the American Revolution. Ironically, many historians of the Alamo and the Texas Revolution are themselves of Irish heritage, but they seem not to have recognized the significance of Irish contributions to the winning of Texas Independence.

SB: Why do you think that is?

PTT: I think primarily because of a lack of existing information and documentation, and how difficult it is to root out this part of the story.

SB: What was difficult about writing this book?

PTT: The years collecting the research and writing the book based upon decades of studying the Irish experience on both sides of the Atlantic.

SB: Were you able to find unexplored primary sources?

PTT: Writing about the forgotten Irish contributions to the Alamo and the Texas Revolution called for digging deeper into primary source material and the overall historical record. Period newspapers in Texas, Mexico, and across America proved invaluable in providing good primary source information. Fortunately, my decades of study (including in Ireland itself) in the fields of Irish history and culture provided a solid foundation from which to embark upon this worthy project, coinciding with my lifelong love of Texas history.

SB: Why did the Irish fight for Texas independence?

PTT: The Irish were motivated primarily by their longtime desire for liberty (long denied to them by the English in their home country), the dream of becoming equal citizens of a new, independent republic, and the acquisition of abundant amounts of Texas land. The legacy of the Irish people battling for independence against a centralized government (England) for centuries played a forgotten role in inspiring the Irish in Texas to break away from the centralized government of Mexico in an armed revolt against a more powerful opponent. And, of course, the autocratic Mexican military strongman and dictator, General Santa Anna, reminded them of centuries of abusive English domination and rule in Ireland.

SB: What happened to the Irish after the Texas victory?

PTT: They gradually merged into the mainstream of Texas and American life, becoming Texans and Americans. However, these developments were a major factor that also led to the loss of an appreciation of Irish heritage and culture. Therefore, a distinct Irish identity in Texas faded away. But what was lost most of all was the memory of significant Irish contributions to the Texas Revolution. And to this day, many people across Texas (including historians) are not fully aware of the importance of the Irish contributions to the making of Texas and how the Texas Revolution was very much of an Irish story on many levels.

SB: Why do you think that it is important to tell this story? How does it stand as a corrective?

PTT: The Irish were the most overlooked and forgotten players in the story of the Alamo and the Texas Revolution. This is a striking paradox because the contributions of the Irish were so important and disproportionate for the winning of Texas Independence. My hope is that readers find this book a timely and much-needed contribution to the distinguished annals of Texas history.

SB: What were some of the contributions of the Irish?

PTT: Their contributions were on every level and virtually endless, including in regard to the issuing of the first Texas Declaration of Independence of the Texas Revolution at Goliad, Texas, in December 1835. Without the significant Irish and Scotch-Irish contributions in so many ways, I believe the Texan revolutionaries would have lost their war for independence, and Texas would have not become an independent republic—at least when it did.

SB: Did any individual fighter's story stand out to you?

PTT: Perhaps the life of David Crockett best represents the overall Irish experience because his family migrated from Ireland, and he became a national figure and is most associated with the Alamo. Despite Crockett's widespread fame and focus on him as a historical figure, no aspect of his life has been more forgotten, unappreciated, and consistently overlooked by historians and Americans than his Irish heritage. Like the Irish in Texas, Crockett became Americanized in a process that obscured the depth of his Irish roots and heritage. He has been long presented as an authentic American hero, but one without a strong Irish connection.

SB: Thank you for talking with us today. Best of luck with your book!

PTT: You're welcome.

Bibliography

Newspapers

Albany Evening Journal, Albany, New York

Arkansas Advocate, Little Rock, Arkansas

Arkansas Gazette, Little Rock, Arkansas

Charleston Patriot, Charleston, South Carolina

Commercial Bulletin and Missouri Literary Register, St. Louis, Missouri

Commonwealth, Frankfort, Kentucky

Dallas Morning News, Dallas, Texas

El Mosquito Mexicano, Mexico City, Mexico

Farmer's Cabinet, Amherst, New Hampshire

Houston Telegraph, Houston, Texas

Maryland Gazette, Annapolis, Maryland

Nashville Banner and Nashville Whig, Nashville, Tennessee

New Hampshire's Portsmouth Journal of Literature and Politics, Portsmouth, NH

New York Evening Star, New York, New York

New York Herald, New York, New York

New York Sun, New York, New York

New York Times, New York, New York

Richmond Enquirer, Richmond, Virginia

San Antonio Daily Express, San Antonio, Texas

Southern Patriot, Charleston, South Carolina

St. Louis Republican, St. Louis, Missouri

Texas Republican, Brazoria, Texas

The Portsmouth Journal and Rockingham Gazette, New Hampshire

The Telegraph and Texas Register, San Felipe de Austin and Columbia, Texas

Vermont Gazette, Bennington, Vermont

Manuscripts

Dimitt, Philip Papers, 1833-1904, Briscoe Center for American History, University of Texas, Austin, Texas.

Galloway, Mary, Briggs, Mary, and Hicks, Marjorie, "The Irish of Stagger's Point, Robertson County, Texas," Paper, internet.

Irish Texans, Institute of Texan Cultures, San Antonio, Texas.

Molloy, Father John Thomas Information, Archives of the Catholic Chancery, Austin, Texas.

Sutherland, John, Narrative, John Salmon Ford Papers, Briscoe Center for American History, University of Texas, Austin, Texas.

12-Irish Texans, Institute of Texan Cultures, San Antonio, Texas.

William B. Ward File, Library of the Daughters of the Republic of Texas, The Alamo, San Antonio, Texas.

Published Sources

Anbinder, Tyler, *Five Points, The 19th Century New York Neighborhood That Invented Tap Dance, Stole Elections, and Became the World's Most Notorious Slum* (New York, NY, 2002).

Asbury, Herbert, *The Gangs of New York* (New York, NY, 1998).

Bannon, John Francis, *The Spanish Borderlands Frontier, 1513-1821* (Albuquerque, NM, 1974).

Barber, Alan, David Kokernot, *Rogue Soldier of the Texas Revolution* (Sandpoint, ID, 2010).

Bartlett, Thomas, Dawson, Kevin, and Keogh, Daire, *Rebellion: A Television History of 1798* (Dublin, Ireland, 1998).

Barlett, Thomas and Jeffery, Keith, *A Military History of Ireland* (Cambridge, MA, 1996).

Barr, Alwyn, *Texans in Revolt: The Battle for San Antonio, 1835* (Austin, TX, 1990).

Binkley, William C., *The Texas Revolution* (Baton Rouge, LA, 1952).

Boatner, Mark Mayo, III, *Encyclopedia of the American Revolution* (New York, NY, 1966).

Boyd, Bob, *The Texas Revolution: A Day-by-Day Account* (San Angelo, TX, 1986).

Bolston, James R., and Wiener, Allen J., *David Crockett in Congress: The Rise and Fall of the Poor Man's Friend* (Houston, TX, 2009).

Bradfield, Jane, *Rx Take One Cannon: The Gonzales Come & Take It Cannon of October, 1835* (Shiner, TX, 1981).

Brands, H. W., *Lone Star Nation* (New York, NY, 2004).

Brown, Gary, *Volunteers in the Texas Revolution: The New Orleans Greys* (Plano, TX, 1999.

Bryan, Walter, *The Improbable Irish* (New York, NY, 1969).

Campbell, Randolph B., *An Empire for Slavery: The Peculiar Institution in Texas* (Baton Rouge, LA, 1989).

Carroll, Michael J., *A Bay of Destiny: A History of Bantry Bay and Bantry* (Bantry, Ireland, 1996).

Carty, James, editor, *Ireland: From The Flight of the Earls to Grattan's Parliament* (Dublin, Ireland, 1957).

Chipman, Donald E., *Spanish Texas, 1519-1821* (Austin, TX, 1997).

Clary, David A., *Eagles and Empire: The United States, Mexico, and the Struggle for a Continent* (New York, NY, 2009).

Crutchfield, James A., *It Happened in Texas* (Helena, MT, 1996).

Cunliffe, Barry, *The Ancient Celts* (Oxford, NY,1997).

Davis, Graham, *Land! Irish Pioneers in Mexican and Revolutionary Texas* (College Station, TX, 2002).

Davis, Graham, "Talking Freedom: The Irish in the Texas Revolution," *Irish Studies Review*, No. 8 (Autumn 1994).

Davis, William, C., *Lone Star Rising: The Revolutionary Birth of the Texas Republic* (New York, NY, 2004).

Davis, William C., *Three Roads to the Alamo: The Lives and Fortunes of David Crockett, James Bowie, and William Barret Travis* (New York, NY, 1998).

De Bruhl, Marshall, *Sword of San Jacinto: A Life of Sam Houston* (New York, NY, 1993).

Derr, Mark, *The Frontiersman: The Real Life and the Many Legends of Davy Crockett* (New York, NY, 1993).

Dickson, Charles, *The Wexford Rising in 1798: Its Causes and Its Course* (London, England, 1997).

Donovan, James, *The Blood of Heroes: The 13-Day Struggle for the Alamo—and the Struggle that Forged a Nation* (New York, NY, 2012).

Doyle, David Noel, *Ireland: Irishmen and Revolutionary America* (Dublin, Ireland, 1981).

Doyle, Danny and Folan, Terence, *The Gold Sun of Irish Freedom: 1798 in Song and Story* (Boulder, CO, 1998).

Edmondson, J. R., *The Alamo Story: From Early History to Current Conflicts* (Plano, TX, 2000).

Fehrenbach, T. R., *Lone Star: A History of Texas and the Texans* (New York, NY, 2000).

Fehrenbach, T. R., *Fire & Blood: A History of Mexico* (New York, NY, 1995).

Fields, Nic, *Roman Conquests: North Africa* (Barnsley: Pen and Sword Books, 2003).

Fleming, Thomas, *Liberty! The American Revolution* (New York, NY, 1997).

Fleming, Thomas, *Washington's Secret War: A Hidden History of Valley Forge* (New York, NY, 2005).

Foster, R. F., editor, *The Oxford History of Ireland* (New York, NY, 1992).

Fraser, Antonia, Cromwell, *The Lord Protector* (New York, NY, 1973).

Gaddy, Jerry J., *Texas in Revolt: Contemporary Newspaper Account of the Texas Revolution* (Fort Collins, CO, 1973).

Garrett, Julia Kathryn, *Green Flag over Texas: The Story of the First War of Independence* (Austin, TX, 1969).

Gleeson, David T., *The Irish of the South, 1815-1877* (Chapel Hill, NC, 2001).

Golway, Terry, *For the Cause of Liberty: A Thousand Years of Ireland's Heroes* (New York, NY, 2000).

Gray, William Fairfax, *Diary of Colonel William Fairfax Gray, From Virginia to Texas, 1835-1836* (Houston, TX, 1965).

Groneman, Bill, *Alamo Defenders: A Genealogy: The People and Their Words* (Austin, TX, 1990).

Groneman, Bill, *Eyewitness to the Alamo* (Plano, TX,1996).

Haning, Peter, editor, *Great Irish Humor* (New York, NY, 1995).

Haltigan, James, *The Irish in the American Revolution and Their Early Influence in the Colonies* (Washington, D.C., 1908).

Handbook of Texas Online.

Hanley, Barry, "The Irish Heroes of the Alamo," *Irish Chronicles*, vol. 5, no. 2. (Winter 2004)

Hanley, James L. *Sam Houston* (Norman, OK, 2002).

Hansen, Todd, editor, *The Alamo Reader: A Study in History* (Mechanicsburg, PA, 2003).

Hardin, Stephen L., Texian Iliad: A Military History of the Texas Revolution (Austin, TX, 1994).

Hardin, Stephen L., *The Alamo, 1836* (Oxford, England., 2001).

Haynes, Sam W. And Wintz, Cary D., eds., *Major Problems of Texas History* (New York, NY, 2002).

Haythornthwaite, Philip, *The Alamo and the War of Independence, 1835-36* (London, England, 1988).

Hinderaker, Eric and Mancall, Peter C., *At the Edge of Empire: The Backcountry in British North America* (Baltimore, MD, 2003).

Hopewell, Clifford, *James Bowie, Texas Fighting Man* (Austin, TX, 1994).

Hoyt, Edwin P., *The Alamo: An Illustrated History* (Dallas, TX, 1999).

Huffines, Alan C., *Blood of Noble Men: The Alamo, Siege & Battle* (Austin: Eakin Press, 1999).

Jackson, Jack, ed., *Almonte's Texas: Juan 1834 Inspection, Secret Report and Role in the 1836 Campaign* (Austin, TX, 2005).

Jackson, Jack, ed., *Texas by Teran: The Diary Kept by General Manuel De Mier Y Teran on his Inspection of Texas* (Austin, TX, 2000).

Jackson, Ron, *Alamo Legacy: Alamo Descendants Remember the Alamo* (Austin, TX, 1997).

King, Richard C., James Clinton Neill, *The Shadow Commander of the Alamo* (Austin, TX, 2002).

Kennedy, Billy, *The Scots-Irish in the Hills of Tennessee* (Greenville, SC, 1995).

Kenny, Michael, *The 1798 Rebellion: Photographs and Memorabilia from the National Museum of Ireland* (Dublin, Ireland, 1996)

Lalor Brian, *The Encyclopedia of Ireland* (New Haven, CT, 2003).

Lack, Paul D., *The Texas Revolutionary Experience: A Political and Social History, 1835-1836* (College Station, TX, 1992).

Lamego, Miguel A. Sanchez, *The Siege and Taking of the Alamo* (Santa Fe, NM, 1968).

Leder, Lawrence H., *The Colonel Legacy, Loyalist Historians*, vol. 1 (New York, NY, 1971).

Levy, Buddy, *American Legend: The Real-Life Adventures of David Crockett* (New York, NY, 2005).

Leyburn, James G., *The Scotch-Irish: A Social History* (Chapel Hill, NC, 1962).

Libura, Krystyna M., Moreno, Luis Gerardo Morales, and Marquez, Jesus Velasco, *Echoes of the Mexican-American War* (Berkeley, CA, 2004).

Linn, John Joseph, *Reminiscences of Fifty Years in Texas* (New York, NY, 1883).

Lord, Walter, *A Time to Stand: A Chronicle of the Valiant Battle at the Alamo* (New York, NY, 1971).

Lundy, Benjamin, *The War in Texas* (Philadelphia, PA, 1836).

MacKay, James, *William Wallace, Braveheart* (Edinburgh, Scotland, 1995).

Marshall, Bruce, *Uniforms of the Alamo and the Texas Revolution, 1835-1836* (Atglen, PA, 2003).

Martin, Joel W., *Sacred Revolt: The Muskogees' Struggle for a New World* (Boston, MA, 1991).

Matovina, Timothy M., *The Alamo Remembered: Tejano Accounts and Perspectives* (Austin, TX, 1995).

McCullough, David Willis, *Wars of the Irish Kings* (New York, NY, 2000)

McDonald, Archie, *William Barret Travis: A Biography* (Austin, TX, 1995).

McWhiney, Grady, and Jamieson, Perry D., *Attack and Die: Civil War Military Tactics and the Southern Heritage* (Tuscaloosa, AL, 1982).

Miller, Edward L., *New Orleans and the Texas Revolution* (College Station, TX, 2004).

Moore, Stephen L., *Eighteen Minutes: The Battle of San Jacinto and the Texas Independence Campaign* (Lanham, MD, 2004).

Moore, Stephen L., *Savage Frontier: Rangers, Riflemen, and Indian Wars in Texas, volume I, 1835-1837* (Plano, TX, 2002).

Murphy, Charles, *The Irish in the American Revolution* (Groveland, MA, 1975).

Nutting, Wallace, *Ireland Beautiful* (New York, NY, 1975)

O'Brien, John A., *The Vanishing Irish Race* (New York: McGraw, 1953).

O'Brien, Michael, *A Hidden Phase of American History: Ireland's Part in America's Struggle for Liberty* (New York, NY, 1920).

O'Toole, Fintan, *White Savage, William Johnson and the Invention of America* (New York, NY, 2005).

Palmer, Alan, *Napoleon in Russia* (London, England, 1997).

Reid, Stuart, *The Texan Army, 1835-46* (Oxford, England, 2003).

Reid, Stuart, *Culloden Moor 1746: The Death of the Jacobite Cause* (Oxford, England, 2002).

Remini, Robert V., *Andrew Jackson and his Indian Wars* (New York, NY, 2002).

Roberts, Randy and Olson, James, *A Line in the Sand: The Alamo in Blood and Memory* (New York, NY, 2001).

Roell, Craig H., *Remember Goliad!* (Austin, TX, 1994).

Rose, Ben Z, *John Stark, Maverick General* (Waverly, MA, 2007).

Santos, Richard G., *Santa Anna's Campaign Against Texas, 1835-1836* (Waco, TX, 1968).

Scheer, Mary L., ed., *Women and the Texas Revolution* (Denton, TX, 2012).

Scheina, Robert L., *Santa Anna: A Curse Upon Mexico* (Washington, D.C., 2002).

Shackford, James Atkins, *David Crockett: The Man And the Legend* (Lincoln, NE, 1986).

Smithwick, Noah, *The Evolution of a State* (Austin, TX, 1983).

Stewart, A.T.Q., *The Summer Soldiers: The 1798 Rebellion in Antrim and Down* (Belfast, Ireland, 1995).

Stout, Jay A., *Slaughter at Goliad: The Mexican Massacre of 400 Texas Volunteers* (Annapolis, MD, 2008).

James K. Swisher, *The Revolutionary War in the Southern Back Country* (Gretna, LA, 2008).

Tanner, Marcus, *Ireland's Holy Wars: The Struggle for a Nation's Soul, 1500-2000* (New Haven, CT, 2001).

Teja, Jesus F. de la, ed., *A Revolution Remembered: The Memoirs And Selected Correspondence of Juan A. Seguin* (Austin, TX, 2002).

Texas Almanac, Texas State Historical Association, internet.

"The Alamo: The Irish Heroes of the Alamo," *Irish Connections* (2004), Internet.

Tucker, Phillip Thomas, *Exodus from the Alamo: The Anatomy of the Last Stand Myth* (Philadelphia, PA, 2010).

Tucker, Phillip Thomas, *The Important Role of the Irish in the American Revolution* (Bowie, MD, 2009)

Wallace, G. Chariton, *Exploring the Alamo Legends* (Plano, TX, 1990).

Walraven, Bill, and Marjorie Walraven, *The Magnificent Barbarians: Little Told Tales of the Texas Revolution* (Austin, Texas, TX, 1993).

Webb, James, *Born Fighting: How the Scots-Irish Shaped America* (New York, NY, 2004).

Weems, John Edward with Jane Weems, *Dream of Empire: A History of the Republic of Texas, 1836-1846* (New York, NY 1995).

Index

About the Author

Phillip Thomas Tucker earned his doctorate in American History from St. Louis University, St. Louis, Missouri, in 1990. He spent more than two decades working as a historian for the Department of Defense, and now writes full time at his southern Maryland home in Upper Marlboro.

Tucker specializes in breaking new ground in multiple fields of American history and overturning outdated views, myths, and stereotypes. He is the author or editor of more than two dozen books devoted to a wide variety of subjects about the American experience, with a special focus on the Irish, the American Civil War, the American Revolutionary War, and Texas. His book *The Confederacy's Fighting Chaplain: Father John B. Bannon* was awarded the Douglas Southall Freeman Award for the best book in Southern history (1993).